OpenStreetMap

Using and Enhancing
the Free Map of the World

About the Authors:

Frederik Ramm and Jochen Topf have been working in the IT industry for over 10 years. They have been with OpenStreetMap since 2006 and are active members of the German and international OpenStreetMap community as mappers, developers, speakers, authors, and conference organizers. Frederik and Jochen are interested in neogeography from a professional angle as well, having founded the Karlsruhe, Germany based Geofabrik GmbH which offers products and services around OpenStreetMap and other free and open geodata.

Steve Chilton is a trained cartographer, and is the current Chair of the Society of Cartographers. He has worked professionally in the field for many years, and has been involved in OpenStreetMap since early in 2006, contributing countless hours to the project since then. He is currently employed as Education Development Manager at Middlesex University. He gets his "map fix" by adding map data wherever he travels in the world, and is also the main designer of the cartographic styling of the default map layer, and now co-maintainer of the stylesheets associated with that aspect of the project.

Contact:

Frederik Ramm <ramm@geofabrik.de>

Jochen Topf <topf@geofabrik.de>

Steve Chilton <steve8@mdx.ac.uk>

Accompanying Web Site:

www.openstreetmap.info

Frederik Ramm

Jochen Topf

and Steve Chilton

OpenStreetMap

Using and Enhancing

the Free Map of the World

Published in 2011 by
UIT Cambridge Ltd.
PO Box 145
Cambridge
CB4 1GQ
England
Tel: +44 1223 302 041
Web: www.uit.co.uk

ISBN 978-1-906860-11-0

The right of Steve Chilton, Frederik Ramm, and Jochen Topf
to be identified as the authors of this work have been asserted by
them in accordance with the Copyright, Designs and
Patents Act 1988.

The programs and instructions in this book have been
included for their instructional value. Neither the publisher
nor the authors offer any warranties or representations in
respect of their fitness for a particular purpose, nor do they
accept any liability for any loss or damage arising
from their use.

The publication is designed to provide accurate and
authoritative information in regard to the subject matter
covered. Neither the publisher nor the authors make any
representation, express or implied, with regard to the
accuracy of information contained in this book, nor do they
accept any legal responsibility or liability for any errors or
omissions that may be made. This work is supplied with
the understanding that UIT Cambridge Ltd and its authors
are supplying information, but are not attempting to render
engineering or other professional services. If such services
are required, the assistance of an appropriate professional
should be sought.

Many of the designations used by manufacturers and
sellers to distinguish their products are claimed as
trademarks. UIT Cambridge Ltd acknowledges
trademarks as the property of their respective owners.

10 9 8 7 6 5 4 3 2 1

Preface

Writing a book about OpenStreetMap (OSM) is almost as difficult a project as OpenStreet-Map itself.

For many, including some mappers who have been with the project almost from the start, the fact that OpenStreetMap actually works is still something of a miracle. How can a project with so few rules, and where so many decisions are left to the individual contributors, ever bear fruit? We had our doubts, too, when we wrote this book: Is it going to be possible to cover such a fast-moving project in something as slow to produce as a printed book – hopefully in a way that will not render the book useless after a year or so? Will we not, after having completed the last chapter, immediately have to begin updating the first chapters?

We think that we have succeeded. The first edition of this book, in German, was published in February 2008 and went through three print runs. The second edition was published in March 2009 and was, with its extended content and some updates, even more popular than the first. Many people from the worldwide OpenStreetMap community asked if we would produce an English version, and here it is. We have completed the English version shortly after releasing the third edition in German.

Once again, we have thoroughly revisited everything we have written, and updated the book to reflect the project's latest developments. The English version has the same chapters and content as the original German one, but we have dropped some material that only made sense for mappers in Germany, and instead added an appendix that discusses some mapping concerns for mappers around the world.

We hope to inspire you with our passion for OpenStreetMap. Discover how much fun there is to be had surveying the planet for such an ambitious project, and what you can do with the wealth of data contributed by mappers around the world!

The English edition would not have been possible without old OpenStreetMap hand Steve Chilton, who made sure that what you read is proper English and not peppered with remnants of a German book, and who also brought a different angle to some of the topics we covered.

Our thanks go to the proofreaders of the first edition in German – Christoph Eckert, Stephan Holl, Christine Karch, Jörg Ostertag, and Thomas Ott – for lots of corrections small and large; to Sebastian Schwarz, Daniel van Gerpen, and Marcus Wolschon who helped us with parts of the second edition; and to Andy Allan, Matt Amos, Shaun McDonald, and Richard Weait, and who proofread the English edition. Many thanks also to the people who have contributed their local knowledge to the "Mapping the World" appendix.

A warm thank you also goes to Christoph Kaeder from our German publisher, Lehmanns Media, who encouraged us in many ways during the three German editions, and to Niall Mansfield of UIT for helping make the English edition happen and for catering to many of our whims. Catherine Jagger has scrutinized this edition with an eagle eye to iron out any remaining issues.

Last but not least, we wish to thank the tens of thousands of OpenStreetMap activists who have created what we discuss in this book. We have also been very pleased with the good feedback and encouragement we have received from the community – our German book was bought and praised by enthusiasts who didn't even speak the language...

Frederik Ramm and Jochen Topf

Karlsruhe, August 2010

About the English Edition

It has been my pleasure to work with Frederik and Jochen on this English language edition of the definitive OpenStreetMap book. The whole of the content has been revised and some sections have been expanded for the international audience. All examples and illustrations have been reviewed and revised as necessary, changing where appropriate the German locations for international ones when illustrating particular points or techniques.

My contribution has been to take Frederik and Jochen's excellent English translations and hopefully to correct any anachronistic phraseology, all the while checking for consistency and accuracy of information. Any quirks of language or tone are thus my responsibility and not directly theirs.

I thought I knew a lot about the intricacies of the project, but doing this work has taught me a whole lot more. I hope it will prove as instructional for you, the reader.

Finally, I would like to give my thanks to all the contributors to the project – for the data, and especially for the amazing tools that have been developed. I have met some of you at conferences, mapping parties, hack days and socials, while some are just names on mailing lists or on IRC. To all of you – the OpenStreetMap community – thanks, for creating such a ground-breaking project, which we hope this book in some small way illuminates.

Steve Chilton

London, August 2010

About This Book

This book aims to give you all the information you need to understand and work with OpenStreetMap data – whether you want to survey data as a *mapper,* to apply your programming skills to writing OpenStreetMap software, or simply to use the existing OpenStreetMap data for your own purposes.

Outline

The book is divided into four main parts:

Part I introduces you to the OpenStreetMap project and its community, and explains how to become part of it.

Part II describes how to use GPS devices to survey data, and how to add that data to OpenStreetMap using any of the project's main editors. This part also explains the OpenStreetMap data structures and includes practical mapping examples.

In **Part III**, creating maps and navigation routes from OpenStreetMap data takes center stage. We highlight the rendering engines Osmarender, Mapnik, and Kosmos, and explain how to convert OpenStreetMap data for use with the popular Garmin GPS devices or for navigation purposes. We also show how you can use just a little HTML and JavaScript to produce interactive maps for use on web pages.

Part IV is aimed at hackers and developers. You don't have to be a programmer to make use of the first three parts of the book, but this part explores in more detail the OpenStreetMap database server and its API (Application Programming Interface), explains how you import and export data, and presents useful and interesting ways to hack OpenStreetMap and its data.

The **Appendix** has an introduction to Geodesy (the scientific discipline that deals with the measurement and representation of the Earth), which explains some of the fundamentals of cartography. Also, there are details about the variations in mapping practices in different countries of the world.

In writing this book, we had two different groups of people in mind. If you simply want to contribute data to OpenStreetMap, you will find everything you need to know in parts I and II. The only prerequisites are that you should be familiar with basic computer tasks (copying files, or downloading them from the Internet). If you want to use OpenStreetMap data in your own projects, however, you will find all the necessary information in parts III and IV – but we still recommend that you read parts I and II in order to understand the basics of the OpenStreetMap project. Part III requires readers to be able to work with a text editor and execute programs (e. g. from the command line). For part IV, elementary programming skills are required.

Accompanying Web Site

The OpenStreetMap project is constantly evolving. While we have tried to make sure that our information was accurate when the book went to press, we can't predict the future. Some likely future developments have been pointed out, but other unforeseeable things will happen, and the book will become out of sync with the project in some aspects. Visit our website `www.openstreetmap.info` every now and then and we will update you on the latest developments. You can also subscribe to an RSS feed there.

Links to the OpenStreetMap Wiki

The OpenStreetMap wiki is a community-maintained web site that provides documentation on all things OSM. Throughout the book, we will point you to articles on the wiki for further reading. Such links are marked like this: Wiki Link. To access the article, you can either enter its name into the search form on `wiki.openstreetmap.org`, or you can go directly to `http://wiki.openstreetmap.org/wiki/Wiki_Link`.

Maps in this Book

All pictures in this book that have been created using OpenStreetMap data are made available under the license "Creative Commons Attribution-Share Alike 2.0". You can freely copy and re-use them under the terms of that license. This freedom does not apply to other illustrations and the other contents of the book, which may not be copied without permission.

Table of Contents

Part IV: Hacking OpenStreetMap

Appendix

Part I

Introduction

In this part we discuss what OpenStreetMap is, and how it compares to other online mapping systems. We introduce you to the OpenStreetMap website and related sites, and show how to get involved with the OpenStreetMap community of mappers.

Making the Free World Web

Part 1

Introduction

1 Making the Free World Map

The OpenStreetMap (OSM) project was started by Steve Coast in England in 2004, and its aim is to create a free world map. The term *free* is used here in the sense pioneered by the Free Software movement. It is not about being free of charge (although this often goes along with it), but being free of restrictions that hinder the productive use of the data.

A traditional cartographer's hair might well stand on end when they hear how OpenStreet-Map intends to achieve that goal: Hobbyists walk, hike, bike, or drive, recording their tracks using GPS devices. These recordings are then meticulously redrawn on a computer screen, furnished with additional information such as street names, and then uploaded to a central database.

For people who tend to be skeptical, and especially for geo-industry insiders, there are lots of reasons why this is bound to fail: The GPS devices are not accurate enough, the people involved are dilettantes, their styles are not consistent, the technical methods are inadequate, and there is no way to guarantee even a minimum level of quality.

These prejudices notwithstanding, OpenStreetMap has already achieved remarkable success. Worldwide, many cities are already mapped to a level of detail unmatched by the web offerings of Google, Yahoo, or Microsoft. Furthermore, OpenStreetMap data is usually more current than any printed map or indeed many web map offerings. You will find some examples of OpenStreetMap mapping in the color section.

In most areas, OpenStreetMap mapping will start from a blank sheet. But sometimes it is possible to import a base dataset from existing sources. The Netherlands, for example, benefited from having an almost complete dataset donated by Dutch company AND. In the US, mapping of the road network was given a head start by importing the freely available TIGER dataset (see color plate 17, and also the appendix), and Canada, Germany, and many other countries also have a number of completed import projects.

These import success stories are often the result of lots of work by local mappers who have to find and convert the data. Sometimes it makes a lot of sense to not only travel around with a GPS in your hand, but to also try other avenues of data acquisition. Chapter 26 has more on data imports.

1.1 The Wikipedia of Cartography

In many ways the OpenStreetMap project is like Wikipedia, the free encyclopedia. Anyone can contribute to Wikipedia, just as anyone can contribute to OpenStreetMap. Wikipedia critics never get tired of pointing out the supposedly inferior quality of the articles because there is no copy-editing, and OpenStreetMap receives similar criticism. While there may be occasions when Wikipedia really is inferior to a classic encyclopedia, overall it is a huge success.

The parallels continue if you look deeper. For example, Wikipedia has deliberately avoided creating rigid structures such as "articles about composers must contain at least their date of birth, date of death, and a list of works". This principle is mirrored in OpenStreetMap, where users can upload data in the form they find most appropriate. For both projects however, time has brought some consensus about "standard operating procedures", which created some degree of structure. Both projects also have a detailed change history, so that anybody can see who made which changes and when.

In other areas, OpenStreetMap and Wikipedia are less similar. Currently, contributors to OpenStreetMap experience a fairly steep learning curve to get to grips with one of the available editors. The structure of the data that is collected in OpenStreetMap is also very different as it is much more interconnected than Wikipedia, which is fundamentally a collection of individual items.

Technologically, OpenStreetMap lags behind Wikipedia (which, to be fair, is also several years older). OpenStreetMap doesn't yet have options to display changes in the map data in an easily understandable form so that contributors can see what happens in their area. Also, reverting changes is currently much more complex in OpenStreetMap than it is in Wikipedia, and often involves tedious manual work.

1.2 Free is more than Free of Charge

OpenStreetMap is not the only source of maps that is available free of charge. Services like Google Maps, Yahoo Maps, or the Microsoft offering Bing Maps have very good mapping available for viewing via the Internet, and they don't require payment.

The idea of community mapping is also being taken up by the geodata industry. The Tom-Tom company, a manufacturer of navigation devices, has recently bought TeleAtlas which is the world's second-largest supplier of map data. Through their Map Share program they already offer (limited) possibilities for users to modify map data. In the summer of 2008, Google unveiled its "Map Maker", an editor that allows users to trace map data from satellite or aerial imagery and upload it to the Google servers. At the moment, Google is using Map Maker primarily in countries where they can't buy suitable map data from the traditional geodata suppliers, but given that in late 2009 they switched from using TeleAtlas mapping to using their own map data in some parts of the world, it may not take long before Map Maker is enabled on a larger scale.

All these offerings give only very limited rights to the users of their maps. If you want to add a "how to find us" map to your printed company brochure, for example, these "free" Internet sources are usually not usable. With OpenStreetMap, on the other hand, any form of reproduction or processing is allowed, and you don't have to ask anybody for permission.

OSM data is published under a Creative Commons license which grants you that freedom. In exchange, the license requires that anything you produce from OpenStreetMap data must pass the same freedom on to its users. For most users it is not a problem to agree to this. If you create your company brochure with a "how to find us" map, you must allow the recipients of your brochure to copy that map. If you use OpenStreetMap data to create a hiking map of the Catskills, then you may sell that map for any price you want, but you can't bar your customers from copying it and distributing it further. We will cover the details of the license in chapter 20.

1.3 Bitmaps, Vector Data, Geodata

Behind all maps there is a collection of data: Roads, forests, rivers, and all other features depicted on the map are loaded from a database during its creation (in the case of computer-generated maps). The art of cartography consists mainly of selecting the right set of features from the database, and deciding how they should be represented on the map – their styles, colors, weightings, etc.

Established online services usually offer ready-made maps, which are the end product of cartography. You don't get access to the data from which the maps are made, even though this would of course give you a much broader range of possibilities. If you have the original data, then you can be your own cartographer; you can select the features you are interested in and you can design your own map. You can even use the data for completely different purposes from drawing maps, for example for statistical analyses or to generate driving directions. OSM gives you this freedom.

Figure 1-1 shows the differences between a bitmap image as typically supplied by a web mapping service, and geodata as supplied by OpenStreetMap. You can easily create vector drawings or bitmaps from geodata, but going in the other direction is almost impossible to achieve automatically – a lot of the conversion has to be done by hand.

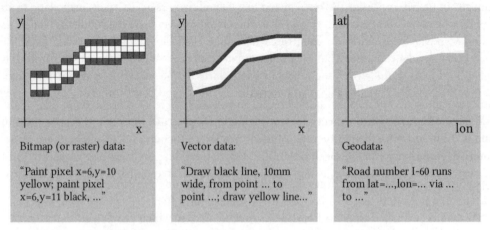

Figure 1-1: Differences between bitmaps, vector data, and geodata.

Many web services try to alleviate their lack of proper geodata by allowing you to create simple custom maps based on the existing material. You can mark important points on the map with symbols, or perhaps draw some picture elements on top of the map. The products of such activity are called *mashups*. Google leads the field in this area; they even have a mashup editor that is supposed to make creating mashups and integrating them in a website easy for non-programmers.

Mashups are not a copy or a derived product of the original map and as such there is no licensing problem with them; but the service provider (for example, Google) could in theory curtail their service at any time. Equally, they could embed advertising into their maps, or start to charge a fee. They could even shut down the service completely, leaving stranded all mashups that were based on their service. But above all, mashups are unsatisfactory from a cartographic perspective because they can never really change the look and feel of the map. Mashups are just "push pins on a map", and you can't do anything interesting, like change the appearance of a road depending on how many accidents happened there.

In contrast to all other data providers, OpenStreetMap offers full access to its geodata. Everyone is free to take it and create whatever type of map (or other artifact) they desire with it.

1.4 OpenStreetMap and Geographic Information Systems

Processing geographic data with computers is, of course, nothing new. The discipline is called GIS (Geographic Information Systems), and there are many commercial and Open

Source software products that can be used. The worldwide GIS community is mainly comprised of people who use GIS professionally. The software used is powerful, but often difficult to get to grips with for the layman and can be very expensive.

The OpenStreetMap project has decided to use its own data formats and custom software that best serve the OSM purpose. For OSM, it is very important that software and data formats can be used by people without prior GIS experience, and the technology must support the free-style attributes for objects (the *tagging*, which we explain in chapter 7) required in an open, international project. It is virtually impossible to create a pre-defined data structure for OSM data and to expect everyone to use the same categories and the same level of detail. Allowing this flexibility is incompatible with the more rigid, top-down structures found in traditional GIS approaches.

OpenStreetMap works on a large, shared database containing data that comes from lots of different sources and that can be used for a number of different purposes. It is important for OpenStreetMap that the road data forms a network which can be operated on automatically, for example to derive driving directions. This is a demand seldom found in classical GIS.

But there are many bridges between the two worlds. OpenStreetMap data can be converted to *shapefiles* (see section 26.3) or imported into PostGIS databases (see section 17.2), formats that are very common in the GIS world. The reverse route may be used for importing data into OpenStreetMap (see section 26.2). Thus, OpenStreetMap can receive data from the classical GIS world, and also serve as a data source for GIS projects.

OpenStreetMap maps can also be used in the GIS world through a Web Map Service (WMS). The project doesn't offer a WMS server because this would put too much strain on the server infrastructure, but there are commercial and non-commercial third-party organizations offering such WMS servers. More detail on that can be found under WMS on the OSM wiki pages.

2 OpenStreetMap on the Web

The central purpose of OpenStreetMap is to collect geodata, and make that data available to anybody in its raw form. In addition to that, the project also offers a number of different maps on the web, which are created from this raw data. By looking at the maps one should immediately be able to get an impression of how well one's local area is represented in OpenStreetMap. People who see that their home town is only partly complete are often tempted to sign up and finish the task.

This chapter explains the main OpenStreetMap website. It's best to read it sitting at your computer so you can try out the various pages. We'll also cover some related websites.

2.1 The OpenStreetMap Web Site

The world map on the OpenStreetMap website (www.openstreetmap.org) can be used just like any other modern map on the web: Drag the mouse to pan the map display, and use the mouse wheel or double clicks to zoom in. (See figure 2-1 and color plate 1.) There is a "+" symbol in the top right corner of the display that lets you select a different map style or *layer;* you can choose Mapnik, Osmarender, or Cycle Map – all three are fully explained later in the book.

The pre-computed OpenStreetMap map images are freely accessible[1] and can be put on any web page with just a few lines of JavaScript code. Chapter 14 covers that in detail.

Data Layer

As we said, one of the differences between OpenStreetMap and other map providers is that OpenStreetMap makes the raw data available. This is visible directly in the *data layer.* Selecting this layer from the same menu as the other map layers loads all data objects for the

---

1 subject to a usage policy, see Tile usage policy on the wiki pages.

current map view and shows them on the map, including those that may be too obscure to show up on the normal map. The data layer is discussed in depth in section 12.1.

Figure 2-1: The main OpenStreetMap website (see also color plate 1).

Exporting from the Web

By using the "Export" tab at the top of the main OpenStreetMap site (figure 2-2), you can directly export OSM data in a variety of data formats. Data is always exported for the part of the map that is currently visible, unless you select with a mouse drag an area to export.

The following data formats are available:

- OpenStreetMap XML Data – a raw data export that you can process with suitable OSM software. This export has a size limit; you can only use it if you are looking at a reasonably small area of the map (approximately 10 km x 10 km).
- Mapnik Image – an image drawn in the same style as the Mapnik map layer. You can select from various image formats (e. g. PNG, JPEG, PDF), and you can specify a scale.

The smaller the scale number, the more detailed (and larger) the image. The default scale number suggested will match the detail on your current map view. There is a limit on how low you can go with the scale number to avoid creating huge PDF files for a whole country that contain even the smallest footpath or other detail.

- Osmarender Image – an image drawn in the same style as the Osmarender map layer. This export only supports PNG and JPEG formats, and you have to select a zoom level instead of a scale number. The larger the zoom level, the more detail you will have in your file. The default zoom level is the one at which you are viewing the map.
- Embeddable HTML – an HTML snippet that you can copy into your own web page to show the map as you see it before you. Users of your web page will be able to zoom and pan the map, and the Export tab even lets you click a position to be marked with a symbol in the generated code.

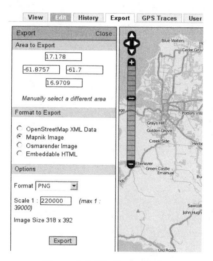

Figure 2-2: The Export tab.

Apart from the print button in your web browser, the Export tab is the second easiest way of printing OpenStreetMap maps. You achieve the best results by requesting a Mapnik export in PDF format and then using any PDF viewer to print that in the desired size. For printing to DIN formats (A4 etc.), make sure that you request a map with an aspect ratio of roughly 1:1.4, and for US Letter format, 1:1.3.

The Search Box

The Search box on the left-hand side (see figure 2-1) can be used to enter any search term, and will then simultaneously search for that term in the OpenStreetMap database and in Geonames, a free location database unrelated to OpenStreetMap. Results are displayed as a list, and you can click on list items to zoom to the location on the map.

Further Controls on the Map View

In the lower right corner of the map display (see figure 2-1) there are a permalink and a shortlink, which you can save as a bookmark or share with others. Using those links will always get you back to the currently viewed map area with the same layers.

In the gray box on the left there is a "Map Key" link which displays a legend for the currently visible zoom level. (This is a general legend for the zoom level you are on; not all objects described in the legend will necessarily be somewhere on your map.)

2.2 OpenStreetBugs

Not everyone is comfortable with editing OpenStreetMap data themselves. In order to engage as many contributors as possible, the OpenStreetBugs website has been created.

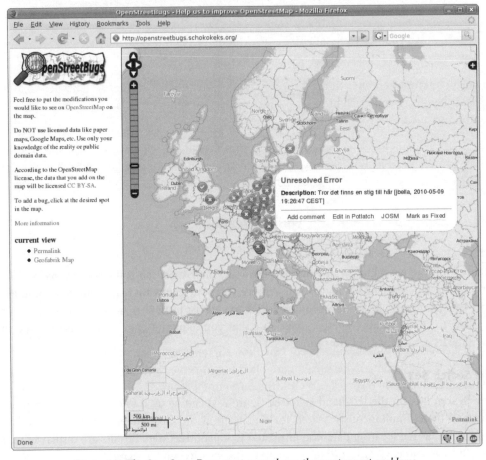

Figure 2-3: The OpenStreetBugs start page shows the most recent problems.

Here, anyone can mark a location on the OSM map by a click of the mouse and add a comment. Others can then read these comments, add their own remarks, or use their OpenStreetMap editing knowledge to repair the problem and close the bug. OpenStreetBugs does not require you to sign up for an account.

When you first visit OpenStreetBugs (`www.openstreetbugs.org`), you see a map with symbols on it (figure 2-3). The red crosses show problems that haven't been corrected yet; the blue check marks show those that have been repaired recently (these expire after a while). Only a small number of symbols are shown so as not to clutter the map, but if you zoom in further you see more. Hover your mouse over one of the symbols to open a bubble with an explanation and any possible comments. Using the links in the bubble, you can add comments, or you can mark the problem as fixed (click once to access the options). If you feel you can repair something, you can jump directly to the Potlatch or JOSM editors[2] to edit the problem in question.

To insert a new bug report, simply click on the map at the relevant location to open an empty "bubble" that will let you enter a description of the problem and give you the option of leaving your OSM username.

If you zoom in far enough, you get three extra links on the left-hand side. Clicking on "RSS feed" lets you set your web browser (or RSS reader) to subscribe to changes in the area currently displayed.

The "GPX export" link gives you a GPX file that has all bug reports as *waypoints* (marked locations). You can load this into your GPS device to check out problems while out surveying. The "GPX export (open bugs)" link does the same, but only for the unresolved issues.

2.3 OpenRouteService and YourNavigation

The University of Heidelberg in Germany runs OpenRouteService. Originally invented at Bonn University, OpenRouteService was the first web-based OpenStreetMap routing service. The `www.openrouteservice.org` website lets you interactively select a start and destination location on the map and quickly finds an optimal route.

You can also enter start and destination addresses (see figure 2-4). If OpenStreetMap has the relevant house numbers mapped, OpenRouteService will take you door to door. It can find you the best route, whether you are planning to drive, walk, or cycle, and allows you to download computed routes as a GPX file for your GPS device.

By marking *avoid areas,* you can force OpenRouteService to find a route that goes around one or more places rather than through them.

---

2 JOSM requires a plugin for that to work, see page 136.

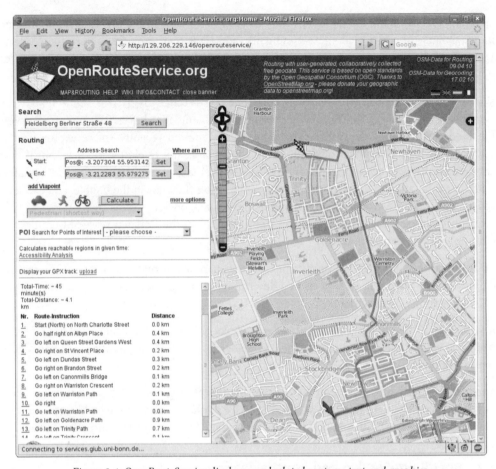

Figure 2-4: OpenRouteService displays a calculated route as text and graphics.

OpenRouteService has some other interesting features, among them a directory service that finds *points of interest* (POI, e. g. post offices, restaurants, etc.) in the vicinity of a given location, and you can perform an accessibility analysis that highlights the area reachable from a given start point in a given time.

OpenRouteService currently covers Europe only.

The OpenRouteService source code is not available, but the service can be used through standardized Open Location Services (OpenLS) interfaces.

There is an alternative Open Source routing service called YOURS, which you can access at yournavigation.org. YOURS is based on the free OSM routing engine Gosmore (see section 19.13). YOURS supports a large number of diverse modes of transportation, such as traveling by car, on foot, by bicycle, motorcycle, or motorbike or even heavy goods vehicle or public service vehicle. The service has worldwide coverage and offers altitude profiles for some areas in Europe.

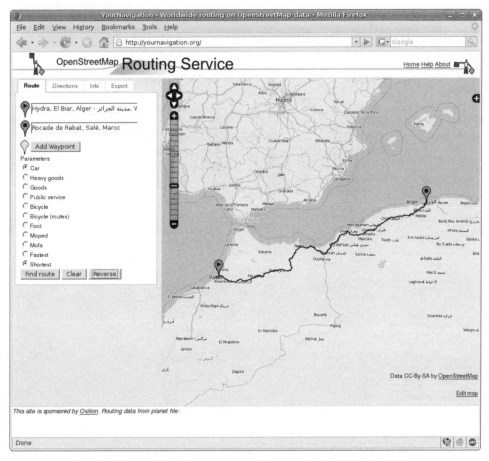

Figure 2-5: Using YourNavigation to produce a route from Rabat to Algiers.

There are also commercial offerings of OpenStreetMap-based routing services, most notably from US-based supplier Cloudmade (www.cloudmade.com) and from Geofabrik in Germany (www.geofabrik.de).

2.4 The Best of OSM

If you are interested in some highlights of OpenStreetMap data collection and mapping, visit www.bestofosm.org, a showcase page that celebrates OSM successes and pioneering events past and present (see figure 2-6). The website collects interesting locations in four categories: "Interesting Places", which are simply well known or famed; "Data Imports", where OSM has successfully imported data from other sources; "OSM History", places that are important to the history of OSM; and "Best of OSM", places that are mapped to an impressive standard.

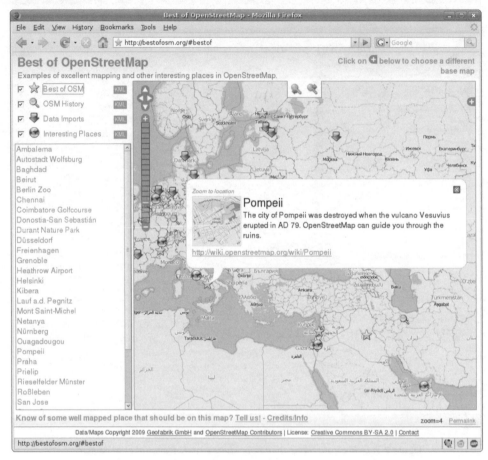

Figure 2-6: Best of OSM shows interesting places on the OpenStreetMap map.

2.5 National and Regional Resources

There are national OpenStreetMap pages in many countries and languages, and the list is growing constantly. Some of these national pages are listed in the table at the end of this section.

Most of these national websites link to local OSM groups and initiatives, and many also have their own map, sometimes with localized rendering styles. These websites are not operated centrally by the project, but rather by community members in their own countries.

They also don't have direct access to the raw data or user data, so lose some of the functionality of the main OSM website (such as map exporting, the "edit" tab, or community services, which will be discussed in the next chapter).

As the main OpenStreetMap page has now acquired multi-language capabilities, the national web pages may have become less relevant, but they are still often the first port of call for people interested in OpenStreetMap in that country and may have information about national events or carry community news. You can find more information about OpenStreetMap in different countries in the appendix.

The following screenshot shows the German OpenStreetMap website, which introduces visitors to the project, links to current events and mapper resources, and pinpoints local groups on the map so that people can join the nearest regular mapper meeting.

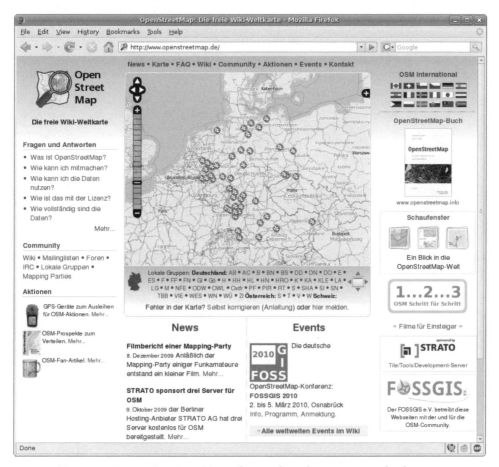

Figure 2-7: German OpenStreetMap website with markers pinpointing local groups.

Countries with national OpenStreetMap sites include:

Canada	`www.openstreetmap.ca`	Philippines	`www.openstreetmap.org.ph`
Chile	`www.openstreetmap.cl`	Poland	`www.openstreetmap.pl`
Czech Republic	`www.openstreetmap.cz`	Slovakia	`www.openstreetmap.sk`
Ethiopia	`www.openstreetmap.org.et`	South Africa	`www.openstreetmap.org.za`
France	`www.openstreetmap.fr`	Spain	`www.openstreetmap.es`
Germany	`www.openstreetmap.de`	Sweden	`www.openstreetmap.se`
Italy	`www.openstreetmap.it`	Switzerland	`www.openstreetmap.ch`
Japan	`www.openstreetmap.jp`	Taiwan	`openstreetmap.tw`
Netherlands	`www.openstreetmap.nl`		

If your country doesn't have a national OSM website yet, why not create one?

3 The OpenStreetMap Community

While the map data and software created in OpenStreetMap are undoubtedly important, the heart and soul of the project is the community, the people supporting the project. Without people to compile and maintain the data, all that has been collected would quickly decay and become much less useful.

This chapter discusses how to join the OSM community, how to communicate with other mappers, and the social aspects of being part of the community.

3.1 Your OpenStreetMap Account

If you only want to read OpenStreetMap data or the wiki, you don't have to register. But as soon as you want to upload something, or become more involved, you need a username and a password. In fact you'll need two username-password combinations, one for the wiki (`wiki.openstreetmap.org`) and another one for the database and the community website (`www.openstreetmap.org`). You can register with each by clicking on the relevant link in the top right corner of the page ("create account" or "sign up").

The Community Website

When you sign up on the community website, you can set the coordinates for your home location, and then you will be shown a list of other mappers in the vicinity. In addition the community website currently lets you:

- Exchange messages with other mappers (whom you only know by screen name, not by e-mail address).
- Upload a small personal profile for other mappers to see.
- Keep a mapping diary (blog), which others can read.
- Upload *GPS tracks* (the recordings of movements from a GPS receiver) and browse the database for tracks uploaded by others.

You don't have to use any of these features of course, but you do need to register before you can upload map data or use an online editor to make changes.

The Wiki

The OpenStreetMap project uses a wiki mainly for the following purposes:

- Documentation of software and procedures; most importantly documentation of data attributes used (the *Map Features,* see chapter 7).
- Event calendar.
- Coordination of local mapping work – many geographical areas have their own pages in the wiki where mapping progress is recorded and issues are discussed.

From time to time we link to the wiki from this book, and we use a dashed underline to mark the names of wiki articles: e. g. Map Features.

Most wiki pages are in English, but this being an international project, people have started to translate pages into other major languages. If the same article is available in different languages, the non-English ones will usually carry the same name as the English ones but will be prefixed with a language code (e. g. "DE:Map Features" is Map Features in German). Pages that are only available in a non-English language will often carry the national language name without language code.

As with most other wikis, the motto is: Be bold! If you find a mistake or if you think something is missing, just fix it. The wiki is based on MediaWiki (`www.mediawiki.org`), which you may already be familiar with from Wikipedia.

Protecting Your Privacy

When you register on the community web page, you have to specify your e-mail address and a *screen name.* You can use any name you want for this; some mappers use a nickname, some their real name. Your e-mail address will never be shown to others, but others may send you e-mail by creating a message through a web form on the community site.

Whenever the OpenStreetMap database is edited, the screen name of the editing user is recorded. The editing history (describing who edited what and when) is publicly available.

When you upload GPS tracks, you can choose how public your tracks should be. Choose "Identifiable" if you want to allow everybody to see the uploaded data (including the complete GPX file). The data will be marked with your screen name and will appear in the list of uploaded tracks. Choose "Trackable" if you don't want other people to see the connection to your screen name and you don't want them to be able to download the complete file. In this case the data is only available as single anonymous points through the API (Application Programming Interface – chapter 22 describes the OSM API in detail), but the points keep their original *timestamp* (the recording time information). Finally, the "Private" option removes the timestamps from the points so that people can only see that somebody was at this point at some time. (Of course you can only achieve real privacy if you don't upload your data at all.) There is also a fourth option, "Public", which has been used in the past to allow others to download your GPX files, but unlike "Identifiable", which is preferred, and also unlike "Trackable", the "Public" option does not expose timestamps on the API. The more data you allow to be accessed, the more useful your GPS tracks are. Timestamps, for example, can be used by editing software to find out which speed the receiver was traveling at and color the track display accordingly. But even "Private" tracks are better than none.

If you are very concerned about your privacy, you may create multiple accounts with OpenStreetMap and, for example, upload data from your vacation under another username than those from home. Nobody in OpenStreetMap will object to that. The most important reason for not allowing totally anonymous edits is that mappers want to be able to contact anyone about their contribution, and that is possible regardless of how many accounts you have.

Contacting Other Mappers

Every mapper's screen name is published together with their contributions to the database. Everyone can see who was active in a given area or timespan, or who made a certain edit.

If you stumble upon something in the database that looks wrong to you, or if you notice that a certain user makes a lot of changes that you disagree with (or that you want to congratulate them on), you can access the URL http://www.openstreetmap.org/user/displayname and use the "send message" link there. The receiving user will be able to see the message in the web interface and also get the contents of your message in an e-mail. The receiving user only sees your screen name, not your e-mail address, and they can respond either through the web interface or by e-mail, which will go back to OpenStreetMap and then be forwarded to you.

When contacting other mappers, always try to keep it friendly, even if you are contacting them because you disagree with an edit that they have made. OpenStreetMap members generally don't make edits with malicious intent – in most cases you will find that there was some misunderstanding or simply a mistake made when using the editor.

The help.openstreetmap.org Site

At help.openstreetmap.org, anybody can ask questions about OpenStreetMap and anybody can answer them. What makes this site special is the ranking system that allows you to find interesting questions and good answers more easily. The site is moderated by its users: If your contributions are voted up by others you get "karma" points. The more points you have, the more moderation options you get.

3.2 Mailing Lists and Forums

A lot of important communications in OpenStreetMap are transmitted through the mailing lists. You can either subscribe to them directly, or participate through the GMANE web service at http://dir.gmane.org/index.php?prefix=gmane.comp.gis.openstreetmap.

A list of available mailing lists can be found at lists.openstreetmap.org. From there, you can directly subscribe to one of the lists or browse their archives.

The following is an excerpt from that list:

Mailing List	Purpose
newbies	list for beginners' questions
dev	list for OSM software developers
talk	generic project mailing list
josm-dev	list for JOSM developers and suggestions
talk-us	specific mailing list for the US
talk-gb	specific mailing list for the UK
talk-ca	specific mailing list for Canada
tail-au	specific mailing list for Australia
legal-talk	list for discussion of licensing, attribution and copyright issues
routing	list for developers and users of OSM-based routing software

There are national mailing lists for dozens of other countries (with discussions usually held in the national language). Communities in countries with most OSM activity, among them Germany, the UK, and the US, have also started to set up local and regional lists.

There is also a web-based forum at forum.openstreetmap.org if you prefer that mode of communication. This forum has a number of thematic and regional boards, some in different languages. In some countries, OSM also has nationwide discussion forums run by the national cyclist or geocaching organizations.

3.3 Keeping Track – Trac and Subversion

OpenStreetMap uses the Subversion (SVN) revision control system. You can retrieve current or older versions of OSM software from svn.openstreetmap.org at any time. If you want to contribute your own software or change existing packages, you will require an account for write access to SVN. This is usually granted without further ado if you write an e-mail to one of the administrators (read more on the wiki page Accounts).

In addition to Subversion, the project uses the issue tracking software Trac to record problems or enhancement requests. Read more on Subversion in section 21.2.

3.4 The OpenStreetMap Chat on IRC

Day and night, you will likely find around a hundred OpenStreetMap project members on the Internet Relay Chat (IRC) channel #OSM (server `irc.oftc.net`). Many have IRC running while they do something else but are alerted if their name is mentioned. The IRC channel is a very good way to get in touch with people quickly if something doesn't work or needs fixing on the server side. If you do not have an IRC client, you can also access the channel with a web browser at `http://irc.openstreetmap.org/`. The wiki has more in the article IRC.

3.5 Mapping Parties

A *mapping party* is a planned event, lasting from an evening to several days, where participants get together to work systematically to improve OSM coverage in a given area. A good mapping party has three important outcomes:

- OpenStreetMap coverage is improved.
- Local people who aren't yet mappers but are interested in the project get a chance to see how it works.
- Local OSMers (or OSM tourists coming in from further afield) get to know each other better, and exchange ideas.

A mapping party usually begins with an introduction to help newcomers understand what is happening. Afterwards tasks are assigned and people start mapping. Later in the day, people meet again to postprocess the GPS tracks that they have collected and to upload their results to the OSM server. When the work is done, participants often head to a restaurant or pub to socialize.

The organization of a mapping party typically involves taking stock of what data is already available and dividing the work to be done into parcels of varying complexity (perhaps even into separate parcels for every mode of transport involved). That way, every participant can find a task that suits them. Newcomers can either be asked to do a small task on their own once they have been told how things work, or they can go with an experienced mapper to learn from them.

The base camp for a mapping party should be a place where people can safely store their belongings (especially laptops) while they map. Ideally, the location should also offer a good Internet connection, and space to do data entry and uploading.

Mapping parties are not organized centrally and you don't have to ask anyone before you set up your own. If you think that there isn't enough OpenStreetMap activity in your area, just run a mapping party! There are a number of tips on running mapping parties on the wiki: Mapping Weekend Howto.

The OpenStreetMap Foundation has a pool of GPS devices that they will loan for community projects if you think that you require some. Attending OSMers often have spare GPS devices for the use of novice mappers.

3.6   Meetings and Conferences

Since 2007, OpenStreetMap has had its own annual conference called "State of the Map" (`www.stateofthemap.org`). The two- or three-day event usually centers around talks by active OSMers about their current area of work, but also has presentations from speakers outside of OSM, discussing other aspects of free map data or possible uses for OSM. The main purpose of the conference is of course the same as for mapping parties or other get-togethers: Socializing (with food and drinks) in the evening, getting to know each other, and matching a face with a name you know only from the mailing list or IRC.

There are other regular international meetings, among them the OSM birthday party, which has until now always taken place in London on a day in August, and the annual general meeting of the OpenStreetMap Foundation, which is often at the same time and place as one of the other events.

Some countries have their own, national conferences. For example, there is the FOSSGIS conference in Germany, a US version of State of the Map, and a national conference in Italy.

3.7   The OpenStreetMap Foundation and its Local Chapters

The OpenStreetMap Foundation (OSMF) is a not-for-profit UK company that aims to support free mapping in general, and in particular OpenStreetMap. OSMF supports OpenStreetMap by doing publicity work, collecting donations for hardware and other things that need to be bought, and helping to organize mapping parties. The Foundation is also the owner of the openstreetmap.org domain name and any registered trademarks, as well as the maintainer of all the OpenStreetMap servers.

In contrast to the project itself, OSMF has (because the law requires it) a board of directors with well-defined decision-making processes. But OSMF decisions are not binding for the project and don't usually concern OSM directly – OSMF usually just decides how to organize itself or how best to spend money on the project.

Currently for UK £15 per annum, anyone can become a member of the Foundation (see wiki article Foundation). However, membership is in no way a pre-requisite for contributing to OpenStreetMap. In some countries there are national organizations that do the OSMF's work there. Check the OSMF website (`www.osmfoundation.org`) to see if there is a local chapter in your country.

Part II

OpenStreetMap for Contributors

In this part, we'll guide you through becoming an OpenStreetMap mapper, starting from choosing a GPS device and collecting data through to editing and uploading to OpenStreetMap. The first chapter discusses various factors about GPS data, then we take you through a typical survey with our mapper Max to introduce you to the processes. The following chapters contain the finer detail on what terms to use for mapping. Then we cover the various editing tools that you can use to enter data into OSM. The final chapter in this part helps you to understand copyright and licensing issues – what you can and can't do.

4 On the Road with Your GPS Device

The "original" way of acquiring data for OpenStreetMap is collecting *tracks* (that is, recorded itineraries) with a GPS device, and then editing and uploading them using a computer. There are other ways of course – data can be traced from satellite imagery, and a lot has been imported from public data sources – but only with a GPS are you truly independent of existing data. Thus the GPS device is still the most important tool for any OSM mapper. This chapter explains how GPS works and has practical recommendations for using GPS devices with OpenStreetMap.

4.1 The Global Positioning System

The US Department of Defense started researching a satellite-based positioning system in the 1970s. This work resulted in the Global Positioning System (GPS), which became fully operational in 1995. Twenty-four satellites[1] were launched into carefully aligned orbits, so that several of them are always visible from any place on earth. The satellites broadcast a timing and location signal, which a GPS receiver uses to calculate its position.

GPS was first and foremost a system for military use, and it is still the Pentagon that foots the operations bill. But today, civilian users vastly outnumber the military ones. GPS is used for navigation in cars, ships, and aircraft; for surveying; for fleet management; and for countless other purposes. And for OpenStreetMap, of course.

In order not to make it too easy for the enemy, military-grade GPS receivers were initially able to perform more accurate positioning than those available on the general consumer market. The civilian devices received an artificially distorted signal. This scheme, known as Selective Availability (SA), was discontinued in 2000, and the Pentagon affirmed that there were no plans to re-introduce it. There are now too many important civilian GPS appli-

---

1 A few more have been launched since to increase accuracy further.

cations, like aviation, that would be jeopardized by a loss of precision. This means that civilian uses, including OpenStreetMap, can now benefit from the best possible GPS precision.[2] There are no usage or license fees for operating a GPS receiver.

There are other satellite-based positioning systems. The Russian Federation operates a system called GLONASS, which is currently used exclusively by the military. The European Union is developing a system of its own under the name Galileo, but this has suffered several political delays and setbacks. At least for civilian, non-commercial use, GPS is expected to enjoy a monopoly for years to come.

4.2 The GPS Signal

The signal that is broadcast by each GPS satellite contains the satellite's current position and a high-precision timestamp. The GPS receiver uses the timing information to calculate how far away from the satellite it is, and if four or more satellite signals are available, this is sufficient for the receiver to determine its current position in three dimensions (a 3D fix).

In addition to the positioning signal itself, GPS satellites also broadcast a list of orbital parameters for all satellites, known as the *almanac,* which the GPS device needs for its position calculation. A GPS receiver that has been switched off for a long time, or has moved a long distance while offline, may require up to 15 minutes to download that information during what is called a *cold start.* If switched on again in the same area as before, the list of satellites is still in its memory, and the receiver will only need seconds to acquire a signal and determine its position. This is called a *warm start.*

A scheme called "Assisted GPS" (AGPS) reduces the time required for a cold start. AGPS devices can load the almanac data from the Internet or over a mobile phone network. If such a network connection is available, this allows for a significantly faster cold start. Only the almanac is downloaded over the network connection; the positioning still uses satellite signals exclusively.

4.3 Satellite Visibility and Positional Fix

The signal quality and therefore the accuracy of the positional fix depends on many factors. The most important ones are how many satellites the receiver can "see", and how strong the signal is when arriving at the receiver. Reception from four satellites is sufficient to determine the receiver's position in 3D space. However, the more satellites that are visible to the receiver, the better the positional accuracy will be.

---

2   There is still a minor difference between the unencrypted civilian GPS signal (SPS) and the encrypted military signal (PPS). The difference in accuracy is minimal, but the military signal is less susceptible to distortion or manipulation.

In a flat, open area, it is not uncommon for a GPS receiver to see eight or more satellites, but in a city with high buildings it can be difficult to find enough satellites. GPS signals are shielded by mountains, walls, and even car bodies and trees – much more than mobile phone signals are. Only high-quality receivers have any reception at all inside buildings (and even then you often have to go near a window to get a position fix). You can generally get a fix in a car, though modern car windows often have a metal coating that interferes with the GPS signal. In trams and trains it will sometimes work. Do experiment – there is often a sweet spot with good enough reception somewhere. In cars this is usually near the rear window, and in sealed modern trains you can sometimes get reception in the passage between two cars.

The positional fix is better if the visible satellites are spread out across the sky. If all the satellites seen by the receiver are in a row or close to each other, precision will suffer. This dispersion or proximity of satellites can be expressed in a numerical value, called the Dilution of Precision (DOP). Often this is further divided into a horizontal (HDOP) and vertical (VDOP) precision value. The smaller the value the better: A value of 1 is best; values greater than 10 mean you can't get a position fix. DOP values are not normally shown on the GPS display, nor are they saved with the track data; to retrieve them, the receiver will have to be connected to a computer that reads the NMEA data stream (see page 36).

In theory, GPS receivers can determine not only their current latitude and longitude, but also their altitude. But since all visible satellites are always above the receiver (or more precisely, those that are below are shadowed by the Earth), it is impossible to get a good altitude fix. GPS is therefore unsuitable for precise altitude measurement. Good GPS receivers often have a built-in barometric altimeter. This allows for precise altitude measurement (a barometric altimeter can easily detect altitude differences of one meter or less). Because barometric pressure is weather dependent, these devices need to be calibrated with reference to a known altitude before each use. For example, if you know the exact altitude of your front porch, you would simply set the altimeter to that altitude before you go on a trip.

4.4 Differential GPS

In a best-case scenario, even a modern GPS receiver won't give you more than ±5 meter accuracy. The limited accuracy that GPS offers led to the development of an enhanced system called Differential GPS (DGPS). DGPS uses two GPS receivers: You leave one stationary at a known location and take the other with you. As long as you remain in roughly the same area as the stationary device, the inaccuracies introduced by atmospheric conditions and the slight signal distortion that goes along with them will be the same for both devices. Special algorithms can then be used to correct the signal from the moving GPS using the distortions measured with the stationary GPS. DGPS allows for sub-meter accuracy, but DGPS-enabled receivers are very expensive, so they are generally only used by professional surveyors.

WAAS (Wide Area Augmentation System, used in the US) and EGNOS (European Geostationary Navigation Overlay Service) are similar enhancements. With these systems, a standardized calibration signal is broadcast from additional satellites. Many consumer-grade GPS devices already support these systems, and while they don't offer the same high accuracy as DGPS, a WAAS or EGNOS signal is still better than just plain GPS reception. Whether or not you can receive such a calibration signal depends on local and atmospheric conditions.

4.5   Is GPS Accurate Enough?

When people hear that OpenStreetMap wants to survey the world using GPS devices, they tend to be skeptical about the accuracy. Being able to measure a position to within ±5 meter accuracy doesn't sound too great. But in practice this isn't really a problem. It may not be sufficient for a large-scale map with highly accurate property boundaries – but for city or area maps that OpenStreetMap produces, an accuracy of ±5 meters is perfectly adequate. Roads are usually a few meters wide and you don't travel down the middle of the road when surveying them. Whether your results are a few meters off to the North or to the South is of little concern – it is much more important to get the topology right. For example, you have to be able to clearly say whether a road is connected to another road or whether it is a dead-end that just happens to be close.

You can achieve sightly better accuracy by surveying the same road multiple times – ideally on different days, when satellite positions and atmospheric influence are different. OSM supports that by allowing (and recommending) that people upload their unedited GPS tracks to the server. When drawing a road, you always have access to all GPS tracks recorded along this road, and you can visually even things out. This is always a manual process though – it can't be done automatically.

GPS accuracy becomes more of a problem when surveying buildings, because reception is bad right next to a wall. The wall tends to shadow half of the available satellites – this is called the *canyon effect*. It is virtually impossible to map all corners and protrusions of a complex building with GPS alone. If there is suitable aerial imagery available for the area then you can use that to draw the building outline.

Large buildings can also be mapped by recording *waypoints* (individual named or numbered locations stored in the GPS receiver) lying a few meters out along the projected sides of the building and later determining the intersection between the lines going through these points (figure 4-1).

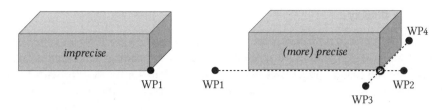

Figure 4-1: Mapping the corner of a building directly (left) or as an intersection (right).

There is no GPS reception in tunnels of course. Many GPS devices will interpolate along the last known trajectory for a few seconds and act as if they still had reception – hoping that the interruption will only be temporary. Shortly after the tunnel exit, GPS tracks created by these devices tend to have a clearly visible jump in them, when the signal was reconnected. But for OpenStreetMap purposes it isn't vital to know where exactly the tunnel is; having good fixes for both ends of the tunnel is sufficient for the initial survey. Someone else with local knowledge or with specialist equipment can refine the data later.

When the GPS receiver is stationary, for example when stopping the car, the position fix is usually less accurate than while moving, because the receiver software is optimized for use in motion. The track then contains characteristic "point clouds", as even though the device was stationary, a slightly different position was recorded every second.

4.6 GPS Receiver Designs

There are a large number of GPS devices available on the market for different kinds of users. This section explains the different designs of receivers and their suitability for OpenStreetMap.

Devices without Display

There are two kinds of GPS receivers without display: Data loggers and GPS mice.

Data loggers use their internal memory to regularly record their position. These tracks can later be loaded onto a computer and processed there. Data loggers are very small and light, and have a good battery life. Data loggers are a good choice if you want to record your track on a trip but don't need to actually read out the current position while on the road.

In contrast, GPS mice don't have any memory of their own; they only consist of the GPS chipset and an antenna. GPS mice have to be used in conjunction with a computer or a PDA, and they transmit the GPS position using Bluetooth or a USB or serial cable. GPS mice are very small and cheap. When operating on USB, they don't need their own power supply. GPS mice are a good choice if you are traveling with a notebook or PDA anyway.

Many devices combine data logger and GPS mouse capabilities.

Devices with a Display

Older or cheaper devices with a display can show the current position as coordinates as well as the track traveled and any waypoints, but they can't show a map. Better and more modern devices can handle maps, and many even have built-in routing (provided that the map data supports it). Many devices are built for specific uses, like walking, aviation, or nautical use.

OSM maps can be installed on nearly all GPS devices designed by Garmin (if they have the map capability – see section 19.3). For Magellan devices, the existing Garmin maps can be converted, or the Mobile Mapper Office software can be used to create Magellan maps directly.

Other Devices

In addition to standalone GPS devices, there is a host of other devices with built-in GPS chips, most notably mobile phones or PDAs. Whether or not these can be used for OpenStreetMap depends largely on the software available for the platform in question. There are already OSM editors developed specifically for mobile phones or PDAs, but not every platform is supported equally well.

Car Navigation Systems

Car navigation systems come in many flavors – from built-in devices for the radio slot, through mobile devices to software for PDAs. Many of these can't be used for OpenStreetMap work because they don't let you save or access GPS data, but it may be worthwhile to check on the Internet what your specific make and model will let you do. For example, there is software that can be installed on most devices made by TomTom to record tracks.

4.7 Choosing a GPS for OSM

This section tells you the features to look out for if you want to contribute to OpenStreetMap and are considering buying a GPS receiver for that purpose. (The following ignores other criteria, like suitability for in-car navigation, which might of course also influence your decision.)

> ☞ *The OpenStreetMap wiki has detailed reports on various GPS units on the GPS Reviews page.*

The first thing you have to decide is how you want to do your mapping. Are you planning to simply let the GPS run while you are on the move, and not take any notes? This calls for a data logger, which you stow away in a pocket and which silently records your track. But if you want to take things further and record waypoints and make notes to improve your surveying, then you might want to go for a device with display, which makes these things much easier.

Below we list some criteria that you might want to consider when choosing a device. If, after reading this, you are still unsure, read about the practical aspects of mapping in chapter 5 to get a clearer picture of what the task involves.

Track Memory

The device needs to have memory to store the track you have traveled. There should be enough memory to save a few hours' worth of track logs without losing older data. (Many devices automatically discard the oldest bits of track when the memory is full without telling you.) Some devices have a slot for a Micro-SD memory card that you can save multiple tracks to.

Setting Waypoints

A method to set and store waypoints is a very important mapping requirement. This lets you mark points of interest along the way, for later processing in the editor. Setting a waypoint should be possible by pressing a single button – devices where you have to navigate through a menu to do this tend to be cumbersome in use.

Waypoints are typically numbered automatically. It is desirable for the GPS device to immediately display the number assigned to a new waypoint, so that you can write it down together with your notes. Some devices have the option of assigning names or special icons to waypoints, but that is a feature you will seldom use while mapping.

Interfaces, Data Transfer, and Data Formats

Being able to process the collected GPS data on a computer is the most important aspect of OpenStreetMap surveying. Modern GPS devices usually have either a USB connector or a Bluetooth interface for transferring data. Older devices may have (RS232) serial interfaces. If your device has a memory card, you can also eject the card and insert it into a card reader on the computer. Any way to access the data is fine. Data transfer protocols and formats differ between vendors. Ideally, the device should support the GPX standard or the NMEA format (see section 4.9 for more discussion on these formats). If the conversion software GPSBabel (see section 4.10) supports the device or its data format then you probably will have no data transfer problems.

Mounting

You need a method of mounting the GPS receiver on your chosen mode of transport. If you are on a bicycle or a motorcycle, you will probably use a handlebar mount. For cars, there are mounts with suction cups that go on the windscreen. Lightweight GPS receivers can also be fitted with a non-skid pad and placed in a corner of the dashboard.

Map Display

GPS devices that display the current OSM map (see color plate 4) are a great help when working in sparsely mapped areas. If you pass a road that isn't on the map, you can quickly follow it to collect the missing information, and if you see a point of interest that the map doesn't have, you can immediately set a new waypoint and make a note.

Modern GPS Chipset

Every GPS device has a built-in GPS chipset that decodes GPS signals and computes the position. Only a handful of vendors make these chipsets, so GPS devices from many different brands all use the same chipset. Newer generations of chipsets are much better than old ones, because they can decode more satellite signals simultaneously and have better algorithms to allow a position fix even when reception is weak. The SiRFstarIII chipset is among those with a proven track record.

External Antenna

Sometimes being able to connect an external antenna makes the difference between getting or not getting a positional fix, for example when metal-coated car or train windows make reception impossible. In these cases, an external antenna can sometimes be taped to (or mounted on) the outside of the vehicle. Consumer GPS devices seldom have the option of connecting an external antenna.

4.8 Types of GPS Data

GPS devices operate on three different types of data:

Tracks, or *traces,* are recordings of the movement of the device. A track consists of track segments and these in turn consist of trackpoints. A trackpoint contains at least a latitude and longitude value, but depending on the type of device, it may also have a timestamp, speed or altitude information, or HDOP/VDOP values. Trackpoints are often saved a fixed number of seconds apart, but some devices also save trackpoints only when the direction changes or the device moves farther than a pre-configured distance. Every time the device loses reception or is switched off it will start a new track segment.

Waypoints are set manually by pressing a button on the GPS device. Much like a trackpoint, the waypoint has a position and possibly timestamp; in contrast to a trackpoint however, waypoints may have a name and an associated icon or even multimedia content. If you don't assign a name, waypoints will simply be numbered sequentially.

Routes consist of a number of points *(routepoints)* that must be visited in sequence to get to a destination. Routes are of no relevance to OpenStreetMap.

4.9 GPS Data Formats

GPS data can be transmitted and stored in various data formats. Many vendors have their own format, but the vendor-independent GPX and NMEA formats are widely understood. There is a free software program called GPSBabel for converting between all kinds of GPS data formats (see page 36). OpenStreetMap generally uses the GPX format.

GPX

GPX (GPS Exchange Format) is an XML-based format for saving GPS tracks, waypoints, and routes. The following example has two waypoints named "001" and "002" as well as a track consisting of four trackpoints.

```
<gpx version="1.1" creator="GPSBabel - http://www.gpsbabel.org"
    xmlns:xsi="http://www.w3.org/2001/XMLSchema-instance"
    xmlns="http://www.topografix.com/GPX/1/1"
    xsi:schemaLocation="http://www.topografix.com/GPX/1/1 ∠
                        http://www.topografix.com/GPX/1/1/gpx.xsd">
  <wpt lat="49.78581670637695" lon="9.26481034667384">
    <time>2007-10-01T11:46:27Z</time>
    <name>001</name>
  </wpt>
  <wpt lat="49.786560191735184" lon="9.265752519584733">
    <time>2007-10-01T11:48:47Z</time>
    <name>002</name>
  </wpt>
  <trk>
    <trkseg>
      <trkpt lat="49.78581670637695" lon="9.26481034667384">
        <time>2007-10-01T11:46:27Z</time>
      </trkpt>
      <trkpt lat="49.78589781442508" lon="9.264705660794853">
        <time>2007-10-01T11:46:32Z</time>
      </trkpt>
      <trkpt lat="49.78591133241991" lon="9.264831283849638">
        <time>2007-10-01T11:46:37Z</time>
      </trkpt>
      <trkpt lat="49.78603382143362" lon="9.264983716253345">
        <time>2007-10-01T11:46:42Z</time>
      </trkpt>
    </trkseg>
  </trk>
</gpx>
```

As usual with XML, the GPX format is quite flexible and can easily accommodate special-use extensions, for example for storing hyperlinks or references to sound recordings.

NMEA

The US National Marine Electronics Association (NMEA), a commercial association of vendors of electronics for marine use, has published a standard (NMEA 0183) for communication between navigational devices and other naval equipment. This standard is widely supported among GPS units, including consumer devices.

If you set the GPS to NMEA mode, it will start sending a continuous stream of different data "sentences", some of which for example refer to the current position, and some to the precision of the fix. Not all GPS devices support all types of NMEA sentences.

4.10 GPSBabel

GPSBabel (www.gpsbabel.org) is a versatile Open Source program for working with GPS tracks, waypoints, and routes. It supports downloading and uploading data from/to GPS devices and can convert between over 100 different GPS data formats. It also has filtering algorithms that allow you to weed out stray trackpoints or exclude everything outside a defined area. GPSBabel runs under Linux (from the command line) as well as under OS X and Windows (it supports a graphical user interface for these).

If you want to use the program with a graphical user interface under Linux, try Gebabbel (gebabbel.sf.net), which is an add-on for GPSBabel.

A GPSBabel command line is formatted like this:

```
gpsbabel [GPS types] -i input format -f input file
    -x filter
    -o output format -F output file
```

For GPS types, the options are tracks (-t), waypoints (-w), or routes (-r). The input and output file names may also be device names if you want to download from or upload to a GPS device. Specifying a filter is optional.

To download a GPS track from a Garmin GPS device, you would for example use the following command line:[3]

```
gpsbabel -t -i garmin -f usb: -o gpx -F myfile.gpx
```

In this example, only tracks (-t) will be downloaded using the Garmin format (-i garmin) from the USB interface (-f usb:). The tracks are then saved to the file myfile.gpx (-F

---

3 Note to users of Garmin GPS devices with memory cards: These devices only save the current end of the track to internal memory, and that's all that GPSBabel can access. Full track data has to be downloaded by connecting the device as a memory drive and directly copying the GPX files from there. These GPX files, however, don't contain waypoints; waypoints are only stored in the internal memory and have to be retrieved through GPSBabel.

myfile.gpx) in GPX format (-o gpx). If you want to download waypoints instead of tracks, replace -t by -w.

One of the helpful filters offered by GPSBabel is the "simplify" algorithm which removes points from a track without affecting its shape too much. Use it like this:

gpsbabel -t -i gpx -f in.gpx -x simplify,error=0.02k -o gpx -F out.gpx

GPSBabel loads a track from the file in.gpx and removes trackpoints as long as the shape of the track doesn't change by more than 20 meters (=0.02 km). The new, simplified track is saved as out.gpx.

GPSBabel has a whole range of other filters and options. Consult the GPSBabel website for a detailed user manual.

4.11 Handling the GPS Unit

When you switch on the GPS device, it can take anything from a few seconds to 15 minutes to find out about its current position (see the explanation of cold start and warm start on page 28). Even high-quality GPS receivers sometimes have trouble getting their initial positional fix when they are moving, so it is best to remain stationary until you get the fix. Once the fix is acquired, they can be moved at any speed without losing it.

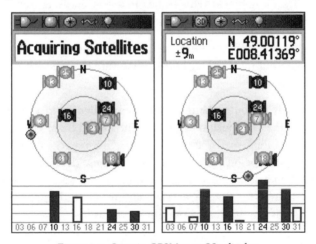

Figure 4-2: Garmin GPSMap 60CSx display.

Figure 4-2 shows two typical screen displays for a GPS device. On the left, the device is shown still searching for a good-enough satellite signal. It has already received data from four satellites, but not enough has been received from satellite 16 (the bar is not yet solid) to compute a positional fix. The height of the bars is an indicator of signal strength, and the circle shows the approximate position of the satellite in the sky. Satellite 21 is almost directly above the GPS receiver, and satellite 10 is on the horizon in the North-East. The satellites shown in light gray (for example 21 and 31) are expected to be in the position shown but no data has been received from them – a possible reason being some obstacle that is obscuring the view.

On the right, a positional fix has been acquired, and the position is shown in a box at the top of the screen. There is also an indication of the estimated accuracy (±9 meters). The four satellites with the solid bars contribute to the positional fix, and those with the outlined bars don't do so yet.

Important Settings

The device must be configured to record a track that can later be used as a basis for editing OpenStreetMap data.

Many devices have the option of saving trackpoints only when a certain distance has been traveled. This saves memory and thus allows for longer trips without having to download data from the device. However, some information is still lost, and tracks are more difficult to postprocess in an editor. GPSBabel (see section 4.10) can simplify tracks in this way even after they have been recorded with a frequency of one per second. That's why we suggest that you have the device record one trackpoint per second, regardless of whether you are walking, cycling, or traveling by car. This results in a very accurate track that, for example, makes a clear distinction between a sharp bend in the road and a smooth curve.

If the device has a memory card, sometimes it can be configured to save tracks either to the memory card or to internal memory (or both). Make sure that enough memory is available at the selected destination.

Some devices with built-in route planners have a so-called *snap to road* function which automatically corrects the GPS position to match the loaded map. The device assumes that it will only ever travel along roads, and thus if the GPS reports a position slightly offset from a road, it is moved to be on the road. As long as these devices only make that correction for displaying the position, all is fine. Care has to be taken however that the track information saved and used for OpenStreetMap editing isn't influenced by the device's proprietary map data, as this might cause copyright problems.[4]

Be sure to set your device to use the WGS 84 map datum, or the reported position may be a few hundred meters out. You can read more about the map datums in the Geodesy appendix. WGS 84 is the default setting with most devices, but it is a good idea to check it.

---

4   A track saved in snap to road mode often has characteristic jumps from one road to another, parallel road, and also lacks the usual point clouds where the vehicle was stationary.

5 Mapping Practice

In this chapter we show you how to get started with mapping. You will see how to survey for OpenStreetMap and how to upload your data to the database.

OpenStreetMap has steadily increased in complexity. The large user community is constantly devising new and clever ways to improve and fine-tune the mapping process. Bewildered newcomers often look at the map display in an editor and ask themselves: How can I ever survey and enter that much detail? But a map is created in many iterations, often by different people. To give you an idea how a map develops, we will pick a hitherto unmapped area for our example, and we will leave out some details at first. The following chapters will then explain things in depth.

5.1 A Typical Mapping Example

We will accompany our exemplary mapper Max as he surveys an area for OpenStreetMap. He takes his GPS receiver, empties the track memory, and checks the settings. Max grabs a notepad and pencil and leaves his hotel room. Outside the hotel, he waits until the GPS receiver acquires a fix, receiving signals from enough satellites to determine its location.

His hotel is called the Mulberry Inn – Max doesn't even have to take one step before he can set his first waypoint. He presses a button on his GPS receiver, and the device responds with "001". Max makes a note of this on his notepad, "001 Mulberry Inn", and walks down the road to his right. It is a residential road; he doesn't have the name yet, but he writes it down as "highway=residential" nonetheless. Experienced mapper that he is, Max knows his "map features" by heart, including all the road types usually assigned to the highway key. For less experienced mappers, we provide an overview of road types on page 64. After a short walk, Max reaches a junction with two road signs: The road he is on is called Castle Way, and the road branching off to the left is Tower Road. Max instructs his GPS to store the current location as waypoint 002 and continues ahead.

After a few meters, Max notes a little stream passing under the road – waypoint 003: Who knows, maybe it will come in handy later. Max continues on Castle Way and finally reaches a busy main road, the name of which he can't find out. He adds another waypoint and decides to turn back and take Tower Road. On his way he passes a post box and marks it as waypoint 005 in his notes, together with its compass direction.

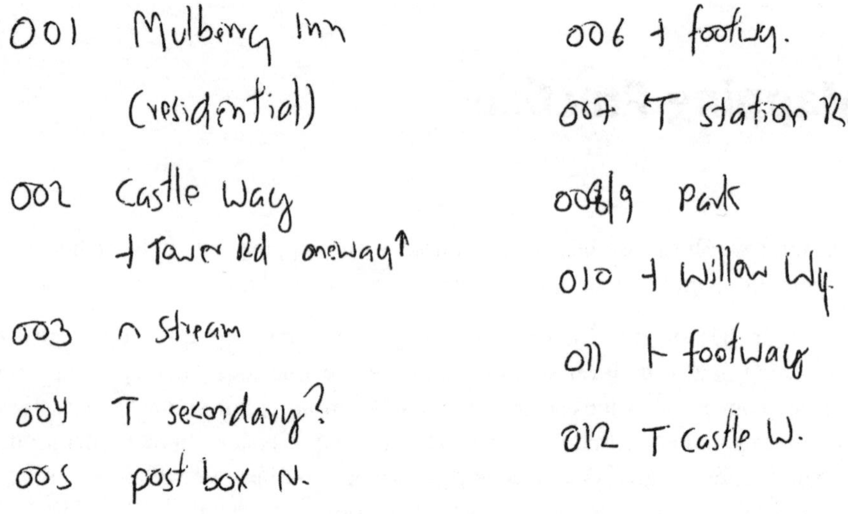

001 Mulberry Inn
(residential)

002 Castle Way
⌐ Tower Rd oneway↑

003 ∩ Stream

004 T secondary?

005 post box N.

006 ⌐ footway.

007 T Station Rd.

008/9 Park

010 ⌐ Willow Wy.

011 ⊢ footway

012 T Castle W.

Figure 5-1: Reference notes for this mapping tour.

Tower Road is a one-way street, and Max duly notes the fact. In between two houses he sees a footpath branching off to the left. He does not follow the path but records a way-point (006) there. Reaching the end of Tower Road, Max turns left into Station Road (007). There is a little park on the right-hand side. Max passes it by at first but then decides to quickly walk down the arc-shaped footpath through the park, recording waypoints 008 and 009 where it leaves and rejoins the road.

He continues on Station Road and then makes a left turn into Willow Way (010). Soon after that he sees the same footpath (011) which he had noticed branching off when walking down Tower Road. Max continues straight on, and soon he is back on Castle Way (012). Turning left, he is quickly back at the hotel.

In the peace of his hotel room, Max inspects the data he has collected. He transfers the GPS data onto the computer where it is stored in a GPX file. Max then uses the upload website http://www.openstreetmap.org/traces/mine to send his raw GPX files to the OSM server. In doing so, he specifies a short description and a number of keywords to make it easy for him (or someone else) to find the file later.

Max now fires up the JOSM editor (see chapter 10) and instructs it to open the GPX file he has saved from his GPS (figure 5-2).

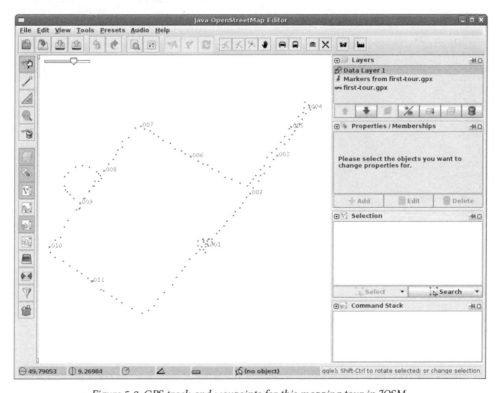

Figure 5-2: GPS track and waypoints for this mapping tour in JOSM.

Max has a decent GPS device, and his steps have been traced accurately, the only exception being a point cloud where Max stood waiting in front of the hotel at the start of his walk. As we said, such point clouds are often recorded while the GPS device is acquiring a signal after being switched on. All waypoints look correct, and they match the entries Max has written on his notepad.

Before Max can begin to enter his data, he has to cross-check what data is already available on the server. When he did so a few days ago, the area was a blank spot on the OSM map, but what will it look like now?

The JOSM Editor automatically selects the currently displayed area when downloading. Max zooms out a little bit to include data in the vicinity, and then instructs JOSM to download data from the OSM server (figure 5-3).

How cool! The busy road where Max turned around is already present in the data on the server, but nothing else is there.

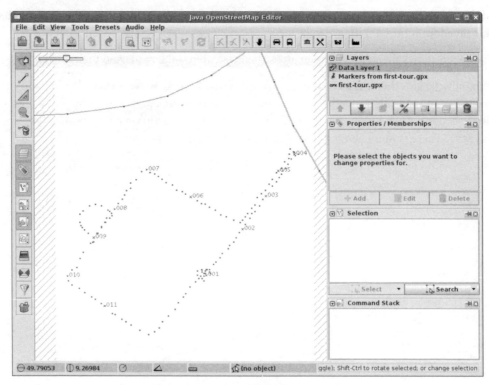

Figure 5-3: Data downloaded from the server.

Max draws the four new roads. Although the GPS trackpoints don't make a perfect straight line, Max remembers that the roads are straight, and he is content with placing one node at each corner rather than one node at every position recorded by the GPS device.

After he has completed the road layout, Max starts entering the attributes. Since all roads surveyed are residential roads, Max uses the tag highway=residential for all of them (see figure 5-4). In addition, Tower Road gets tagged with oneway=yes. And of course he also enters the names from his notepad for each of the roads. There is more about road tagging in section 7.1.

Figure 5-4: Adding a tag to an object.

In the North-East, Max connects his newly surveyed Castle Way to the existing road he has downloaded.

Figure 5-5 shows the map on screen after Max has entered the roads and their attributes.

Max now tackles the next items on his list, which are a bridge over a small stream, and the post box. To map the bridge he inserts two nodes into Castle Way and splits the road into three sections. Then he can tag the middle section with the additional tags bridge=yes and layer=1. There is more about tagging bridges and tunnels in section 7.1.

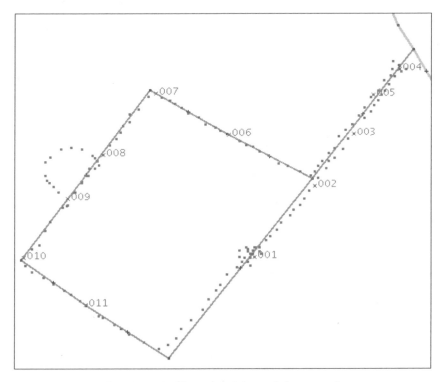

Figure 5-5: Max has entered the roads he surveyed.

Max doesn't have any information about the path of the stream, but nonetheless he draws the section he could see from the bridge. Maybe he (or someone else) will find some aerial imagery later that can be used to complete the stream, or the mapping of further bridges will lead to someone making a reasonable guess about where the stream runs, and map more of it.

For the post box, Max inserts a node, but he can't remember the correct tag to use so he opens the "presets" menu in the JOSM editor. There is a "man made" section, and in there he finds an "amenities" menu, which then offers the option "post box". Selecting this option, Max is asked about the operator of the post box (in many countries there is no mono-poly so it makes sense to specify that). The node is then tagged amenity=post_box. The same tag could have been entered manually; there is nothing special about using presets. For amenity=post_box, the editor displays a letter symbol at the location. Read more about tagging points of interest in sections 7.4 and 7.6.

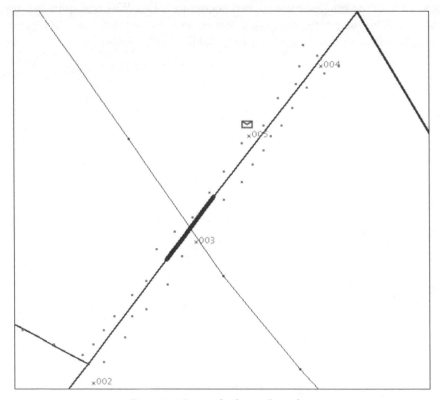

Figure 5-6: Stream, bridge, and post box.

There are three remaining items in the south-western part of the area surveyed: A park with a footpath, a hotel, and a path connecting two roads but without a GPS track.

Max adds the park with a rectangle tagged as leisure=park. More about tagging natural and leisure areas in sections 7.2 and 7.4. The footpath leading through the park is recorded as highway=footway and connected to the road.

The path connecting Tower Road and Willow Way is also recorded as highway=footway. Max doesn't have a GPS track, but on passing each end it was obvious that it was reasonably straight and direct. Since Max is aiming for perfection today, he adds source=extrapolation – which means "this isn't really surveyed but rather guesswork". This could prompt someone to refine it at a later date.

Finally, Max enters a node where his hotel is: tourism=hotel, name=Mulberry Inn. At reception, Max had seen a leaflet with a building outline; if the TV gets too boring then he might even draw it and tag it building=yes to make the map even more complete.

Figure 5-7 shows Max's final results in the editor.

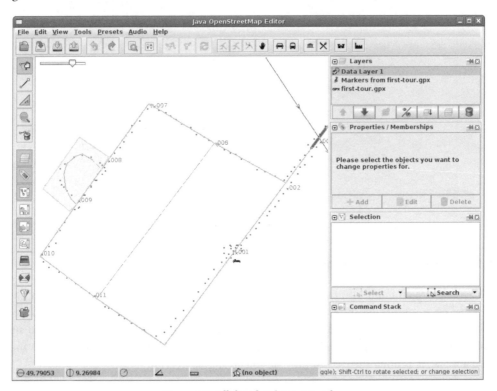

Figure 5-7: All data has been entered.

Max is happy with what he has achieved, and with a click on the upload button (fourth from left in the button bar at the top) he initiates the data upload to the OSM server.

Other users who download data for this area will see the new features immediately. Additionally, the changes will be made available in a change file on the server within minutes, and this file will be downloaded and processed by a number of mirror servers around the world. Other systems that carry current OpenStreetMap data perhaps only receive data changes in daily batches, so they will get Max's data in their next daily update.

Many map image servers, including the main tile server at www.openstreetmap.org, will automatically be aware of the changes and re-draw the map for the area within hours or even minutes. The work Max has done is in high demand!

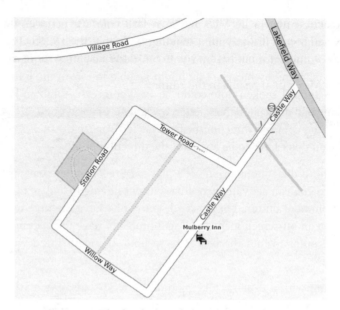

Figure 5-8: The finished result (see also color plate 6).

5.2 Notes and Recordings

GPS tracks are an important basis for mapping, but they are of little use on their own; they need to be accompanied by extra information like street names, road types, and points of interest. Newcomers to OSM are often surprised about this, because the press likes to simplify everything and is prone to claiming that OSM collects GPS tracks and combines them into a map. As is often the case, things are not so simple in reality!

You can record additional information in various ways. How you do it depends on your personal preferences, as well as your mode of transport. You can conveniently make notes on a slip of paper when you are traveling by train, but you will be less inclined to attempt this when riding a bicycle or motorcycle.

Mappers typically use paper to prepare written notes, or they record spoken notes on a voice recorder or an MP3 player. Some also use a digital camera to record street names and other interesting bits of information.

Mapping with a notepad (and, perhaps, a clipboard) gives you the ability to make quick sketches, for example when mapping a complex junction. If you are mapping an area that already has basic coverage in OpenStreetMap, you can print out the existing data and scribble notes on that. But be aware that making notes that you can still decipher at your PC a few hours later does require a certain diligence – it is easy to forget this when you are on the road and want to map things quickly!

If you use a voice recorder or an MP3 player, record your waypoint on the GPS first and then speak the number of the waypoint together with the description. This is a very efficient way of recording information, and you can describe things in more detail than on paper. If you are mapping by bicycle, you might be able to record the information without even stopping. A typical spoken note could be "waypoint 17: Abraham Road, residential" (consider spelling out difficult names letter by letter), or "waypoint 23: post box South-East". Specifying the compass direction instead of "left" or "right" makes postprocessing of the data easier; you don't have to be aware of the direction of travel.

When shopping for a dictaphone or an MP3 player to record spoken mapping notes, try to get a model where you can activate recording without having to look at the device – ideally by pressing a prominent button. On the road, you won't have the time or patience to find the right option in an on-screen menu. You will probably have to perform a number of test mapping rides in order to find the best way to hold or mount the device and operate it while mapping.

If you are mapping with a camera, take pictures of road signs and anything you want to put on the map later. The camera will record the exact time the picture was taken, and by matching the timestamps with the GPS track later you can determine the location of the picture.[1] If you tend to forget the direction in which you shot the photo, here's a trick to help you. Imagine that you're driving past a restaurant that you want to map. Then take three photos – one of the road in front of you, one at 45 degrees to show the road and the restaurant, and then a 90 degree shot of the restaurant so you can read the name.

Blurring can be a problem when taking photos of road (or other) signs, especially when moving. A big advantage of photos, however, for recording mapping data is that you won't introduce spelling errors with difficult names, and a camera release button can usually be operated even with motorcycle gloves on.

The OpenStreetMap editor JOSM, which we will cover later, has a built-in function to match photos or MP3 sound files to GPS locations, and to display or play them from within the editor. See chapter 10 on page 116.

Be aware that using a camera to photograph road signs could look a little strange: Be prepared to answer questions from worried residents and to explain OpenStreetMap to them.

5.3 Working with the Map

When you go out mapping, it is really useful to carry an OSM map of the area to see which bits are covered already. This map could be a paper printout, or it could be on your PDA or

---

1 There are cameras that record the current GPS position together with the photo, but they aren't widely used. Mobile phones equipped with both a camera and GPS often offer this option, too.

GPS device. A printed map is good if you want to scribble your notes directly onto it. Some people also use different colors to distinguish between road types or other features, to save on writing.

Obviously an electronic map that automatically shows the current area and the track already traveled is very convenient. Such a map lets you see instantly which parts are mapped already and which are still missing. Many Garmin GPS devices can display maps, for example, and there is software to convert OSM data into their map format, and to download sections of map to the device.

For a number of mobile devices there is also editing software that lets you directly enter and upload new data. It is often difficult to accurately map road geometries with these mobile editors, but they are very convenient for recording points of interest, road names, house numbers or similar information.

You find more about using OSM with Garmin and other mobile devices in chapter 19.

The Walking Papers Project

The Walking Papers project (`www.walking-papers.org`) is a great help for people who use printed maps as a basis for mapping. It simplifies the process of aligning data recorded on paper with was is already in the database.

Figure 5-9: Walking Papers map for parts of Halle, Germany.

On the project web page you can select an area from OpenStreetMap and generate a PDF file to print out. Take the printout with you and add things that are missing, just like you would do if you had printed the map directly from OSM.

Using a scanner, you load the map back into your computer, and send it to the Walking Papers website. Walking Papers will now analyze the QR code (the strange looking rectangle in the bottom right corner of the map), and use that information to georeference and straighten the document. After that, you can load your handwritten notes into your favorite editor[2] as a background layer and transfer them into tags on OpenStreetMap.

5.4 Working with Aerial Imagery

Instead of moving about with your GPS device, you can often map roads, rivers, or lakes conveniently from home by tracing them from aerial imagery. OpenStreetMap currently has two important sources for such imagery: The NASA Landsat images, and the satellite or aerial imagery from Yahoo.

The Landsat images are of rather coarse resolution, but they are in the public domain and so they can be used without license issues. While unsuitable for discerning features in an urban environment, they are a good source for drawing the outlines of lakes or forest areas. Rivers, railway lines, or major roads can usually be seen as well.

The Yahoo satellite and aerial imagery is copyrighted. However, Yahoo has declared that their terms of use do allow tracing features from them, and that these traced features may then be distributed under the OpenStreetMap license. The Yahoo imagery is of varying quality; in some areas you can see every single road even in a city, while in others they aren't any better than the Landsat images.

Generally, roads and building outlines can be traced from aerial imagery very well. Note, however, that these images aren't always positioned correctly: Depending on the provider, they may be mislocated by several hundred meters. In the major editing tools, you can correct such problems if you have a reliable GPS track (for JOSM see section 10.8; for Potlatch see section 9.9). Also remember that these images may well be several years old, and that the detail may have changed since they were taken.

Aerial imagery is ideally suited for creating a basic grid of features in an unmapped area so that you have something to start with when you head out into the field. Working in the field can't be avoided – the images don't tell you the name of a street, or whether it is a one-way street, and you can't copy that information from other maps (see chapter 13). Remember that OpenStreetMap is allowed to use Yahoo imagery but not Yahoo maps!

---

2 The Walking Papers web site has instructions on how to do this with your particular editor.

5.5 More Mapping Tips

OSM mapping is, in most cases, a two-stage process: First you collect raw data in the field, and then you improve the database with it. No matter how you make your field notes, it makes sense to think about how you will later convert them to OSM objects. For example, when you travel along a road, you usually record the name and determine the value of the highway tag that best matches the road classification (see chapter 7 for established highway types).

How you travel along a grid of roads can also be optimized for later track processing. For example, if you make a left or right turn at an intersection, then it will be difficult later to see whether there was a bend in the road there or an intersection. If you go straight on and later cross your own track, then the GPX trace shows clearly that there was an intersection there. If that isn't possible, then you should at least record a waypoint and make a note saying that there was an intersection. If you have to push your bicycle for a short way to get from one road to another, be sure to note that down, lest you might be tempted to enter a road or cycleway later when in reality there was only a footpath.

It is usually a good idea to routinely set a waypoint at each intersection so that you can refer to that in your notes ("post box North-East intersection 37"). If you are mapping a fairly rectangular grid of roads then you can probably skip many of the connections and just note down that there was a road connecting two waypoints – just as Max did with the footpath in our example.

And one last tip: It is almost impossible for a beginner to think of everything during their first mapping trips. With time, you will get more experienced, and things will become much easier. Don't aim too high initially. Perhaps just map the streets on your first outing, and skip the footpaths and points of interest. Go mapping for just half an hour and then enter the data into an editor. On your next trip you will already have a clearer idea of what to look out for to make the editing work easier. With experience you will soon become faster. Mapping a complex intersection might be too much for you during your first days as a mapper, but don't be afraid to leave it out, and return to the area when you feel more confident.

6 The Data Model

You have now seen quite a few maps that use OpenStreetMap data, and you have followed an editing session with the JOSM editor. But how does OpenStreetMap store all that information?

In this chapter weth describe in detail the data model used by OpenStreetMap. The basic data model is fairly abstract. It provides mechanisms to describe real-world objects, but it does not specify how they are to be used – much like a word processor, which provides a mechanism to store characters but doesn't make assumptions about whether you use it to write a computer program or a poem. How the OpenStreetMap data model is used in practice is something we discuss in the following chapters.

The data model is the basis for the organization of the central OpenStreetMap database. It also forms the basis of the XML data format that is commonly used to exchange OpenStreetMap data. Every OSM object has an XML representation – we'll present examples in this chapter.

6.1 Basic Object Types

The two most important object types in OpenStreetMap are *nodes* (also called *points,* some people use the term *vertices* as well) and *ways.* Attributes assigned to these objects in order to describe what they represent are called *tags.* A tag consists of a *key* and a *value*[1] and is usually written with an equals sign between both parts: "key=value". In addition there is a *relation* data type that can be used to model relationships between objects. Together, nodes, ways, and relations make up the editable data world that is OpenStreetMap.

---

1 This is different to the concept of tags as used in the Web 2.0 world; there, tags are usually single words or phrases without a key/value structure.

Every node, every way, and every relation in the database is assigned a unique numeric identifier (ID) when it is first created. This number is used to identify the object when retrieving or modifying it. IDs of deleted objects are not re-used. Every object type has its own number space, so there can be both a node with an ID of 1 and a way with an ID of 1.

Figure 6-1 shows a simplified schematic of the data model. The numbers in the diagram indicate how many of each element can be linked to each other element.

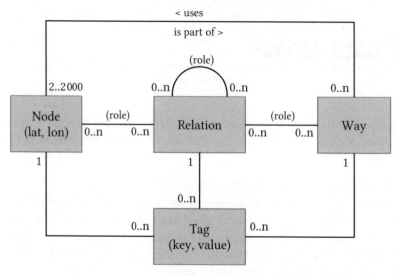

Figure 6-1: Simplified schematic of the current data model. "0..n" means zero or more.

Nodes

A node consists of the following information:

- Geographical coordinates (latitude and longitude).
- Timestamp of the last edit, user ID and username of the last editor, version number, and number of the changeset in which the change was made (see page 55).
- Zero or more tags.

Latitude and longitude are stored in degrees (with negative values used for the western and southern hemispheres). The OpenStreetMap database uses seven decimal places for these values, allowing a resolution of ±1 cm (at the Equator, where one degree covers the greatest length; even better in other regions). This should be sufficient for all currently conceivable uses – especially considering the fact that consumer GPS devices seldom allow measurements more precise than ±5 meters (see page 30).

Nodes can be connected to form ways, and thus serve as vertices in a linear geometry (for example a road) or a polygon outline (for example a lake).

Nodes are also used to map "points of interest" (POIs) – for example to mark the position of gas stations, restaurants, or movie theaters. (When mapping in great detail, these may instead be mapped as polygons.)

The XML code for a node might look like this:

```
<node id="463165820" lat="42.4052664" lon="-71.141967" version="2"
      changeset="2126558" user="fiveisalive" uid="58305" visible="true"
      timestamp="2009-08-13T05:52:29Z">
  <tag k="name" v="Cambridge Savings Bank"/>
  <tag k="amenity" v="bank"/>
  <tag k="source" v="survey"/>
  <tag k="addr:housenumber" v="190"/>
  <tag k="addr:street" v="Massachusetts Avenue"/>
  <tag k="addr:city" v="Arlington, MA"/>
</node>
```

Some nodes may serve both purposes at the same time. For example, if you have a cattle grid on a road, then instead of drawing the cattle grid as a separate entity, you might just use one of the nodes making up the road, and tag this node as cattle grid.

Ways

A way consists if the following information:

- An ordered list of at least two nodes.
- Timestamp of the last edit, user ID and username of the last editor, version number, and number of the changeset in which the change was made (see page 55).
- Zero or more tags.

Ways are mainly used to depict linear features such as roads, railways, or rivers. Ways always have a direction (even though it isn't always relevant). If the first and last node of a way are identical and the tags allow this interpretation, then a way is treated as an area. So you can also use ways to map forests, lakes, or buildings (see section 6.3).

The XML code for a way might look like this:

```
<way id="44174838" version="1" timestamp="2009-11-12T14:01:32Z" uid="165"
     user="Richard" changeset="3098347">
  <nd ref="22918443"/>
  <nd ref="264737192"/>
  <nd ref="264737193"/>
  <nd ref="264737194"/>
  <nd ref="31418238"/>
  <tag k="highway" v="secondary"/>
  <tag k="maxspeed" v="70"/>
  <tag k="ref" v="B6273"/>
  <tag k="source" v="survey"/>
</way>
```

Relations

A relation consists of the following information:

- An ordered list of members together with a role for each member.
- Timestamp of the last edit, user ID and username of the last editor, version number, and number of the changeset in which the change was made (see p. 55).
- Zero or more tags.

Relations are the most recent addition to the OpenStreetMap data model. They are used to make connections between different objects in the database. The database server doesn't know about the meaning of these connections, but it can ensure referential integrity so that there are never any broken links between related objects. In practice, relations are frequently used to model complex areas, or to join multiple roads to form a named route. There are lots of other uses as well. We discuss relations in depth in chapter 8.

The members of a relation can be nodes, ways, or indeed other relations. The role assigned to every member is a free-form string (which you can leave empty if it doesn't make sense to use it with a certain kind of relation). A relation must have at least one tag or one member. The list of relation members is ordered. The same object may be member of a relation more than once – think of a relation describing a bus route, and there is a loop in the route that makes the bus use a certain bit of road when going into the loop and when returning from it.

The XML code for a relation might look like this:

```
<relation id="365795" version="1" timestamp="2009-12-18T15:43:52Z"
          uid="110450" user="gosausee" changeset="3401326">
  <member type="way" ref="37102583" role=""/>
  <member type="way" ref="40697301" role=""/>
  <member type="way" ref="26961355" role=""/>
  <member type="way" ref="823144" role=""/>
  <member type="way" ref="41210130" role=""/>
  <tag k="name" v="Gosausee-Adamek"/>
  <tag k="route" v="hiking"/>
  <tag k="type" v="route"/>
</relation>
```

Tags

Nodes, ways, and relations can have any number of tags. Tags consist of a key and a value, both of which can be any string of up to 255 characters. Tags are UTF-8 encoded in order to allow all sorts of special characters. Keys must not be empty; values may be empty but this seldom makes sense and is usually treated as an error by editing software.

An object can't have multiple tags using the same key. (Keys are compared in a case-insensitive way, so that having two keys that differ only in case is not valid either.)

Tag values don't have different types like "boolean", "numeric", and so on; they are always just strings. Usually the values "yes" and "no" are used if a tag is conceptually boolean, but software processing OSM data must be able to handle "true", "1", "false", and "0" as well.

A colon is often used as part of the key to specify a namespace. Namespaces are used to distinguish an identical tag used in different contexts. For example, some people will tag a place with population=2500, and then add a source:population tag indicating where they retrieved that information from. The database itself doesn't support namespaces; for the database, the whole name including the colon in the middle is just a string like any other.

Changesets

If you refine a road geometry (layout), this will probably include moving several nodes, and adding new nodes to the way. You might also delete some existing nodes or split a way in two. Someone else who later reviews a list of changes in the neighborhood won't be interested in a full list of all your individual actions – they will be content to see a high-level description like "changed road geometry". A changeset represents such a group of edits and may be annotated with just such a description.

The OpenStreetMap server requires that you open a changeset before you can change any objects. After that, you can add any number of individual edits to the changeset, and you can close the changeset after having uploaded your changes.

A changeset roughly corresponds to an editing session. Everything you change within one session, before uploading your changes, will normally form one changeset. A changeset contains:

- User ID of the person performing the changes.
- Timestamps when the changeset was opened and closed.
- A rectangular area encompassing all the changes.
- Any number of tags, among them usually one named comment.

Changesets are designed to help people keep track of who has performed edits where and when. The project website www.openstreetmap.org has a "history" tab which displays all changesets whose rectangle intersects the current map view.[2] Also, the object history you can retrieve on www.openstreetmap.org will always list the comment tag for all changesets in which an object was edited, and anyone can check the list of changes performed by a given user. It is strongly recommended that use a meaningful changeset comment in everything you do because it makes all these functions more valuable to other mappers.

---

2 This function currently suffers from the fact that there are many changesets with edits on various continents. Since the change rectangle for these covers half the planet, the changeset will likely show up even if someone only looks at the history for a small area. Improvements are being developed.

Examples for good and helpful changeset comments are "refined roads in North Spring-field", "added POIs and buildings in Ravenshill reserve", "reverted erroneous edits by user HumptyDumpty near Colmar Bridge", or "fixed county boundary, added footpaths from aerial imagery". These make it clear to anybody what the change was about. Examples for useless changeset comments are "some changes", "edit", "afternoon mapping", "fixed stuff", or the classic "...". Comments such as these indicate that the mapper is not interested to help others understand what they are doing.

6.2 The OSM XML Format

OSM XML files (usually ending in .osm) consist of an <osm> element, and therein an op-tional <bounds> element followed by a list of OSM objects. Usually nodes come first, then ways, and then relations:

```
<osm version="0.6" generator="OpenStreetMap server">
  <bounds minlat="..." minlon="..." maxlat="..." maxlon="..."/>
  <node id="2347839" ...>
  </node>
  ...
  <way id="9836255" ...>
  </way>
  ...
  <relation id="325465" ...>
  </relation>
  ...
</osm>
```

The version attribute specifies the version of the database API or the XML format. As this book went to press, version 0.6 was the current one. (Don't get this confused with the version attribute given with nodes, ways, and relations, which contains the version num-ber of the individual object, starting at 1 when it is first created.) The generator attribute gives the name of the software that created this OSM file.

The <bounds> element is optional. It specifies the rectangular area for which data has been requested. Because the API will always hand out complete ways even if only a part of them is contained in the area requested, the file may contain nodes outside the area described by <bounds>. The JOSM editor uses this element when saving data to a file, so that even when re-opening the file later it can give you a visual hint about the area in which you can rely on the completeness of the data (see also page 119).

The OsmChange Format

An OSM XML document as discussed above describes a static situation. There is another XML format called OsmChange, which can be used to record changes to an OSM dataset. OsmChange files have the file extension .osc.

An OsmChange document can have any number of <create>, <modify>, and <delete> blocks; these, in turn, contain the same objects as a normal OSM document:

```
<osmChange version="0.6" generator="Osmosis 0.31.1">
  <modify>
    <node id="12050350" timestamp="2007-01-02T00:00:00.0+11:00"
        lat="-33.9133118622908" lon="151.117335519304" uid="238"
        user="sandmann" version="17">
    </node>
  </modify>
  <delete>
    <way id="30755420" timestamp="2009-02-02T23:55:58Z" uid="16079"
        user="saharadesertfox" version="13"/>
  </delete>
  <create>
    <node id="340141676" timestamp="2009-02-02T23:55:11Z" uid="57437"
        user="Canley" version="1" lat="-38.212792" lon="145.0555682"/>
  </create>
</osmChange>
```

OsmChange files usually carry the full representation of an object in the <create> and <modify> blocks; the <delete> blocks may just list the object type and ID depending on the method used to create the OsmChange file.

6.3 Modeling Areas

The OSM data model has no specific data type for areas (polygons). Instead, areas are just another type of way. A circular (i. e. closed) way that has tags suitable for an area is automatically treated as an area. Looking at just the fact that the first and last nodes are the same is not enough, because there are circular ways that don't describe areas (for example circular roads). Only by taking a look at the tags can you tell the difference between an area and a simple circular way.

Areas with holes, for example a building with a courtyard or a forest with a clearing, have to be constructed using relations. First you create two circular ways, one for the area and one for the hole. Both are then made members of a relation tagged as type=multipolygon, one with a role of outer and one as inner. You can find out more about multipolygons in section 8.1.

6.4 Tracks and Trackpoints

In addition to nodes, ways, and relations with their tags, which form the OSM geodata set, OpenStreetMap also stores raw GPS tracks and their trackpoints. One reason for doing this is that it lets OpenStreetMap "prove" that data has really been collected using GPS receivers, and not simply copied from elsewhere. Making GPS tracks available to mappers

57

also allows them to cross-check with tracks collected by others and to average out erroneous GPS readings. GPS data is stored completely separate from the other OSM data.

GPS tracks are assigned a unique numeric identifier when you upload them to OSM. The file name, uploading user, description, and keywords are recorded together with the track data. Each trackpoint is stored with its latitude, longitude, and timestamp. Additional information contained in the track, for example the separation into track segments or extended GPX elements, are not stored in the database. However, any GPX file uploaded as "Identifiable" (see page 20) is downloadable in full from the server, so this information isn't lost – just more difficult to access.

6.5 History of the OSM Data Model

If you are just interested in the status quo then you can skip this section. But knowing how things were handled earlier and how the database has developed over time may help you to understand a few things more easily.

The Simplest Thing That Could Possibly Work

Doing the simplest thing that could possibly work has always been a principle of OpenStreetMap, and this applied to the first version of the data model as well. It allowed three kinds of objects: trackpoints like the ones we still have today, nodes, and segments. Segments were short lines connecting (exactly) two nodes.

These basic building blocks were sufficient to record road networks. People were not inclined (and too eager to get started with mapping) to spend their time making up a catalog of objects to map, and existing standards were deemed too complex. OSM didn't want to create rules about which kinds of roads, points, or areas should be mapped. Instead, nodes and segments were allowed to be tagged by adding key-value combinations. People could now map any kinds of objects and describe them.

Initially, a raw classification of objects was achieved by using a tag named class. Roads were class=highway, railways were class=railway, and a telephone booth was tagged class=telephone.

The basic characteristics of this approach are still with OpenStreetMap even now. At the core, we have a geo object with a certain geometry, which derives its identity from tags ("this object is a ..."). This makes OpenStreetMap different from many established data models in the GIS world, because there you often have an abstract object at the core ("this represents a road"), which derives its location from geo attributes ("the location of this object is ...").

From Segments to Ways

In order to be able to map longer roads, the segment approach required splitting them up into a large number of straight bits – and every single one had to be furnished with information like the street name. That meant a lot of work and was error-prone, and led to the introduction of ways. Ways could be used to connect a number of segments into a continuous road. At the same time, an area data type was introduced, but it was never really used and removed again later.

This data model was used in OpenStreetMap for a long time (from early 2006 until October 2007). It is often referred to as the "n/s/w" model, for "nodes/segments/ways". When it was phased out in October 2007, OpenStreetMap had 20 million nodes, 20 million segments, and four million ways.

October 2007 saw a big change with the introduction of version 0.5 of the data model. Segments were taken out, and ways now consisted of an ordered list of nodes. At the same time, the new concept of relations was introduced, so that logical connections between objects could be stored.

API 0.6: Seeing What Happens

In March 2009 there was another big change in the OpenStreetMap data model – the change to API version 0.6. The most important new feature were the "changesets". For the first time, users were able to comment on their changes in a way similar to revision control systems in IT. Someone who reviews changes in a certain area will now see a single changeset, instead of lots of individual changes: "user Hummingbird, 3rd March 2009 16:10h – fixed geometry of river Rhine near Koblenz. 345 changes". Reversing changes now became much easier through changesets.

Another important change in API 0.6 was the ordering of relations. Because relation members were unordered before, the role attribute had to be (mis)used to create an order where desired. In the case of a bus route, for example, this led to mappers using role designators of "stop_01", "stop_02" and so on when including the bus stops in the relation. With API 0.6, they could now all share the role designator "stop", and be saved in the correct sequence.

6.6 Future Development

OpenStreetMap grows with the demands of its users and contributors. For example, a major driving force behind the introduction of relations was the desire to create turn restrictions and other complex rules that are required for proper routing.

There is no concrete timeline for the introduction of the next data model and API version, but it will certainly be required at some point. One often-discussed change could be the creation of two distinct types of points – one with a life of their own ("POI nodes") and one that exists solely to build the geometry of a way. Some people have called for a simplification of the concept of ways so that ways only have "connectors" at their endpoints, and ways would never extend past an intersection (a concept that would make building routing graphs easier). Another idea being floated is the ability to modify only parts of a complex object, without actually having to download and upload the full object.

Tags could also be subject to change. Other data models used for describing road geometries often allow *constrained attributes,* attributes that are only valid for a certain vehicle type, during certain hours, or only for the left lane of a road. It isn't inconceivable that OpenStreetMap will introduce mechanisms to constrain the validity of tags similarly.

Finally, the way in which OpenStreetMap currently handles areas is rather unusual and might some day make way for a proper area data type, which would then be the fourth native data type next to nodes, ways, and relations.

7 Map Features – What We Map

Objects drawn on an OSM map are called *map features*. A map feature has a geographic position and extent, and a type. In OpenStreetMap, map features are represented by a node or a way combined with one or more tags. To get an object (for example a road, a post box, or a lake) onto the map, you therefore need to know whether to draw a node or a way, and which tags to use to describe the object in question.

Each node and way can have an arbitrary number of tags. All tags assigned to an object are valid for the whole object. If you draw a road that changes properties along the way – for example if there's a 500-meter pedestrian section in the middle – then the road must be modeled as several ways joined together. The tag for pedestrian streets (it is called `highway=pedestrian`) can only be assigned to a way as a whole, and not to a part of the way.

A tag consists of a key and a value ("key=value"). Both can be arbitrary strings. OpenStreetMap doesn't have an exhaustive list of "allowed" tags; you may use whatever keys and values you like. That sounds potentially chaotic, but it is an important feature of OpenStreetMap's success. This open specification has enabled mappers to create and use most of the tags in use today, without needing to refer to a central authority or complex decision-making processes.

Of course it makes a lot of sense for mappers to agree on a common tagging scheme. Traditionally, the developers of *renderers* (programs that draw maps from OSM data) have always had a strong influence on which tags became widely used, because everyone wanted "their" area to look nice on the map. For example, a tag for bridges had been in limited use for quite a while, but only as bridges actually became visible on the maps (by the renderers adding them to their stylesheets) did people start to map them in significant numbers.

The wiki page Map Features lists most commonly used tags with descriptions and often also photos. Figures 7-1 and 7-2 show some typical tags assigned to nodes and ways.

highway=motorway (page 64)

highway=motorway_link (page 64)

highway=primary (page 64)

highway=cycleway (page 65)

natural=water (page 73)

natural=wood (page 73)

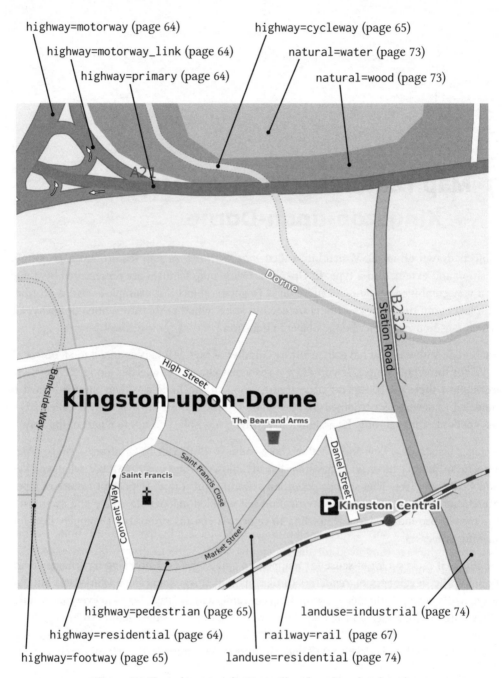

highway=pedestrian (page 65)

highway=residential (page 64)

highway=footway (page 65)

landuse=industrial (page 74)

railway=rail (page 67)

landuse=residential (page 74)

Figure 7-1: Typical tags in a fictitious village (see also color plate 7).

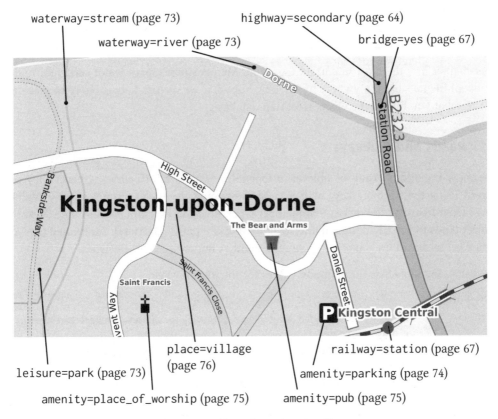

waterway=stream (page 73)

waterway=river (page 73)

highway=secondary (page 64)

bridge=yes (page 67)

place=village (page 76)

railway=station (page 67)

leisure=park (page 73)

amenity=parking (page 74)

amenity=place_of_worship (page 75)

amenity=pub (page 75)

Figure 7-2: Typical tags (continued).

Proposals for new tags are published and discussed on the wiki page Proposed Features, and they can be voted upon. Once a new tag has been accepted, it is added to the Map Features page.

However, in reality only a very small number of people are interested in this process. Many just create the tags they need for their mapping work, without discussion or a vote. Often they simply consult their peers on one of the mailing lists or on IRC: "How would you tag this and that?" and if the answer sounds sensible, then the mapper will follow the advice – no matter whether the suggested tag is on the Map Features page or not, or whether anyone has ever cast a vote on it.

When you are new to OpenStreetMap, it is likely that you adhere closely to the existing Map Features. But don't hesitate to show some creativity if the existing schema doesn't suit your needs. You can propose something on the Proposed Features page and hold a vote on it, but a sensible new idea will be accepted by the community without a vote, and a tag that isn't well thought out won't be used, no matter how many votes it has garnered. The Map

Features page is a recommendation – it is neither exhaustive nor binding. Nobody can tell mappers who spend their free time working on OpenStreetMap what they have to do – the only avenue is discussion and persuasion.

This chapter lists the most important tags from Map Features. Space is not sufficient to describe all the tags used anywhere by anyone, but what we discuss here is likely to make up 90% of what you find in the OpenStreetMap database.

7.1 Roads and Railways

The most important group of objects in OpenStreetMap are, of course, streets. They are tagged using the highway key, with a value describing the type of street or way. Values range from freeways (motorway – remember OpenStreetMap was founded in the UK so the project tends to use UK-designated terms) down to footpaths (footway). Additional tags are then used to record the name of the street and other important characteristics.

The following table lists the common values for the highway key:

Value	Used for
motorway	Large, grade-separated, limited access freeway (or motorway). Each carriageway is drawn separately.
motorway_link	On/off-ramp or lane that connects different freeways; often part of a larger intersection.
trunk	Large, freeway-like road, often a divided highway (dual carriageway). In the UK, a primary A road with green signs.
trunk_link	On/off-ramp or lane that connects different "trunk" type roads.
primary	Major long-distance (intercity) road. In the UK, an A road with black and white signs.
primary_link	On/off-ramp or lane that connects different "primary" type roads.
secondary	Other major highways. In the UK, a B road.
tertiary	Smaller but significant regional road, arterial road.
residential	Residential street. Most innercity roads use this type unless they are through ways.
living_street	Extra traffic-calmed residential road found in many European countries.
unclassified	Minor roads that are not residential roads. Note: "unclassified" doesn't mean "this still needs to be sorted out" – it is a proper highway type originating from the official UK road classification. Compare with road.
service	Access roads usually paved but not meant to be used by the general public – for example, access to parking or particular buildings.
track	Forest or agricultural path, often unsurfaced and with restricted access. Usually accompanied by the tracktype tag (see the next table). Only used for ways wide enough for four-wheel vehicles.
bridleway	Bridleway (i. e. for horses).

Value	Used for
cycleway	Cycle way (or bike way).
footway	Footpath *(highway=footpath is not used!).*
path	Alternative tagging for ways that have insufficient width for a track. Additional tags describe the intended use (see discussion of motorcar/bicycle/foot/horse in the next table). This type is often used for ways that are shared-use and can't be adequately described as footway, cycleway, and the like.
pedestrian	Pedestrian area or street.
steps	Steps.
road	Road of unknown type. This tag is used for example when tracing from aerial imagery where it is impossible to determine the exact type of road.

The original road classification in OpenStreetMap was based on the road types found in the UK. Meanwhile mappers in most countries have created some kind of mapping of the respective national highway system to OSM tags. We discuss these preferences for several countries in the appendix, and you should find an up-to-date list on the Key:highway wiki page. But remember that the last word always lies with the local mapper: If you think that the village main road is a "primary" road, then that's what it is.

Dual carriageways (divided highways) are usually created as two individual ways in Open-StreetMap, each drawn in the direction of traffic flow. With the exception of highway=motorway (where this is the implicit default), such ways should be tagged oneway=yes. Individual lanes of a multi-lane road will usually not have their own ways in OpenStreetMap, but the tag lanes= can be used to specify the number of lanes (per direction).

Likewise, cycle ways and footpaths attached to a road without proper separation won't be drawn as individual ways – see the section on *bundled ways* in the following chapter.

Areas which are accessible to traffic, for example a city square, are drawn as a closed way, tagged with the appropriate highway tag and additionally with area=yes.

The following table shows tags often used together with the highway tag:

Tag	Used for
name=...	The name of the road (see remarks on page 76).
ref=...	The official road number. There are variations of this, like int_ref, nat_ref, and reg_ref (for international, national, or regional road numbers where they deviate from what is normally used). European freeways, for instance, often have an Europe-wide E number in addition to their national number.
oneway=yes (formerly also true or 1)	Used for tagging one-way streets. Traffic is allowed only in the direction of the way. There is also the rarely used oneway=-1 for situations in which traffic is allowed only against the direction of the way (when the way can't be reversed due to another direction-dependent tag). Freeways (highway=motorway) are always assumed to be one-way streets even if this tag isn't present.

Tag	Used for
bicycle=..., foot=..., horse=..., motorcar=... = yes / designated / private / permissive / no	Access restrictions that specify what kinds of traffic are allowed on the road or the way. A yes value means "allowed", and no means "not allowed". The value designated is sometimes used in conjunction with highway=path to convey that a way is explicitly dedicated to a certain kind of traffic: A way tagged bicycle=yes simply means that it can be used by cyclists, but a way tagged bicycle=designated is explicitly (often using special signage) meant for cyclists. A footpath with an additional "cyclists allowed" sign could be tagged as foot=designated, bicycle=yes, whereas a combined foot and cycleway would receive foot=designated, bicycle=designated.
	For most road types the permitted uses are enshrined in national law. In Europe, freeways must not be used by cyclists (not so on some US freeways) and therefore European mappers don't usually place a bicycle=no with highway=motorway. A residential road can trivially be used by pedestrians, so adding foot=yes is superfluous. These tags become important where roads deviate from what is usual, or where the highway type doesn't carry enough information (e. g. when using highway=path).
	There are further access tags for motorcycles, trucks, etc., and in addition to yes, no, and designated, there are the values permissive (meaning: You don't have a legal right but you can use it nevertheless) and private (for private access only).
access= agricultural, delivery, destination	Further access restrictions. access=agricultural is common for countryside tracks in parts of Europe and means that vehicular traffic is restricted to agriculture. access=delivery means you can only use the road for deliveries and access=destination is another expression for "no through traffic". For further options, see the wiki under Key:access.
maxspeed=...	The permitted maximum speed where it deviates from what is usual for the road type. The value is assumed to be in kilometers per hour, unless followed by an explicit "mph".
tracktype= grade1...grade5	Used to give more detail about the usability of a way (normally in combination with highway=track).
	A grade1 track is almost like a proper road (with an asphalt surface or heavily compacted hardcore), grade2 is a firm gravel track, grade3 a generally firm track with occasional soft bits, grade4 already has plants growing in the middle, and grade5 means that you probably have to look twice to see that there is a track at all.
surface= paved, unpaved, gravel, cobblestone, asphalt, ...	Describes the surface of the road or way. The values paved and unpaved can be used if more detail isn't available; otherwise, detailed values like asphalt, cobblestone, gravel are preferred. An exhaustive list is given on the wiki page Key:Surface.
	This tag shouldn't be used to describe the default situation (like surface=asphalt for a freeway).

For traffic lights (stop lights), use a node tagged with highway=traffic_signals; pedestrian crossings are mapped by tagging a node as highway=crossing.

Railways (Railroads)

Railway tracks are mapped using the railway key. The most common values are rail (for freight and long-distance tracks), light_rail (for urban railways, unless they use the same tracks as long-distance railways), tram (for tramways or streetcars), and subway (for underground railways). Railway stations and halts are mapped by tagging one of the nodes making up the track. Tram stops are tagged as railway=tram_stop; all other railways use either railway=station (for a proper station) or railway=halt for the much smaller ones.

When rail tracks directly cross a road, create a node that is part of both the road and the railway, and tag it railway=level_crossing. Crossings for pedestrians only are mapped as railway=crossing. There is currently no distinction between guarded and unguarded crossings.

Where tram tracks are embedded in a road, they are often drawn as a separate way, but reusing the same nodes on which the road is built.

For more details, see the section on public transport in the next chapter.

Bridges and Tunnels

When a road or railway track goes through a tunnel or over a bridge, the affected section is cut out of the way and tagged with bridge=yes or tunnel=yes. Additionally, the key layer is applied with a value of 1 (for bridges) or -1 (for tunnels).[1] This tag specifies the relative level for the object. The default value is 0, and values from -5 to 5 are allowed. This tag can be used to influence the drawing order for everything, but it is most important to make bridges and tunnels look right in the map.

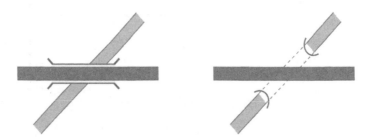

Figure 7-3: A grade-separated crossing as bridge and tunnel.

---

1 More precisely: The layer for a tunnel should be one smaller and the layer for a bridge should be one larger than the layer for the road that is being crossed. There are situations, for example complex freeway interchanges in the US, where you can easily have a bridge with layer=4 crossing another bridge with layer=3.

When drawing bridges or tunnels, make sure that they don't begin or end directly at an intersection, but a small distance away.

It isn't always obvious when looking at a grade-separated crossing whether something is a bridge or a tunnel – sometimes even a civil engineer has to look twice. We will get back to this when we discuss mapping a freeway junction towards the end of this chapter.

Roundabouts

Draw roundabouts (traffic circles) just like a circular road and give them the usual tagging for the highway type, plus the additional junction=roundabout. An explicit oneway=yes isn't required (but make sure to draw the circle in the direction of the traffic flow). If a roundabout is just a painted or slightly elevated circle in the middle of an otherwise normal junction, you can just tag the junction node with highway=mini_roundabout (do not use junction=...!).

Junctions

The following figures 7-4 to 7-6 depict some common types of road junctions together with a sketch of how they are typically mapped in OpenStreetMap. Where the flow of traffic is important, we have assumed that traffic drives on the right; invert all the arrows if you live in a country that drives on the left.

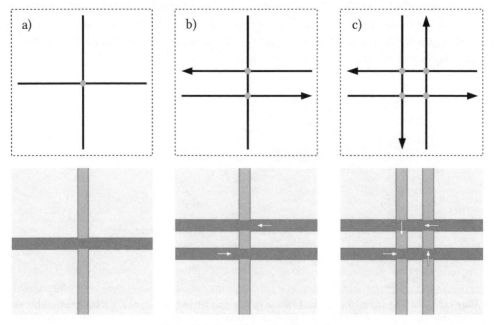

Figure 7-4: Typical junctions (part 1).

a) A plain intersection of two roads. Simply uses one junction node, part of both roads.

b) A simple road crosses another road that has physically separated lanes for each direction. This uses two junction nodes, and the lanes are tagged with oneway=yes. The little bit in the middle connecting the two junction nodes doesn't have to be a separate way; it can simply be part of the road running from North to South. If the road going North is a different road than the one going South, then the middle bit should be a separate way tagged primary_link, secondary_link, or unclassified, depending on the road types. Typically you would use the link class matching the highest road class involved.

c) An intersection between two roads that each have separate lanes for each direction of traffic. We use four junction nodes; see b) for how to treat the four connecting ways in the middle.

When intersections such as a) to c) have lights, we generally tag the junction node(s) with highway=traffic_signals, instead of placing extra nodes near, or in the middle of, the intersection.

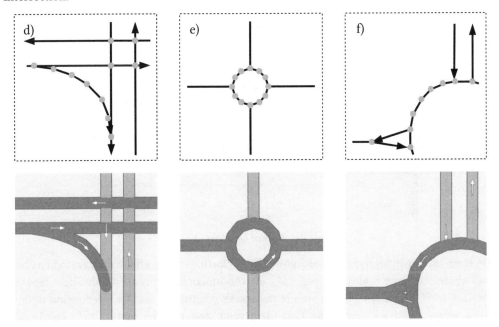

Figure 7-5: Typical junctions (part 2).

d) An intersection between two roads, each with physically separated lanes for both directions, and a turning lane. Draw the turning lane (oneway=yes) by using multiple nodes to get the curve right, and tag it as link just like the little bits of road discussed for the previous intersections.

e) A simple roundabout. It uses the same road class as the connecting roads (the highest of them all if they are different), and additionally the tag junction=roundabout. The curvature is achieved by using several nodes.

f) Special features with roundabouts: The road leaving to the North already has individual lanes for each direction of traffic. The road leaving to the West uses a *fan-out* where both lines split up just before reaching the roundabout. Such fan-outs are very common, but their sizes vary wildly. It is up to you whether you explicitly map the fan-out or not. When the fan-out is only painted or consists of a mini concrete island, most mappers choose to ignore it.

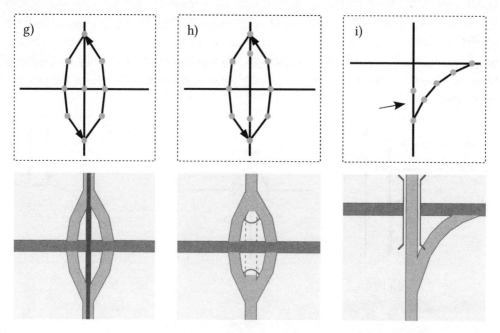

Figure 7-6: Typical junctions (part 3).

g) A tram (or streetcar) uses the road going from North to South (the highway and railway ways share the same nodes, see page 67). At the junction, the road divides into separate lanes for each direction of traffic, while the tracks go straight on. An intersection node is placed where the tracks cross the East-West road, and may be tagged railway=level_crossing (although this is often assumed to be implicit when tram tracks are involved).

h) The road going from North to South crosses under the East-West road. Its middle part is tagged with tunnel=yes and layer=-1, and does not have an intersection node with the East-West road. It is important that start and end of the tunnel are not at the same nodes where the individual lanes branch off as this would not only misrepresent reality but also lead to undesirable rendering results.

i) The same holds true for bridges. The section of the North-South road tagged as bridge=
yes must not extend to where the turning lane branches off; a little stretch of way must
exist between this point and the start of the bridge (marked with an arrow in the picture).

Dead-ends and Turning Areas

Whether or not a road is a dead-end should be obvious from the map. Nevertheless, such
roads are often explicitly tagged with noexit=yes to make clear that they really end like
that and are not just incompletely surveyed. This tag becomes more important when the
road ends near another passing road (see middle of figure 7-7). Such situations might in fact
have arisen from mapping errors (the mapper wanted to connect the roads but clicked
incorrectly). Because of this, some verification tools will check for the existence of a
noexit=yes when they encounter a road layout like that, and issue a warning if none is
found. If, on the other hand, the two roads in this scenario are connected by a little bit of
footpath or steps, then you can just record that connection; you don't use the noexit=yes
tag in this case, even if it obviously applies to motorized traffic.

Where there is a turning area at the end of the road, this is usually mapped by tagging the
end node with highway=turning_circle. This translates to a small circle on detailed map
renderings (lower left example in figure 7-7).

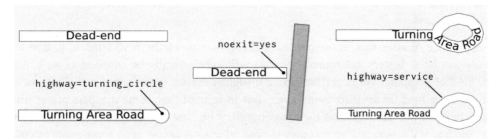

Figure 7-7: Dead-ends and turning areas.

Large turning areas with an "island" may be drawn as separate ways and tagged with
highway=service (lower right example in figure 7-7). If you don't create a separate way for
the turning area and instead just close the road to form a loop at the end, this may lead to
undesirable results in rendering (upper right example in figure 7-7).

Barriers and Traffic Calming

Gates, bollards, and similar obstacles to traffic are mapped by inserting a node with a
barrier tag into the affected way. A gate is tagged with barrier=gate,[2] a boom with
barrier=lift_gate, and a bollard with barrier=bollard. The barrier tags can also be

---

2 You might still encounter an older, now obsolete tag highway=gate tag for a gate.

used on ways to map fences, hedges, city walls, and other linear features. Details on these uses can be found in the wiki, under Key:barrier.

Measures for traffic calming are mapped using the traffic_calming tag (for nodes). There are a number of different traffic calming methods; the most common values for this tag are yes (for unspecified methods), bump (for a short elevation in road surface), or hump (for a prolonged, plateau-like elevation in road surface).

Intersections of Roads and Other Features

We have already mentioned inserting intersection nodes that are placed for non-grade-separated intersections between roads and railways. The same holds true for roads that go through streams or rivers in a ford (the intersection node is tagged highway=ford).

In all other cases, the intersection of a road or railway with another, non-related feature such as power lines, forest edges, or administrative boundaries, will not be mapped with an intersection node.

Nodes Shared by Multiple Features

If an area – for example a park or a forest – is bordered by a road, then it may make sense to re-use the existing nodes of the road for the area as well. This results in two ways that share some nodes.[3]

This practice ensures that, if anyone edits the geometry of the road later, e. g. due to a newly available, better data source, the area will automatically be adjusted as well. Also, this kind of mapping will never lead to an unsightly empty space between the edge of the area and the road on detailed zoom levels. But in spite of that, some mappers prefer using separate nodes for the road and the area boundary because it is clearer in the editor. Neither method is discouraged, so you may choose whichever seems most appropriate to you.

7.2   Forests, Lakes, and Rivers

Colored areas go a long way to making a map look good, and they generally help map users recognize places. You can often map forests, lakes, and rivers from freely available aerial imagery – you don't have to travel around the world with your GPS to add these valuable features to OpenStreetMap.

In contrast to other GIS data models, OpenStreetMap doesn't have a special data type for areas. An area is simply a circular way with tags that denote an area. For areas that are

---

3   If the area is complex enough to warrant a multipolygon relation, the road can be used as-is for an outer way in the relation. See section 8.1 for details.

very large, consist of multiple disjointed bits, or have holes, you can use multipolygon relations – we'll discuss these in section 8.1.

Tag lakes or ponds with natural=water, and forests with natural=wood (alternatively landuse=forest; strictly speaking natural=wood is meant for unmanaged and landuse= forest for managed forests, but that distinction isn't widely understood or used). Innercity parks and gardens are tagged with leisure=park. You can either tag agricultural areas as a whole with landuse=farm, or if you have more information, you can make a distinction between landuse=farmland (where produce is grown), landuse=meadow (where animals graze), and landuse=farmyard (for the smaller area surrounding the farm and its outbuildings).

Map small rivers using a single way down the center, tagged waterway=river. If it isn't large enough to be called a river, use waterway=stream (rule of thumb: You should be able to jump over a stream). For canals, use waterway=canal. Always draw the way in the direction of the flow. Also, add a name tag to give the name of the river (or canal).

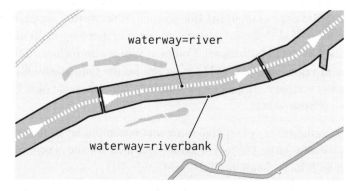

Figure 7-8: Tagging large rivers.

For larger rivers, still use waterway=river for the central way, but in addition to that, draw the banks of the river and tag them waterway=riverbank. For these riverbanks to look correct when rendered, you currently have to create them as a sequence of closed areas. If you don't have enough information to map the river banks but do know where the river changes width significantly, you can draw the river as multiple ways, tagging each with its width (in meters) by adding the width tag.

7.3 Coastline and Islands

The coastline requires special handling. If you were to try and map the oceans of the world as one large natural=water area, you'd end up with an object far too large for editing. Instead, the coastline is tagged as natural=coastline using simple, non-closed ways. The rendering software will later make sure that the area on the sea's side of this line is filled in blue. This requires that all coastline ways go anti-clockwise around a land mass (so that the water is always on the right-hand side of the line).

Coastlines must not be interrupted: If one coastline way ends at a node, then the next coastline way has to start at the same node.

Today, coastlines in OpenStreetMap are mostly complete. But they are still far from perfect, and often lack detail around archipelagos or areas with a very rugged coastline. As with everything else in OpenStreetMap: If you have better information than what is there, don't hesitate to correct or improve the existing coastline.

You can give a name to islands (whether in the sea or in a lake) by placing a node near the center of the island and tag it with place=island and an appropriate name tag.

7.4 Buildings and Land Use Areas

Areas (in the land utilization sense) are represented in OpenStreetMap by the landuse tag. Its most popular values are residential (for housing or residential areas), industrial (industrial parks), commercial (business parks), and retail (shopping malls or innercity areas predominantly used by retail businesses). Common values also include allotments for detached gardens and vegetable plots, village_green for the quintessentially English grassy area in the center of a village, or quarry for quarries. The wiki page Map Features has lots of other possible landuse values.

If you do a rough initial survey of an area using low-resolution aerial imagery, it is perfectly acceptable to use one large landuse=residential area for the whole of a village, until someone maps it with more detail locally.

Car parks (parking lots) are another commonly mapped area type. You can use the amenity=parking tag on a node, but is more commonly found on areas. Streets or parking aisles inside a car park are often tagged as highway=service and additionally with service=parking_aisle to distinguish them from normal service roads.

When people started mapping buildings in OpenStreetMap, they mostly used a single node for each building – a so-called POI (point of interest). With growing demand for more precise and more visually satisfying maps, many mappers started mapping buildings as areas instead. Building outlines are often derived from aerial imagery, and are given the building tag, mostly in the form building=yes. You can use more precise values (e. g. building=church) but remember that this only describes the building – a church in active use would also need to be tagged amenity=place_of_worship. You can add other tags to the building, e. g. amenity=pharmacy or house number tags. Remember that if you draw a building outline, you shouldn't place a POI node as well – do one of them, but not both.

The following table has common tags for various kinds of buildings.

Building	Common tag	Building	Common tag
airport terminal	aeroway=terminal	monument	historic=monument
arts center	amenity=arts_centre	mosque	see below
bakery	shop=bakery	movie theater	amenity=cinema
bank	amenity=bank	museum	tourism=museum
barracks	military=barracks	nursery care	amenity=kindergarten
beer garden	amenity=biergarten	pharmacy	amenity=pharmacy
bunker	military=bunker	physician	amenity=doctors
bus station	amenity=bus_station	playground	leisure=playground
bus stop	highway=bus_stop	police station	amenity=police
café	amenity=cafe	post office	amenity=post_office
car park	amenity=parking	prison	amenity=prison
car rental	amenity=car_rental	pub	amenity=pub
cemetery	landuse=cemetery	railway station	railway=station
church	see below	restaurant	amenity=restaurant
court house	amenity=courthouse	ruins	historic=ruins
dentist	amenity=dentist	school	amenity=school
disco, night club	amenity=nightclub	stadium	leisure=stadium
fast food joint	amenity=fast_food	supermarket	shop=supermarket
filling station	amenity=fuel	swimming pool	leisure=water_park
fire station	amenity=fire_station	synagogue	see below
fitness center	leisure=sports_centre	tourist information	tourist=information
gas station	amenity=fuel	tower	man_made=tower
halt (railway)	railway=halt	town hall	amenity=townhall
hospital	amenity=hospital	university/college	amenity=university
hotel	tourism=hotel	water tower	man_made=water_tower
kiosk	amenity=kiosk	windmill	man_made=windmill
library	amenity=library	youth hostel	tourism=hostel
lighthouse	man_made=lighthouse		

Buildings used for, or dedicated to, religious purposes are tagged with amenity=place_of_worship, no matter whether they actually host any kind of religious service. In addition, you can use the tags religion and denomination to specify which religion uses the facility.

A catholic church is tagged religion=christian, denomination=catholic; a protestant church would be denomination=protestant. A synagogue is tagged religion=jewish and a mosque, religion=muslim. Further examples are on the wiki pages Key:religion and Key:denomination.

7.5 Villages, Cities, and Borders

In order to put the names of a village, city, neighborhood, or other entity on the map, place a node roughly where the name should appear. Give the node a place tag for the type of entity, and a name tag for its name.

Tag	Type of entity
place=suburb	Suburb, or quarter[4].
place=hamlet	Hamlet (very small village).
place=village	Village.
place=town	Town (population roughly 10,000 or more).
place=city	City (population roughly 100,000 or more).
place=farm	Detached farm.
place=island	Island.

The name tag should contain the common name of the entity. If it is known by another name internationally or locally, you can use the tags int_name and loc_name as well. Places that have different names in different languages can be tagged using keys in the form name:language (e. g. name:fr=Bâle, name:de=Basel, name:en=Basle). The language is encoded using ISO 639-1.[5] You should write names in full, not abbreviate them. We write "Russell Street", not "Russel St", and "Woburn Place", not "Woburn Pl". It's much easier to abbreviate something later (for example if it doesn't fit on the map) than to guess whether "St" in a certain context was meant to be "Street" or "Saint". OSM uses Unicode, so you can (and should) include national language characters in a name.

Borders of cities or city quarters can be entered as multipolygon relations with a suitable admin_level; see the discussion in section 8.2. In the past, some mappers used the is_in tag with roads or other objects to denote the administrative unit that the object belonged to, but with more and more boundaries tagged, this is becoming unnecessary.

It is always a good idea to add a population tag to a place node (the value being a plain number, no punctuation, no letters), even if the value is just a rough guess. This makes it easier for rendering engines to give priority to the important places.

7.6 Other Points of Interest

The following table has a list of widely used POIs. There are even more listed on the wiki, but the ultimate OSM gospel is always the database itself – where hundreds of others are

---

4 While proper suburbs are often residential communities within commuting range of larger cities, this tag is also used for city quarters.

5 http://en.wikipedia.org/wiki/List_of_ISO_639-1_codes

already using a certain tag, you could do worse than just follow them, no matter whether that tag is listed on the wiki or not.

POI	Widely used tag
ATM	`amenity=atm`
camp site	`tourism=camp_site`
car sharing station	`amenity=car_sharing` and `operator=organization name`
clothes recycling	`amenity=recycling` and `recycling:clothes=yes`
fountain	`amenity=fountain`
glass recycling	`amenity=recycling` and `recycling:glass=yes`
golf course	`leisure=golf`
park bench	`amenity=bench`
phone booth	`amenity=telephone`
picnic site	`tourism=picnic_site`
post box	`amenity=post_box`
power pole/line/station	`power=tower`, `power=line`, `power=generator`
soccer pitch	`sport=soccer` (usually used with `leisure=pitch`)
tennis court	`sport=tennis` (usually used with `leisure=pitch`)
toilets	`amenity=toilets`
tourist attraction	`tourism=attraction`
viewpoint	`tourism=viewpoint`
zoo	`tourism=zoo`

The `operator` tag specifies who owns or operates an amenity and you can add this to many types of POIs. When the name of an outlet is a chain brand – like "McDonald's" for a fast-food restaurant or "Shell" for a gas station – you can use the `operator` tag to record the actual franchisee. In countries without postal monopolies, post boxes are often tagged with the respective operator (and no name tag).

7.7 Annotations and Missing Information

Sometimes you might need to store additional information for an object but it won't be immediately clear which tag to use, or the information will be too complex to write formally. The `note` tag comes to the rescue:

`note=road usually closed in winter`

If anyone encounters such a tag and knows of a better way to structure the information, they can always edit it.

Many mappers also use the `todo` tag to indicate objects that require further work. Debugging tools usually highlight such objects:

```
todo=road geometry needs to be revisited
```

Sometimes people specify a road name as "FIXME", "unknown", "tbd" or something similar. However, using such names isn't a good idea as they will often show up like that on the map. A missing name tag is more than enough indication of, well, a missing name!

7.8 Links

If you want to link to a website from an OpenStreetMap object, you can add the url tag. You can tag a hotel and its website like this:

```
tourism=hotel
name=Red Bear Inn
url=http://www.red-bear-inn.com/
```

This is not, as some might assume, a spam risk, as the publicly available OpenStreetMap maps will not actually make the hotel icon or building clickable – the link information is there in the data for users to access but it doesn't have an effect on the map.

There is a special tag for linking to Wikipedia articles, wikipedia, which may be combined with a language specification:

```
tourism=attraction
name=Brandenburger Tor
wikipedia:de=Brandenburger Tor
wikipedia:en=Brandenburg Gate
```

These tags only use the Wikipedia article name generally, but sometimes people also enter the full Wikipedia URL.

7.9 Data Sources

The source tag is commonly used to specify the origin of the data. Popular values include yahoo imagery or landsat where people have traced data from aerial imagery, or survey if data has been based on your own GPS tracks. Sometimes you will simply guess where a road is, and in these cases source=extrapolation is a valuable hint for other mappers.

Specifying your sources is important for two reasons. Firstly, it allows others who are thinking of improving or modifying your data to assess its precision; a lake with source= landsat will usually be less precise than the GPS track from the shore walk. Secondly, proper source specifications will help to dispel concerns that data might have been copied from copyrighted sources.

It is usually sufficient to tag ways with a source – you don't have to put the tag on every node. Also, if you make a lot of changes that are all based on the same source, you can put the source tag on the changeset (for information on changesets see page 55) when you upload your changes instead of tagging individual objects.

If you change existing data based on other sources than those specified on the object(s) in question, then you should also change the existing source tag or remove it altogether. A way that was originally traced from Landsat but which you have completely revised based on a GPS track should no longer carry source=landsat.

7.10 A Practical Example

This section uses the example of a freeway junction to show how complex objects are mapped step by step in OSM.

Figure 7-9: A freeway junction in Germany (A60 and B51 near Bitburg).

Many large road junctions around the world use a "cloverleaf" layout. There are four basic ways for each of the four directions, and then four inner and four outer ramps. Figure 7-9 shows an aerial image of such a junction. Mapping it in OpenStreetMap requires the following steps (see figure 7-10 – note that we are assuming the traffic drives on the right):

1. Map the four basic ways for the two intersecting roads as highway=motorway or highway=trunk; don't place intersection nodes.

2. Draw the outer ramps as highway=motorway_link. Since this is an intersection between a freeway and a trunk road, and the most important road type determines the type of link roads used, we use motorway_link throughout.

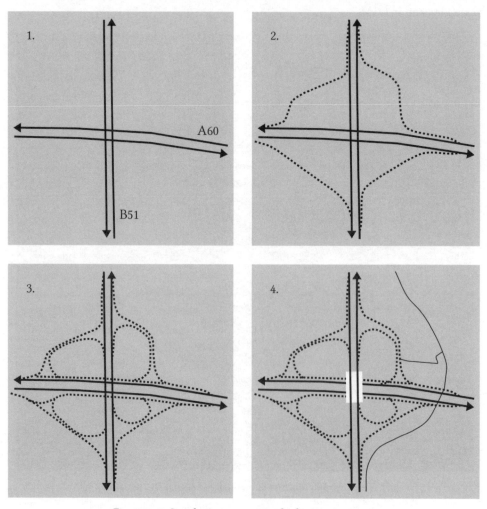

Figure 7-10: Step-by-step mapping of a freeway junction.

3. Now create the four inner ramps (the clover leaves), and tag them also with `high-way=motorway_link`. In parallel to the freeway running West to East, this junction has extra exit/entry lanes that need to be modeled in order to allow for proper automatic navigation – a motorist coming from the West might otherwise be led to think that they can remain on the main freeway lane until they have passed under the bridge. There are no such extra lanes in the North-South direction.

4. Split out the middle section of the two North-South ways and mark it as being a bridge (`bridge=yes`, `layer=1` – symbolized by a bright rectangle in the sketch). Also add any special features of the intersection – in this example there is a small road east of the junction that uses a tunnel to pass under the freeway, and a highway maintenance yard that could be mapped as an extra area with a building sitting on top.

Freeway exits are often mapped as `highway=motorway_junction`. Place the tag on the node where the off-ramp leaves the freeway proper, and you can also use `ref` or `name` to name the exit.

In the example above we wrote without further explanation about a road that "uses a tunnel". And it looks like a tunnel on the aerial image – slightly east of the junction center. But a civil engineer would probably disagree. No hole has been dug underneath anything, and in a technical sense what we named a tunnel is more like a bridge! In practice it is, as always, the mapper who decides what is a bridge and what is a tunnel. If a civil engineer comes by later and takes offense, let them fix it.

7.11 Tagging Priorities

Facing the sheer multitude of objects in OpenStreetMap, newcomers are often perplexed: Where to begin if you start on a hitherto unmapped area? Especially if you are new to OpenStreetMap, you won't be able to map everything in one go – just concentrate on the essentials. Even experienced OSMers will usually need multiple passes until they can declare an area "finished". But of everything we have discussed in this chapter, what is essential, what has priority?

Every mapper has their own ideas about what is important on the map, and needs to decide for themselves what to map and what to ignore. Here is our attempt at suggesting sensible mapping priorities; you may find it helpful to use this hierarchy for your first mapping tours, until you find your own style.

I	
very important	• Record geometries of roads and ways.
	• Highway type (motorway, primary, residential, ...).
always map these	• Map bridges and tunnels, and assign proper layer to them.
	• Road names.

II	
important	• One-way streets, plazas.
	• Road numbers.
try to map these	• For cycleways, footpaths: designated yes or no?
if possible	• Distinctive points of interest (churches, restaurants, fire or police stations, pharmacies, playgrounds, parking) – as nodes only, initially.

III	
of interest	• Traffic restrictions like speed limit (maxspeed), maximum heights, and entry restrictions.
	• Streetcar tracks and lines.
map these if possible	• Perhaps add information about road quality (surface, tracktype).
	• Simple areas (parks, village greens, parking).

IV	
free style	• Lights, pedestrian crossings.
	• Cycleways and walkways running parallel to the street, perhaps even with their own geometry.
on the second visit,	• Bus stops and bus lines.
or if time left	• Distinctive buildings mapped as areas.
	• Other areas (cemeteries, woodland, land use).
	• Bodies of water.

V	
luxury	• House numbers.
	• Turn restriction relations.
if you really have	• All buildings.
a lot of time	

8 Advanced Map Features

You now know how to record simple point and line structures and areas. This chapter shows you how to cope with much more complex objects like country borders, bus routes, or turn restrictions. These objects are usually modeled as relations. We introduced the data model for relations in section 6.1; they are the newest OSM data type, so are still very much under development.

Relations are a very flexible and powerful tool. We show you some tasks that are already a well-established use of relations, but other uses are still too new for a tagging scheme to have become widely accepted yet. So have a look at the Relations wiki page for the latest information.

The main OSM editing tools support relations, though sometimes the way they handle them is still a bit clumsy. However, with more widespread use of relations, the methods for editing and analyzing them slowly improve, and we are beginning to see easy-to-use specialist editors for certain types of relations, for example turn restrictions.

8.1 Complex Polygons

Unlike most other geographic information systems, OpenStreetMap doesn't have a polygon data type for mapping areas. Instead you use one of the following two methods:

1. Simple polygons are created by adding a closed way and tagging it to show it is an area (e. g. landuse=...).

2. More complex polygons and multipolygons are created using the multipolygon relation to group ways that make up the object's outer (and possibly inner) boundaries.

Multipolygon Relations

A multipolygon is an area (figure 8-1a), but it could have one or more "holes" (figure 8-1b). These could be an internal courtyard of a large mansion, or islands in a lake. It can also consist of one or more individual polygons (figure 8-1c). The land area of the United Kingdom, for example, is a multipolygon consisting of one large polygon for the island of Great Britain, plus extra polygons for Northern Ireland and the smaller islands.

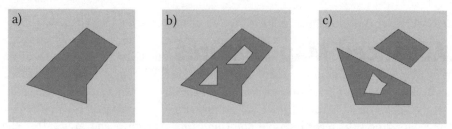

Figure 8-1: Multipolygons can a) be simple; b) have holes; or c) have multiple parts.

To add a multipolygon to OpenStreetMap, you create a multipolygon relation (a relation tagged with type=multipolygon). The members of the relation are the ways that form the polygon outlines. Ways forming the outer rings are given the role "outer", and those forming the inner rings are given the role "inner". Outer and inner rings can consist of multiple ways. Figure 8-2 shows a multipolygon that consists of two polygons. The outer boundary of the left polygon is made up of ways 1 and 2, and it has two holes delimited by ways 4/5 and 6 respectively.

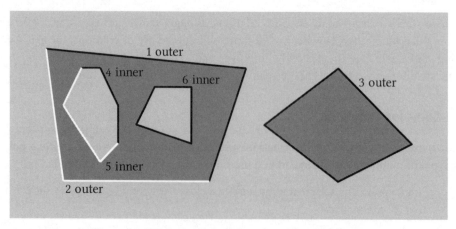

Figure 8-2: Using several ways to construct a multipolygon.

The multipolygon relation can be used to map very long border lines or objects that are very large and complex. Rendering or other processing software is programmed to combine the ways into areas according to the description contained in the relation. A large collection of multipolygon examples and also algorithms that can be used in software that has to deal with multipolygons can be found on the wiki, under Relation:multipolygon.

Note that you can't let the polygons that form a multipolygon or the holes within a polygon intersect or touch one another.[1]

8.2 Boundaries and Land Area

Multipolygons are used to map administrative boundaries (such as state or county borders). They allow the correct mapping of enclaves and exclaves and of shared boundaries. Boundaries enclose administrative areas, which vary in importance. We assign levels of importance by number, with the lowest value representing the most important. National borders always have admin_level=2,[2] but levels within a country vary. Levels 4 and 6 usually represent the higher-level administrative structures, and city boundaries are around level 8. For full details, look at Key:boundary on the wiki.

In tagging boundaries, the following rules are generally used:

All boundary lines are mapped as ways, and tagged with boundary=administrative and admin_level=#. Where different boundaries share a stretch of way, for example a county and a country border, only one way is created and tagged with the most important admin_level. When the boundaries diverge, a new way is started for each one.

All the ways making up a boundary are then collected into a multipolygon relation, with an empty role or role=outer. The relation is then tagged as type=multipolygon, boundary=administrative, and admin_level=#. (Initially some people also used type=boundary but that isn't common any more. The fact that this is a boundary is obvious from the boundary=administrative tag, and using the established type=multipolygon makes it clear that this is just a special case of a multipolygon and has to be treated as such.) A name tag is added to name the area enclosed by the boundary, and where required, further tags describe an official classification or numbering of administrative areas.

At the coast, country borders extend into the sea to demarcate the country's territorial waters. When mapping a boundary=administrative relation, follow these maritime borders. For mapping just the land area, you can use a second relation and tag it land_area=administrative. Inland borders are part of both this relation and the boundary relation. Along the coast, however, the coastline (natural=coastline) delineates the land_area relation, and the boundary relation includes territorial waters. Landlocked areas have just one relation carrying both tags (for example County Monaghan in the Republic of Ireland as shown in figure 8-3).

---

1 Many programs make an exception for inner rings, so in fact they may touch, but not intersect.
2 Level 1 is not really used.

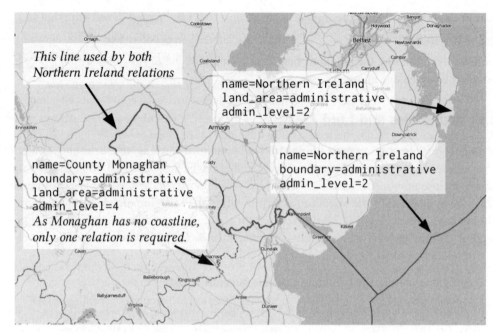

Figure 8-3: Various boundaries in Ireland.

8.3 Addresses and House Numbers

There are several different ways to record address data. For a long time there was no gener-ally agreed method to do so in OpenStreetMap, and this unfortunately led to people not en-tering addresses at all. But today the Karlsruhe Schema is widely used, and this is how it works:

A number of tags describe the address of an object, all of them beginning with the addr: prefix. Common ones are listed in the following table. If you want to tag a single residen-tial property, just place a node and tag it with as many address tags as required. If you have a POI node already, for example because there is a restaurant or pharmacy at the place, then just add the address tagging to that existing node. You can also add address tags to ways that represent a building outline.

Address nodes shouldn't be part of the road – they sit on their own, on the correct side of the road.

The following table lists common address tags. Of course you don't have to add all of them when recording an address – use the appropriate tags for what you know about the ad-dress, and ignore the rest.

Key	Example Values	Usage
addr:housenumber	17 43a 19-21	The house number. Appendixes like "a" are allowed. The number should be written exactly like it is written on the house. If a house entrance bears a number range like "19-21" then use that. If the same house has multiple entrances, give each entrance its own node.
addr:street	Miller Street Woburn Place	Name of the street, if part of the address. Always write it in full – don't use "Miller St" or "Woburn Pl". The street tag is optional; if not specified, data processing software will normally assume that this address is linked to the nearest named street.
addr:city	Kidderminster Long Beach	Name of the town or city.
addr:postcode	B5 4HX 76133	The postal code (ZIP code in the US).
addr:state	CA	State or province abbreviation for countries like the US or Australia that have this in their addresses.
addr:country	DE GB FR	The country, as a two-letter code according to ISO 3166-1 ALPHA-2 (capital letters). The example has codes for Germany, the UK, and France. The country tag is optional; software should be able to determine the country from the location of the object on the map. See http://en.wikipedia.org/wiki/ISO_3166-1 for a list of country codes.
addr:full	5 Braes Poolewe Achnasheen IV22 2LN	The full postal address. Usually this isn't needed, as it can be derived from combining other addr: tags. However, since the way that this is done may differ from country to country, and there may be some special cases, you can use this tag to specify the full, textual address as it would appear on an envelope.
addr:housename	Rose Cottage Bellmouth Castle	House names are used instead of, or in addition to, house numbers.
addr:...		Additional address tags can be added where required.

You don't have to map and tag every single house along a road; the Karlsruhe Schema has a shortcut. First map the houses at each end of the road (or at intersections) and tag them as described above. Then connect them with a new way and tag it addr:interpolation=.... House numbers are then assumed to lie along that line. The value of the tag determines the numbering. Use "even" to denote even house numbers, "odd" for odd house numbers, or "all" to simply count. Where "even" or "odd" are used, make sure that the houses at both ends have even or odd numbers, respectively. You can't use this shortcut if there are anomalous numbers in the street such as 9a. You can use it, however, to fill an alphabetic range such as 9a, 9b, ..., 9f when you tag the way addr:interpolation=alphabetic.

This house number interpolation only works for nodes. You can't connect two building outlines with an `addr:interpolation` way.

As an alternative, or in addition, streets can be tagged with `postal_code=...` to assign a postal code to all houses along that street. This doesn't work if houses on both sides of the street have different postal codes. Sometimes, in countries with large postal code areas, whole villages are assigned a `postal_code` tag.

The OSM Inspector (see section 12.2) has an address view that helps you to check for problems when working with addresses.[3]

As the name implies, the Karlsruhe Schema was devised in Germany, by people thinking mainly about addresses in the way they are used in Western Europe. The schema isn't intended to cover every possible type of address in the world, and if you are mapping in a country where that system doesn't work, then go ahead and think of something that will.

8.4 Routes

Streets and paths can be part of many different kinds of routes. A bus route uses a sequence of streets; a cycle route follows certain streets or cycle ways; or a street can be part of a tourist walking route.

Ways that together form a route can be grouped using a `type=route` relation. The `route` tag then specifies the type of route. Tags that apply to the route as a whole, such as the cycle network reference number for a cycle route, are added to the relation. If only part of a way is used by a relation, then the way has to be split. A road used by many routes will become a member of many such relations.

Tag	Usage
`route=bicycle`	Cycle routes: For (usually signposted) cycle routes, such as the Sustrans National Cycle Network routes in the UK or the ACA routes in the US.
`route=foot, hiking, walking`	Hiking trails and similar. The terms "foot", "hiking", and "walking" are used interchangeably; a standard usage pattern has not yet evolved.
`route=bus, tram, subway`	Bus, tram (streetcar), or subway lines (see the next section for more details on public transport).
`route=railway`	Railway line.
`route=ferry`	Ferry link.
`route=road`	Sometimes used to connect the numerous parts of a long-distance road such as a freeway.
`route=detour`	Signposted detour (sometimes part of the long-distance road network).

---

3 At the time of writing, this address view is only available for Europe.

Additional tags often seen on route relations:

Tag	Usage
name=...	Route name, e. g. "Thames Valley Cycle Route" or "Air Rail Bus Service".
ref=...	The number of a road, route, or line.
operator=...	The route's operator (e. g. "Transport for London" or "Sustrans").
network=...	Some routes belong to a route network, the name of which can be given here, e. g. "NCN" for National Cycle Network in the UK.

Here's an example for a cycle route relation: The relation itself is tagged type=route, route=bicycle, and name=Thames Valley Cycle Route. All ways used by this route are members of the relation. The role attribute can be left empty (one-way sections of a route are often added with the roles forward or backward, but this seldom makes sense for cycle routes).

For other types of route relations and the latest developments on their use, look at the Relation:route wiki page.

8.5 Public Transport

Drawing maps of public transport information is a challenge for any cartographer. How do you map two bus platforms which are hundreds of meters apart yet form one bus stop? Or a large subway station with multiple entrances and tunnels? These sort of issues arise in any mapmaking system and OSM is no different. As well as making them look good on the map, you need to enter the data into OpenStreetMap in a form that also allows it to be used for route planning.

Even operators of public transport don't use a common scheme to model their data. In OpenStreetMap, a comprehensive mapping scheme has been proposed based on a diploma thesis produced in 2009,[4] but the details of public transport mapping are still under discussion. Doing such mapping really thoroughly is probably asking too much of the average OpenStreetMap contributor; a complex tagging schema would run the risk of only a small elite being able to maintain that data in OpenStreetMap. So a scheme must be found that allows everyone to contribute whatever their level of expertise.

A good way of checking public transport mapping is available through the "public transport" views of the OSM Inspector (http://tools.geofabrik.de/osmi/), which highlights various aspects of public transport such as routes, stations, and track infrastructure. The

---

4 Sebastian Schwarz: "Öffentlicher Personennahverkehr in OpenStreetMap", http://kahlfrost.de/dateien/diplomarbeit.pdf. See User:Oxomoa/Public transport schema on the wiki for a concise English version.

www.öpnvkarte.de website[5] also has a very nice rendering of public transport, displaying simple as well as advanced public transport tagging (see color plate 22).

Public transport features usually fall into one of three categories: They are either linear structures (e. g. tracks or roads), points (e. g. stops), or abstract network information (e. g. routes or areas of transport authorities).

Linear Features

When mapping tracks, we record the mode of transportation (railway, tram, monorail...) and often also the type of use (main line, branch line, industrial rail, ...). The most important tags are:

Key	Value	Usage
railway	rail	Railway tracks.
railway	light_rail	Light rail tracks.
railway	subway	Subway tracks.
railway	monorail	Monorail track.
railway	tram	Tram (streetcar) tracks.
railway	funicular	Funiculars (cable cars).
railway	abandoned	Abandoned rail tracks.
usage	main, branch, industrial, tourism	Main line, branch line, industrial or tourist railway. This tag is used in addition to railway=rail.
tracks	[number]	Number of tracks (unless each track has been mapped individually anyway).
electrified	yes, no, rail, contact_line	Whether or not the track is electrified; if known, also specify the type of electrification.

Also you can use established tags like bridge=yes or tunnel=yes. For subways, always specify tunnel=yes or tunnel=no (where the subway runs above ground) to avoid any misconceptions. Use name or ref to record the name or number of a railway track; don't confuse this with the name or number of a transport line using that track.

For buses, the line infrastructure is simply roads. The lanes at large bus stations are often tagged as highway=service.

Point Structures

The point structures in public transport are stations, halts, stop points, waiting areas, and anything else that belongs to a stop.

---

5 Also accessible at www.openbusmap.org, if your keyboard doesn't have the "ö" character.

Initially, in OpenStreetMap we used a node for any type of halt, tagged variously as `railway=station` (for proper railway stations), `railway=halt` (halts), `railway=tram_stop` (tram/streetcar stops), or `highway=bus_stop` (bus stops). A bus station was `amenity=bus_station` (using a node or area). These tags are still widely used today but they aren't very precise. For bus stops especially, it wasn't clear whether to place the node on the road or next to the road.

A more recent tagging scheme lets you add more detail at stops. You tag the place where the vehicle actually stops as `public_transport=stop_position`, and the platform or waiting area as `public_transport=platform` (whether it's a node, way, or area). You can also tag the platform with a number or name using the `ref` tag. You can then combine a group of stop points, platforms and additional amenities (like shelters or access paths) in a relation tagged `public_transport=stop_area`.[6]

Network Information

The basic railway infrastructure is not enough for a public transport map. It needs to show the railway network or the bus routes. Such network information is mapped using relations on top of the infrastructure. Relation members are tracks (or roads) and halts (or stops), in the sequence in which they occur on the route.

A public transport route relation is tagged like this:

Key	Value	Usage
type	route	To define the relation as a route.
route or line	bus, tram, subway, light_rail, rail	Type of route.
from		First stop, or place where the route comes from.
to		Last stop, or place where the route goes to.
ref		Name or number of the route.
network		Name of the network this route is part of.
operator		Name of the route operator.

If an identical route is used for outward and return journeys, you only need a single relation to map it (and you don't need the `from` and `to` tags). In most cases, however, you need separate relations for each direction of travel, plus perhaps additional relations for variants in the route. If multiple relations are used to describe all possible directions and variations of one route, these are often collected into one further group relation to show that they are all variants of the same route.

---

6 A large-scale data import in the UK (see NaPTAN) uses `public_transport=stop_place` to group these elements instead.

Remember that tagging for public transport routes is still not standardized across the Open-StreetMap project. If you are planning to do public transport mapping, look at how others in your area are doing it and follow suit.

8.6 Turn Restrictions

Navigation systems need to know which turns are allowed at a given intersection in order to generate turn-by-turn navigation instructions for motor vehicles. Originally in OSM it wasn't possible (or at least extremely cumbersome) to express the fact that if you have arrived at an intersection on way A, you can't leave on way B. But thanks to relations, we can now do it.

Relations provide a logical representation of such rules. Three objects have to be included in such a relation: The way on which you enter the intersection (role from), the node that represents the intersection (role via), and the way on which you have to, or must not, leave the intersection when traveling that way (role to). If one of the roads involved in such a restriction continues past the intersection then it must be split into two ways so that the correct part can be made a member of the relation.

The turn restriction relation is tagged type=restriction, and the restriction=... specifies the exact type of restriction. It can have any of the following values:

- no_left_turn
- no_right_turn
- no_straight_on
- no_u_turn
- only_left_turn
- only_right_turn
- only_straight_on

You can also use a name or note tag (e. g. "turn restriction at Park Avenue/Bond Street") which may help to identify the relation in the editor, lest many editors will simply list the relation by its ID which is more difficult to work with.

Many European countries use a blue sign with white arrows to show the direction in which you can go (see figure 8-4). Depending on the signs, you can create an "only something" relation or one or more "no something" relations (e. g. you could set up the left example in figure 8-4 as relations no_left_turn and no_right_turn).

Other countries often use white signs with a black arrow and a red strikethrough to indicate what is forbidden rather than what is mandatory, but this doesn't affect how you represent things in OpenStreetMap.

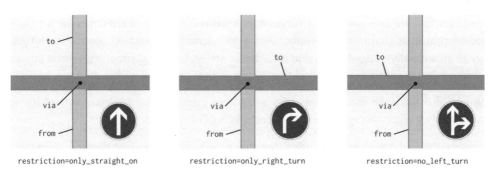

restriction=only_straight_on   restriction=only_right_turn   restriction=no_left_turn

Figure 8-4: Three examples of turn restrictions.

You might start to think that the `restriction` is redundant as it should be obvious from the combination of "from" and "to" ways whether the relation describes a left or right turn or traveling straight on. But it isn't always obvious what angle constitutes a turn, and so it's better to explicitly tag the relation matching the signs on the ground rather than trusting a renderer or other processing software to make the right decision based on the angle of the roads.

At complex intersections, where making a turn involves using extra turning lanes or other small ways, you can enter these ways as "via" members into the relation. Just make sure that there is a continuous path from the end of the "from" way to the start of the "to" way that uses all "via" nodes or ways.

8.7 Life Cycle Concepts, History, and Construction

A topic often discussed on the mailing lists is how we can describe the *life cycle* of objects in OpenStreetMap, i. e. the time when they come into existence and the time when they vanish or change their status. The situations that provoke these discussions are quite diverse: How to map historic objects (that have long ceased to exist); how to map temporary amenities (such as a plaza that becomes a bullfighting arena for one month each year); how to add restrictions based on the time of day or the season (cars prohibited between midnight and 6:00, road closed in winter); how to deal with roads under construction. A related, if not time-dependent, issue is how to record restrictions relating to the type of vehicle (e. g. speed limit for heavy trucks).

There is no standard way to handle many of these concepts in OpenStreetMap yet, but some ideas are catching on, and we list them here.

Construction Sites and Ruins

Mapping of sites under construction (usually roads) is quite well developed. We usually tag such a site with `highway=construction` and `construction=road_type` (for example construction=primary) – meaning a road under construction that is known to be a primary road when opened. Sometimes, people also use the attribute construction=yes as an addition to a normally tagged road, but this tends to lead to confusion with software that doesn't understand this extra tag and then assumes that there is a usable road.

You can also tag large construction sites as an area using the landuse=construction tag, plus possibly a note=xx tag to indicate what is being constructed.

Ruins or disused buildings are often tagged as disused=yes. Tag disused railways as railway=disused if there are still tracks, or railway=abandoned if the tracks have been removed.

Many OpenStreetMap surveyors are working on ideas about mapping things that are under construction, disused, or don't even exist any longer. Read the wiki article Comparison of life cycle concepts for more detail on the subject.

Temporal and Vehicle-Type Restrictions

For attributes or restrictions that only apply at certain times or for certain types of vehicles, we often derive a suitable tag from one that already exists, as in using the maxspeed key as maxspeed:hgv=50 to describe a speed limit for HGVs (heavy goods vehicles). Time restrictions are often expressed by combining an established key with hour_on/hour_off or day_on/day_off. For example if a speed limit of 100 km/h applies between 22:00 and 8:00, we set:

```
maxspeed=100
maxspeed:hour_on=22
maxspeed:hour_off=8
```

This approach struggles to handle more complex restrictions, but it is a start, and it can be converted into something else once someone comes up with a better idea for encoding this kind of information.

Historical Interest

At the moment, OpenStreetMap software is not well suited for storing historical data in parallel to current data. If you map an ancient Roman road right across a modern town, then everyone who loads that area for editing will wonder what the line is that runs through everything else. (Chances are that the road will not show up on most maps because they will not evaluate whatever tags you have used for the old road, but an editor always loads all the data regardless of the tags.) The occasional historian among OSM users might set up a database server of their own, and use OpenStreetMap software and tools to create a historical dataset. Maybe the situation will change one day, when OpenStreetMap tools become powerful enough to work with different datasets without conflict.

You can use the `historic` tag to map objects of historical relevance that still exist today (even if only as ruins). For more details, look at the wiki articles Tag:historic and also Tag:historic=castle.

8.8 Ways Parallel to Roads

When OpenStreetMap began, mappers created one way for each road, with the exception of dual carriageways (divided highways), which received one way for each direction.

In reality, roads consist of a number of different lanes, some of which may be reserved for buses, taxis, cyclists, or other road users. There can be walkways or cycleways on one side of the road or on both, and these extra lanes are separated from the road by a curbstone, a grass verge or perhaps even a lane for parking cars.

Mapping all this detail is desirable, as it makes the dataset more useful. For example, software for automatic route planning from OSM data could be set to prefer roads with more than one lane per direction when computing a car route. Navigation systems could provide detailed instructions like "use the left lane". Cyclists might prefer to use segregated cycleways if they knew where they existed. Even pedestrians might want detailed information about safe walkways – the average pedestrian may always be able to muddle through, but how do you find a secure route to school for a young child?

Unfortunately, OpenStreetMap hasn't yet found an elegant way to deal with this wealth of information. We don't want mapping to become so complicated that only a few people can master it. If we create individual ways for all lanes of a road, which is sometimes referred to as *line bundles,* then an average residential road would have four ways (two lanes for cars and two walkways), and a larger thoroughfare with cycleways could easily reach eight or ten parallel ways. That would become almost impossible to handle in an editor – especially at an intersection of two such roads, or if you need to edit the shape of the road slightly.

So how do you decide how much detail to map? Here's a rule of thumb until something better is proposed: If a way runs parallel to the road, separated from it only by a painted line or a curbstone, then don't map the way separately, just tag the road to indicate its presence. If, on the other hand, the way is separated from the road in such a fashion that you can't switch back and forth between the two at any time, then map the way separately.

Here are a number of tags for mapping cycleways along roads:

Tag	Usage
cycleway=lane (or shared)	This road has a cycle lane.
cycleway=track (or segregated)	There is a segregated cycleway running along the road. Seldom used; most people will map the cycleway as a separate way.

95

Tag	Usage
cycleway=opposite	This road may be used by cyclists traveling in both directions even though it is a one-way street (oneway=yes).
cycleway=opposite_lane	This road has a cycle lane which may be used by cyclists traveling in both directions even though it is a one-way street.

Sporadically, similar schemes are applied to tags such as pavement or busway to map walkways or bus lanes. Currently, however, OSM lacks a good mechanism to describe where on the road – most importantly, on which side of the road – any of these described lanes are located.

8.9 Other Kinds of Relations

Several other possible uses of relations are being discussed and tried out, such as for bridges, tunnels, divided highways, complex buildings and junctions. We cover them briefly, but before you use any of these, you should consult the current discussion on the wiki or on the mailing lists; and remember that editing tools and renderers will not always understand the newest types of relations.

Bridges and Tunnels

Using relations lets you model a situation where multiple roads or railway tracks share a tunnel or bridge. You can even map the outline of the bridge itself as a separate way and included in the relation. The relation for bridges is tagged type=bridge, and the roles are across for ways that go over the bridge and under for those that pass beneath. Tunnels use type=tunnel.

The system currently used in OSM (see page 67) results in rendering software drawing multiple bridges or tunnels for each way passing over or under, even if they actually share the same infrastructure.

Dual Carriageways (Divided Highways)

Currently, a divided highway is modeled in OpenStreetMap as two separate, parallel ways, one for each direction of traffic, drawn individually and each tagged with the road's name or number. Rendering software therefore doesn't realize that both ways form part of the same road. Relations let you group the ways, and better rendering is possible. These relations are tagged type=dual_carriageway; roles for the members are not required.

Junctions

Relations of type junction group all on/off-ramps, turning lanes, and other connecting roads that together make up a complex junction. Then a rendering engine knows to leave out this detail when drawing the map at small scales, for example drawing the whole junction as a filled dot.

Complex Buildings and Sites

Relations give structure to buildings or sites by grouping property boundaries, floor plans, or entrances to a complex building or site, for example a railway station or an university campus. The usual relation type for this is site, but compound is also used.

8.10 Who Else Maps, and How?

There are some online mapping projects similar to OpenStreetMap, and of course there are authorities and businesses who create and maintain map data. The other online projects are often just active in a small region, or focus on a particular topic. A significant portion of map data on the market doesn't contain topological information. Other mapmakers store their data in the highly complex GDF format. Let's briefly look at these two alternative methods of mapping.

Topology

You don't need topological information if you just want to draw maps, but you do need more information about roads and intersections for route planning. Figure 8-5 shows the difference between map data with and without topology. Without topology (illustration on the left), it looks as if you could turn left when approaching from the South-West; only by looking at the topology (illustration on the right) can you see that this is not an intersection, but a bridge or tunnel, and you have to follow a different route to get onto the road you want.

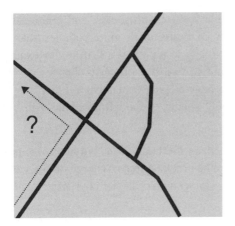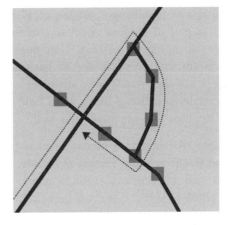

Figure 8-5: Topology for route planning. The boxes in the right image are connection nodes.

Some datasets are just collections of GPS tracks that haven't taken the additional step of creating a topologically correct structure manually from that data, as we do in OpenStreet-Map. These collections are popular because they are easy to create – just upload your GPS track to a central server and that's it. Theoretically it might be possible to construct a road network from such tracks using software, but this is seldom done in practice, and would never yield results as rich as the data in OpenStreetMap. Still, for thinly populated areas where users want to know whether there is any way at all rather than what kind of road it is and what name it has, these approaches can be a quick and useful alternative to the thorough mapping done in OpenStreetMap.

The GDF Format

GDF (Geographic Data Files) is an ISO standard for modeling road network data. It is often used for data exchange between providers and users of map data. The structures used in GDF aren't unlike those in OSM, but are far more complex. Here's a brief overview:

GDF uses "nodes", "edges", and "faces" to encode the basic infrastructure. GDF nodes are similar to OpenStreetMap nodes; edges are connectors between two nodes, but may addi-tionally have any number of "points" that aren't nodes. Faces are areas delineated by a number of edges. These basic elements make up what is called "level 0" in GDF – they en-code geographic information but have no meaning or identity.

On "level 1", these elements are combined into "features". A feature may be a point, line, or area, and it may have any number of "attributes" and belong to a class. Typical features in-clude for example "junction" or "road element". Thus, "level 1" gives elements a meaning. It also encodes relations between simple elements, like turn restrictions.

Finally, there is "level 2", where simple features can be aggregated into complex features.

There is a comprehensive catalog of all allowable features, attributes, and relationships, which is part of the ISO standard. Attributes in GDF are much more complex than the simple tags in OpenStreetMap. They might only relate to a part of a feature, for example. This means that a feature doesn't have to be split in two if a property changes partway along it. On multi-lane roads, attributes can also have a "lane dependent validity", so that you can describe things like a speed limit that only applies to the leftmost lane. Attributes that vary over time are possible as well.

The ISO GDF standard (version 4.0) is published as ISO14825:2004, but it is not freely available. The previous version (3.0), however, can be accessed free of charge on the web, at http://www.ertico.com/en/page_archive/gdf_-_geographic_data_files.htm. Read the wiki article GDF if you want to find out more.

9 Potlatch, the Online Flash Editor

The Flash editor Potlatch, originally developed by Richard Fairhurst, is ideal for OSM novices and casual users because you can use it directly from the OSM web page, without having to install any OSM specific software on your computer.

9.1 First Steps

To use Potlatch you need a web browser that has the Adobe Flash player plugin (version 8 or later) installed. If you zoom in close enough on `www.openstreetmap.org`, the edit tab becomes available (changing from white lettering on a gray background to black lettering on an off-white background). Click on it and you see a login dialog, and after filling that out, Potlatch starts inside the browser window and loads the section of the map that you were viewing.

Before you can start editing, Potlatch asks you to choose which of its two operating modes you want to use (see figure 9-1): The "Edit live" mode immediately saves any change you make to the OSM database; the "Edit with save" mode collects all your changes and only saves them when you ask it to. We recommend that you always use "Edit with save" mode as it's easier to correct mistakes (though this does have the disadvantage that if your browser crashes, you lose your changes). In fact, "Edit live" mode will soon be scrapped completely (see section 9.11 for information on Potlatch 2).

On first use, Potlatch will show a Yahoo satellite image background (if data is available for the region). This background may be varied by using the "set options" icons in the bottom left (a square with a check mark in it).

While working with Potlatch, you can access online help at any time through the "Help" button in the bottom left.

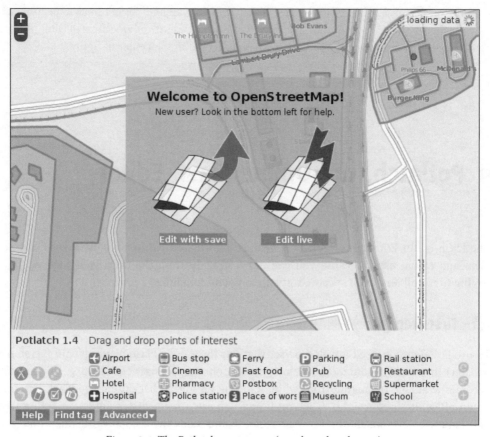

Figure 9-1: The Potlatch start screen (see also color plate 10).

You can move the map by holding down the left mouse button and dragging the mouse, or with the arrow keys. To zoom in and out, use the mouse wheel or the "Page Up" and "Page Down" keys, or the map controls ("+" and "–") in the top left corner of the screen. If you select large or densely mapped areas, working with Potlatch can become a bit slow because each moving of the map leads to large downloads from the OSM server. Zoom in further to speed things up. In the top right corner Potlatch will tell you what it is doing: If it says "loading data" then it is still retrieving data from the server. However, you can actually edit right away – you don't have to wait for the download to finish.

Potlatch makes a distinction between POI and non-POI nodes. If a node represents a point of interest, then Potlatch either displays a matching icon or at least a slightly larger green dot if it doesn't have an icon for that type of POI. In figure 9-1 some different POI nodes are visible in the upper right corner of the screen.

If, on the other hand, a node is only used to construct a way and doesn't have a meaning of its own, then Potlatch usually doesn't show the node at all; it only becomes visible if you select the way that it is on, like the small stream selected in the center of figure 9-2.

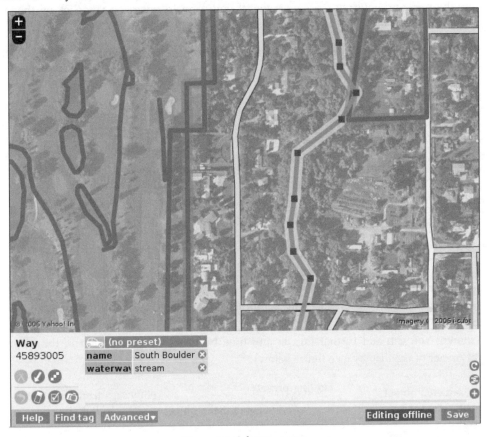

Figure 9-2: Selecting a way.

Ways are colored roughly the same as they are on the OpenStreetMap site: Blue, green, dark red, and orange for the major roads, white for residential roads, brown for tracks, black for railways. Cycleways and waterways are also blue. Objects with a purple outline are relation members (see section 9.7), and those in bright red are locked (see section 9.6).

If you click on an existing way, Potlatch highlights it with a larger underlayed yellow line. All nodes contained in the way are drawn as red squares, and below the map view you can see all the tags belonging to the way. Potlatch calls them *attributes*.

> ☞ *If there are multiple ways on top of each other, sharing the same nodes, you can select one of them and then use the "/" key or the "+" key on the numeric keypad to cycle through them.*

9.2 Editing Tags

If a node or way is selected, you can change its tags by clicking into the relevant field below the map and entering the new value. If you want to remove a tag, click on the "x" symbol next to it.

Potlatch has a number of different preset themes. The little symbol above the tag list tells you which one is selected:

🚗	roads	📷	tourism
🚶	footpaths and bridleways	⛑	sports
🚲	cycleways or tracks	🏛	education
🚢	rivers and canals	🗺	land use
🚆	railways		addresses
🌲	woods and lakes		

Clicking on this symbol cycles through the presets for this theme, shown to the right of the symbol. Depending on your selection, additional input fields will appear – for example if you choose "residential road" from the "roads" theme, an input field for the road name will be shown. You can add further tags at any time by using the plus button in the bottom right corner of the display (see figure below).

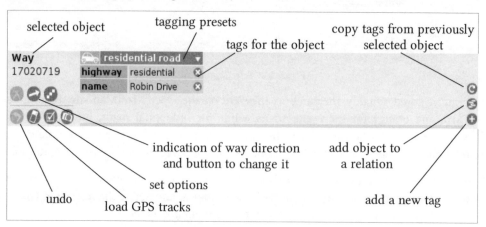

Figure 9-3: Important user interface elements in Potlatch.

If you click on the icon showing a circular arrow on the right, the currently selected object receives the same tags as the one selected before. This action can also be executed by pressing "R" (for "repeat tags"). The key combination "Shift"+"R" will repeat all tags except name and ref.

9.3 Creating Nodes and Ways

To place individual nodes (POIs for post boxes for instance), simply use your mouse to drag one of the POI symbols shown below the map (see figure 9-1) to the correct location on the map. This creates a node and automatically tags it according to the icon you have chosen, and you only have to complete additional input fields, e. g. for the name. Alternatively, you can place a POI by double-clicking the correct location on the map and setting all the tags yourself.

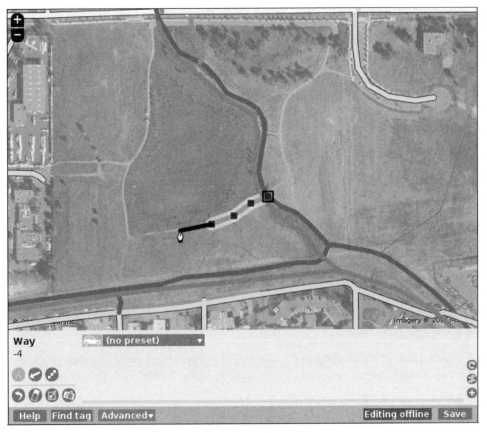

Figure 9-4: A new way being drawn.

To create a new way, click on an empty space on the map. A red square is shown, and a black line connects the mouse cursor to that point. Each additional click places one more square, and double-clicking places the last one and stops the drawing. You can also use the

"Enter" key to finish the new way. If you are entering an area, click the start node again to finish it. You can cancel the edit with the "ESC" key. If you want the new way to branch off from an existing way instead of starting in the middle of nowhere, you have to select the existing way first. If the way already has a node where you want to branch, shift-click that node (hold the Shift key down while clicking with the mouse) and then continue to draw the new way. If the existing way doesn't yet have a node where you want to branch, insert a new node at that position by shift-clicking, then shift-click to select it, and continue as already described (see also figure 9-5).

If you are drawing a new way and want its endpoint to connect to an already existing way, simply click into the existing way while drawing. The target way's nodes will be highlighted in blue while the mouse is over the way. If a node already exists where you click the mouse, it will be used; otherwise a new node, shared by both the existing and the new way, will be inserted.

Potlatch beginners sometimes make the mistake of tracing roads on an aerial imagery background, but not connecting the resulting roads, forming not a grid but a jumble of individual ways. Be careful to make the right connections. When you select a way and its nodes are drawn as red squares, Potlatch draws a black outline around those that are connected to something else.

Figure 9-5 recaps the process of connecting two ways:

a) A way has been selected, and a branch is to be drawn from a location where the way doesn't yet have a node.

b) A new node is inserted by shift-clicking.

c) A second shift-click selects the newly inserted node and activates the way drawing mode. Nodes can now be added to the way by clicking on the empty map.

d) The end of the way is to be connected back to the old way. This figure shows the mouse cursor hovering next to the old way. As soon as the mouse cursor is on the old way, all nodes will light up in blue.

e) A mouse click on an existing node connects the way to that node; a mouse click in between two nodes inserts a new connection node. Pressing "Enter" ends the process.

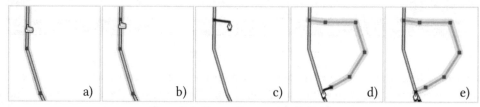

Figure 9-5: Connecting ways in Potlatch.

9.4 Editing Nodes and Ways

This table tells you how to perform editing tasks on existing ways and nodes.

Task	Execution
Move a node.	Click on the node and drag it with the mouse. If the node is part of a way, the way has to be selected first in order to make its nodes visible.
Delete a node.	Select the node and press the "Delete" key. If the node is part of a way, the way will automatically be modified.
Insert a new node into a way.	Hold the Shift key and click on the way where you want the new node to be placed.
Remove a node from a way.	Select the node in the way and press the "–" key. Both the way and the node will remain, but the way will not be using the node any longer.
Extend an existing way.	Select the way's end node and then continue drawing the way just as usual.
Connect a new way to an existing way.	Select the existing way and, while holding the Shift key, click on the node where you want to connect. Then continue drawing the new way as usual (see also figure 9-5).
Split a way in two.	Select the node in the way where you want to split. Then press the "X" key or click on the scissors icon in the bottom left.
Delete a way and its nodes.	Select the way and then press "Shift"+"Delete".
Reverse a way's direction.	Select the way and click on the straight arrow icon in the bottom left.
Undo last action.	Press the "Z" key or click on the curved arrow icon in the bottom left.
Combine two ways.	Select the first way. Hold Ctrl, then click on the second way. Both ways are now merged into one, provided that both ways have been sharing an endpoint before. (Internally, one of the ways is deleted and the other extended by the additional nodes.) Potlatch tries to combine the tags of both ways sensibly but you should still check the result.

The Potlatch/Keyboard_shortcuts wiki page has a list of keyboard shortcuts for Potlatch.

9.5 Saving Changes

If you want to save your changes, click on the "Save" button in the bottom right. Potlatch asks you for a short edit comment – this will become the changeset comment that helps other OpenStreetMap users to understand what you have been doing.

Potlatch then uploads all your changes to the server and tells you when it has finished.

Remember: In the "Edit live" mode there is no save button; Potlatch uploads every change as you make it.

9.6 Reverting Changes

When you save your changes to the server, a new version is created of each object that has been modified. If you select a way in Potlatch and then press "H" (for history), a list of all older versions of that way is shown – all versions, not only ones that you have created. From this dialog (see figure 9-6), you can revert to an older version with the "Revert" button. The "Mail" button allows you to write a message to the author of the selected version, and "More" shows the object history on a web page, in considerable detail.

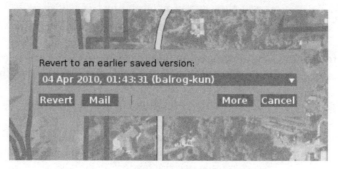

Figure 9-6: Selecting an old version for revert.

If you press "U" (undelete), all deleted ways in the current view are loaded from the server and shown as red lines. If you select one of these ways, a padlock symbol is displayed along with the message "click to unlock" (see figure below).

Figure 9-7: A deleted way is marked with a padlock icon.

Ways locked in this manner won't be uploaded to the server when saving, but you can unlock them by clicking on the padlock icon, and this will then reactivate the way once you save your changes.

9.7 Relations in Potlatch

Unlike other editors, Potlatch doesn't treat a relation as an object in its own right. Instead, it is treated as if it were an attribute of a node or way. If you click on the icon with the chain links in the bottom right, a dialog appears that lets you add the currently selected object to an existing relation, or create a new relation (figure 9-8).

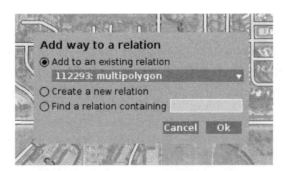

Figure 9-8: A way is being added to a relation.

Objects that are part of a relation are highlighted with a blue or purple halo, and the relation details are shown in the second line of the attributes display (figure 9-9).

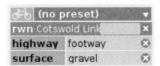

Figure 9-9: Properties of a way belonging to a relation.

The small text box next to the relation name can be used to specify the role of the object in the relation. Clicking on the relation name brings up a window with the relation's tags. New tags can be added here by clicking on the "+" in the top right of the dialog. Clicking "x" next to the relation name removes the object from the relation.

9.8 Working with GPS Tracks

The "G" key or the button in the bottom left that looks somewhat like an eraser activates the display of GPS tracks from the central database. All tracks in the currently visible area are shown, up to a maximum of 10,000 GPS points. Pressing "G" again loads more. Using "Shift"+"G" brings up only your own tracks. If you pan to another area, you will have to use "G" again to load GPS tracks for that area.

Opening Potlatch and displaying GPS tracks is not the only way of working with them. You can also go to the list of uploaded GPS tracks on the community website (see section 3.1) and click on the "Edit" link next to a track. This starts Potlatch with only that track displayed. In this mode Potlatch even displays the track's waypoints. The Potlatch start screen offers a third option, "track", which automatically converts the selected GPS track into ways. Because these ways usually require manual corrections, they are in a locked state initially (with the padlock symbol – just like the deleted ways discussed before). You have to unlock them if you want to make corrections and upload them.

9.9   Background Images

By default, Potlatch comes up with Yahoo aerial imagery in the background. If you only want to work with GPS points or with already existing data, you can completely switch off the background using the "F1" key. "F2" then re-activates Yahoo imagery. The other function keys are mapped to other background imagery – the exact selection varies from version to version. If you hold Shift while selecting a background image, it will be shown lighter than usual. This, and several other options, can also be changed with the "set options" dialog (accessed by the check box icon in the bottom left).

In some areas, Yahoo imagery isn't quite aligned correctly and will have to be adjusted to existing OSM data or GPS tracks before it can be used to derive further information. If you hold the space bar while moving the map with your mouse, only the aerial imagery background moves so that you can carefully align it with existing data.

You can also temporarily disable the map display by pressing "Caps Lock". This shows the map background with only a faint data overlay.

9.10   Additional Functionality

In addition to what we have described in this chapter, you can do a number of other tasks with Potlatch, including:

- Automatically smooth ways and create roundabouts (traffic circles).
- Automatically create parallel ways.
- Upload changes to Twitter or other microblogging services.
- Photo mapping.
- Save tag combinations to a paste buffer and apply them later, as well as automatically add source tags depending on the background image.

Details about these functions are in the online help, or in the wiki under Potlatch.

9.11   Upcoming – Potlatch 2

A version 2 of Potlatch is expected to be released during 2010. Editing in Potlatch 2 isn't going to be significantly different from Potlatch 1, but it will offer major improvements regarding tagging presets – for example, clicking on a traffic sign will be sufficient to set a speed limit or other restriction. Potlatch 2 will have a much improved rendering engine, called Halcyon, which will show the map almost in the same style as the "real", Mapnik-rendered OpenStreetMap map. Halcyon styles are written in MapCSS, which is modeled after the well-known CSS style sheets used with HTML. Relation handling will be rewritten completely for Potlatch 2. Furthermore, Potlatch 2 won't have an "Edit live" mode.

10 JOSM, the Offline Java Editor

JOSM is the editor for OpenStreetMap power users. Using JOSM, you can modify all objects easily through basic editing functions, and a large number of plugins help with specialist editing tasks. If you only want to contribute occasionally to OSM, you might prefer to use the less-powerful Potlatch online editor, which we covered in the previous chapter.

Editing in JOSM resembles the way you use most standard drawing programs. If you've ever worked with Inkscape, Illustrator or the like then JOSM will seem familiar. Data in JOSM is presented on multiple layers: One layer could, for example, show a GPS track loaded from disk, another some data from the OpenStreetMap server, and the third an aerial imagery background. You only edit, however, in the layers containing OSM data.

JOSM is continuously under development. There is a lot of documentation, in several languages, on JOSM's own wiki at josm.openstreetmap.de. Be sure also to check the list of latest changes displayed on that website, as documentation doesn't always keep up with recent developments. You can access relevant pages of this documentation from within JOSM by pressing the F1 key.

JOSM always uses a local copy of OSM data, which you have to synchronize with the server before and after working on it. Having collected data with your GPS device, this is the typical procedure to follow:

1. Start JOSM.
2. Load GPX file with track data into JOSM.
3. Download OSM data for the selected area.
4. Add new data, or modify existing data.
5. Upload your changes.

This chapter guides you through each step in this process.

10.1 Installing and Running JOSM

JOSM runs on Linux, Windows, and Mac OS X. It requires Java 1.6. Download the current version from `http://josm.openstreetmap.de/josm-tested.jar`.[1] On Linux, start JOSM by typing

```
java -jar josm-tested.jar
```

or, on Windows or OS X, double click the icon for `josm-tested.jar` file. If you have any problems, look at the JOSM wiki page.

You can use command line arguments to change default launch settings, though to use these you will have to run JOSM from the command line even if using an operating system that would normally let you run JOSM by double clicking the icon. Here are some of the command line arguments you might wish to use:

JOSM supports many languages and, when it starts, tries to select the language matching your system settings. You can ask for a different language by adding the command line argument `--language=xx` (e. g. `--language=de` for German). Some messages may still show up in English because the newest features are not always translated right away.

If you are working with large datasets, let JOSM use more memory than Java makes available by default. To allow JOSM to use 1 GB of RAM, for example, use

```
java -Xmx1024m -jar josm-tested.jar
```

You can also add the names of OSM or GPX files to load on the command line:

```
java -jar josm-tested.jar cycletour.gpx
```

There are more command line arguments, for example you can also request loading of a specific map section or preset the window size. Run this to see details:

```
java -jar josm-tested.jar --help
```

The application saves its settings and plugins in a special directory. On Linux and OS X this is called `.josm` and is located in the current user's home directory; on Windows the directory is `C:\Documents and Settings\Username\.josm`. In that directory, a file named `preferences` stores various JOSM settings, and a subdirectory named `plugins` contains all the plugins that have been downloaded and installed.

Getting Started

Once started, JOSM loads and displays the start screen (figure 10-1) including a "message of the day" that points out important changes relevant to the version you are running.

---

1 You can also download `josm-latest.jar` to retrieve the latest nightly build.

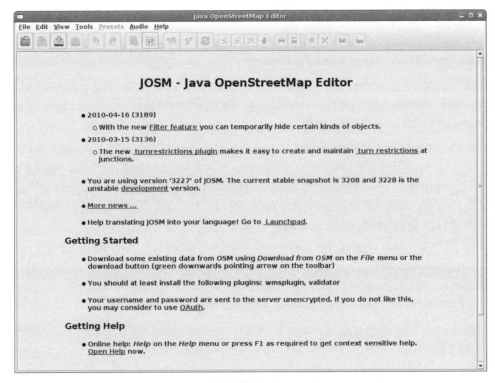

Figure 10-1: JOSM start screen.

Figure 10-2 shows the most important buttons from JOSM's standard button bar which is always displayed across the top of the editor window.

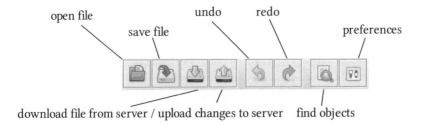

Figure 10-2: The standard button bar.

10.2 Loading Local Files into JOSM

JOSM can read the following file types:

- OpenStreetMap files (XML files with the extension .osm).
- GPS tracks and waypoints in GPX format (XML files with the extension .gpx).

- Compressed OpenStreetMap or GPX files (.osm.gz, .gpx.gz, .gpx.bz2, .osm.bz2).
- GPS logs in NMEA format (*.nmea or *.txt).

You'll normally be working with GPX files.

While OpenStreetMap data can be saved in, and loaded from, local files, the usual work flow consists of loading data for an area from the OpenStreetMap server and then uploading any modifications directly to it.

To load local data, use the "open file" button. JOSM creates a new map layer and displays it. If the file is a GPX file, two layers are created – one for the track itself and one for associated waypoints. Neither of these layers is editable; only by downloading data from the server or creating an empty OSM layer (using the "New" action from the "File" menu) will you get an editable layer.

Once a layer has been created, the JOSM user interface becomes visible (figure 10-3).

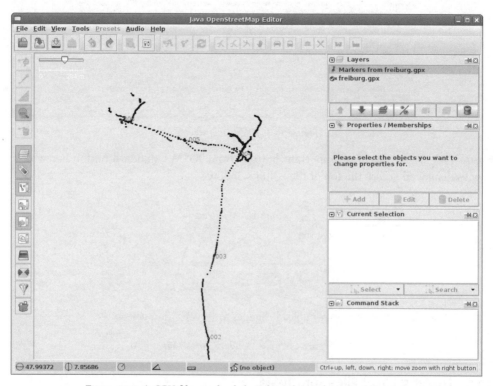

Figure 10-3: A GPX file was loaded, and two layers have been created.

The map view always occupies the center of the screen. Above it you see the menu bar and a row of buttons for accessing the most important features. The column on the left (figure

10-4) has buttons for the various editing modes and switches to open and close dialogs containing the layer list, object properties, and other information required for editing.

	Selection mode (also for moving and rotating)
	Drawing mode
	Rectangle drawing mode
	Zoom mode
	Delete mode
	Layer dialog (activated)
	Properties/Memberships dialog (activated)
	Selection dialog (lists selected objects; activated)
	List of relations
	Command history (activated)
	Display of author's names
	Object change history
	Conflict dialog
	Object filters
	List of changesets

Figure 10-4: Mode buttons and switches for dialogs.

The column on the right contains the open dialog windows. Clicking on the small pin button in the top right corner lets you detach it from the panel, move it around the screen, and resize it. The dialogs visible in figure 10-3 (Layers, Properties / Memberships, Current Selection, and Command Stack) are the ones that are open when you run JOSM for the first time. After that, it remembers which dialogs you have closed or opened, so the interface may look different on successive launches.

Across the bottom of the screen, there is a row showing the latitude and longitude of the mouse cursor and additional information about the object being drawn. There is also a mini help line which gives an indication of possible editing actions, such as "double-click to finish creating the way".

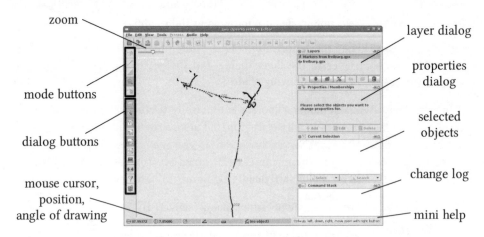

zoom

layer dialog

mode buttons

properties
dialog

dialog buttons

selected
objects

mouse cursor,
position,
angle of drawing

change log

mini help

Figure 10-5: JOSM controls. The screenshot is a downscaled version of that shown in figure 10-3.

To modify how the GPX layers display, open the "Preferences" dialog from the "Edit" menu (see figure 10-6).

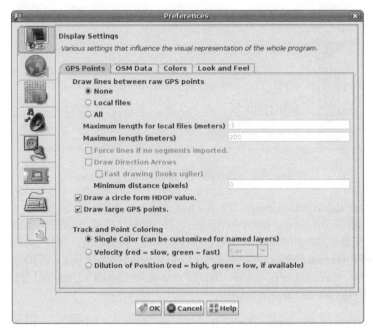

Figure 10-6: The "Preferences" dialog with GPX settings.

In the Preferences dialog, you can change the color, choose the size of the displayed track-points, or set consecutive points to be connected by lines. It is even possible to have JOSM color the tracks depending on the speed at which the GPS receiver was moving, so that you can make out which tracks were recorded by motorcar and which were recorded while walking.

Alternatively you can change the settings for coloring and line drawing of each GPX layer, by right-clicking on that layer in the layer dialog and then selecting the relevant option from the context menu.

Setting lines to be drawn between trackpoints is especially useful if the points are spaced far apart or if you want to zoom in a long way. It isn't always so useful when working with GPX layers loaded from the OSM server, however, as you sometimes get a strange zigzag pattern where trackpoints from different tracks get mixed up. You can avoid this by using the "maximum length" setting in "Preferences" (see figure 10-6) to tell JOSM to draw lines only where points are not too far apart.

Looking at the Map

When loading data for the first time in a session, whether from a file or from the server, JOSM will set the view port (map window) so that all data is visible. To zoom in or out, use the mouse wheel to zoom in or out, or select the "zoom" mode by clicking on the magnifying glass icon on the left and then select the rectangle you want to view. You can also use the "+" and "−" keys on the keyboard or click on the zoom bar (figure 10-5, top left of view port) to change the zoom factor.

To pan in any direction, hold down the right mouse button and drag the mouse,[2] or hold down the Ctrl key and use the arrow keys to move around.

Loading more data later won't change your current view port settings, so if the newly loaded data lies outside your current view port then you won't see it immediately. To bring the full dataset into view, select "Zoom to data" from the "View" menu. Some menu options can be accessed through shortcut keys; the shortcut key for "Zoom to data" is the plain "1" (one) key.

> ☞ *If your GPX file happens to contain a few left-over waypoints from your last holiday on the other side of the world, then JOSM will select a view port encompassing half the planet, and every GPS track will only show up as a single dot. If this happens you might want to split up your GPS track using a program like GPSBabel (see section 4.10).*

---

2 This is different from the OpenStreetMap web page, where you pan with the left mouse button.

Different Layers

For every file loaded, JOSM creates a new layer (two for GPX files, as we said earlier). Downloading data from the server will create an OSM data layer if there isn't one already. The active layer is highlighted in the layer dialog.

By default JOSM only knows about data and GPS layers, but many plugins add their own layer types.

Figure 10-7: The Layer dialog.

The layer dialog (see figure 10-7) has a number of buttons allowing you to change the drawing order of layers, switch the active layer, make a layer invisible, merge layers, duplicate, or delete them. Right-click one of the layer entries to bring up the context menu, which gives access to layer-specific settings, for example setting colors for a GPX track.

Remember that when you are saving data to a file, only the active layer is saved.

Loading Images and Audio Files

A waypoint in a GPX file can have supplementary information in addition to a name and geographic position, among them a link element pointing to a URL or a file. This is a good way to reference audio or image recordings taken while mapping, as long as you can get the GPX file to contain the proper links. (Only few devices are capable of that.)

When JOSM encounters such waypoints in the GPX file, it displays a small button at the position of the waypoint on the map. Click the button, and either a web browser opens to display the content of a link, or audio files (in WAV format) and images (JPEG or PNG files) open directly in JOSM.

Alternatively, JOSM can load photos directly and attempt to correlate the timestamps in their JPEG headers with the timestamps in the GPS track in order to find the correct location for each photo. To import photos in this manner, select "Import images" from the context menu of the GPX layer, and then choose any number of JPEG files. JOSM displays a synchronization dialog that allows you to specify your time zone or a time offset to account for a clock difference between the camera and the GPS device. A useful tip is to take a photo of your GPS device displaying the time before you set out on a mapping trip; comparing the camera's timestamp for this photo and the time displayed on it tells you the exact clock offset.

After a successful import, a new layer named "georeferenced photos" becomes visible, showing a little camera symbol at the locations where the photo timestamp and the GPS timestamp coincide. Clicking on one of these opens the image viewer dialog if it isn't open already, and has it display the photo. You can add the image viewer dialog to the right column on the screen or leave it in a window of its own.

There is a similar feature to load audio recordings ("Import audio") and synchronize them with the GPS track for georeferenced playback.

10.3 Loading Data from the OSM Server

Use the download button (see figure 10-2) to call up the download dialog (see figure 10-8). In this dialog you can specify which area, and which kind of data, you want to download from the OpenStreetMap server. The server's Internet address is already known to JOSM through the default configuration, and you don't need a username or password for downloading data.

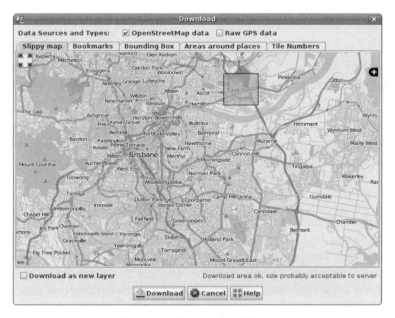

Figure 10-8: The download dialog.

Next to "Data Sources and Types" you can choose whether to download OpenStreetMap data (meaning nodes, ways, and relations) or raw GPS data that has been uploaded by other mappers. Raw GPS data is the less useful of the two since it doesn't carry any additional information, but sometimes it can be useful to look at tracks recorded by other users, especially if your own GPS tracks are patchy.

If you select the "Download as new layer" check box (bottom left), then JOSM will create a new layer for downloaded data. Otherwise the data will be added to an existing OpenStreetMap data layer. In general, leave this box unchecked as it's easier to work with only one OSM layer.

Selecting the Area to Download

Now you've chosen your options, you just need to select the area you want downloaded. By default, JOSM has five tabs for this: "Slippy map", "Bookmarks", "Bounding Box", "Areas around places", and "Tile Numbers". Some plugins provide more options. The default view is the slippy map view, which works more or less like the OpenStreetMap map you know from the website.[3] JOSM won't download the whole visible area, just the bit inside the red rectangle that you draw by dragging with the left mouse button.

Entering Coordinates and Tile Numbers

On the "Bounding Box" tab you can enter the download area as a coordinate range. As discussed earlier, the bounding box preset in this dialog is always the area currently visible in JOSM. To select a different area, change the minimum and maximum values for latitude and longitude.

The "Tile numbers" tab is similar, but on that tab you can enter a zoom level and the x and y coordinates of a range of map tiles in order to chose the area. Map tiles are the bitmaps from which a map on the web is assembled; we discuss them in chapter 14.

The text area titled "URL from `www.openstreetmap.org`" allows you to paste an openstreetmap.org map URL, and JOSM will then decode that URL to extract the download area.

Bookmarks

If you regularly work on particular areas, you can save the bounding box for them in a bookmark. To do this, first select an area using one of the other methods and then switch to the "bookmarks" tab. Then click on "Create bookmark" to save the area as a new bookmark (JOSM will ask for a name). At any later time, you can select one of the bookmarks you have created and JOSM downloads the current version of the data for that area.

Download by Place Name

The "Areas around places" tab lets you enter a place name and then conducts a search on the OSM database. A list of results is displayed. If one of the results is what you were looking for, select it to download the surrounding area.

---

3 Remember you have to use the right mouse button to pan the map in JOSM, not the left.

Error Messages when Downloading

Apart from network problems, JOSM could display an error message during download for the following reasons:

- The OpenStreetMap server is currently unavailable because of planned maintenance or technical problems. You usually find details about such issues on the wiki page Plat-form Status.
- The area you requested was too large. The OpenStreetMap server currently allows downloads of 0.25 degrees squared – the product (max_latitude-min_latitude) * (max_longitude-min_longitude) must be smaller than 0.25. At the equator this corresponds to an area of approximately 50 km x 50 km, and roughly half that at extreme Northern and Southern latitudes. If you need a larger area, you have to download it in multiple steps (but see API usage policy on the wiki) or retrieve the data using an extract or a mirror. The download dialog will normally show a warning in the bottom right corner if the area is too large.
- The area you requested contained more than 50,000 nodes. In densely populated areas this limit can be reached for areas as small as 10 km x 10 km.
- The area you requested was empty.

If the server is too busy, the message "contacting OSM server" may remain indefinitely. If this happens, just try again at a later time, or check the aforementioned Platform Status. wiki page for known problems.

When downloading data for an area that overlaps with data already loaded, conflicts can occur. This happens when you and somebody else have been editing the same objects simultaneously. JOSM has a sophisticated mechanism to resolve such conflicts; we discuss it in "Conflicts During Download" on page 130.

Objects Outside the Downloaded Area

JOSM sends requests for rectangular areas to be download from the OpenStreetMap server. What the server returns is usually a ragged area only roughly resembling that rectangle, because any object partly contained in the rectangle will be included in full, even those bits that lie outside the requested area. In its default setting, JOSM shows a yellow hatching outside the requested area to remind you that in that area, not everything present in the database is also on your screen.

For example, the database could contain a house at the location marked with a question mark in figure 10-9. That house wasn't downloaded because it was completely outside the requested area, but the roads to its East and to its West go into the requested area so were downloaded. Without the yellow hatching you could easily forget that the area containing the house is incomplete.

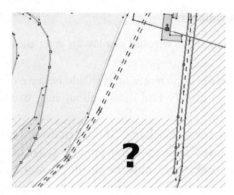

Figure 10-9: Objects can extend into the hatched, non-downloaded area.

Loading Data along a GPS Track

In the context menu of a GPX layer (which you can access by right-clicking the mouse on the layer in the layer dialog), you can choose "Download from OSM along this track". This function downloads a narrow corridor of data in the immediate vicinity of the GPS track. This is useful as it downloads much less data compared to downloading the complete bounding rectangle for the track which might well be over the allowed size limit.

10.4 Editing the Map

Adding Nodes and Ways

Downloading data from the OpenStreetMap server makes JOSM create a new data layer which can be edited. If you want to create an empty data layer to edit without downloading things, choose "New" from the "File" menu.

Now you can start editing. To create a new way, switch to drawing mode (by clicking on the appropriate button shown in figure 10-4, or using the shortcut key "A"). Now click at the position where the way is to start, and then click to continue the way. Every click creates a new node, extending the way (see figure 10-8).

During this process, the way that you are drawing is selected (highlighted), and a yellow rubber-band line connects the last placed node to the current mouse position.

If instead of clicking on empty terrain you click on an existing node, JOSM will connect the new way to the existing node. If you click on an existing way (but not near one of its nodes), then a new node will be inserted into the existing way and be used as the starting point for the way being drawn. Conclude the way creation by double-clicking the last node, or by pressing the ESC key.

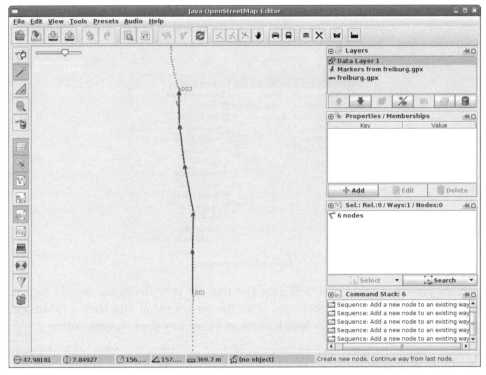

Figure 10-10: Creating a new way between GPS waypoints 001 and 002.

The modifier keys Shift, Alt, or Ctrl change the behavior we have just described, according to the following table:

Modifier	Function of left mouse key
Shift	JOSM places a new node but doesn't connect it to the way being drawn; the new node is isolated. Use this to start a new way at another location, or to place a POI node.
Alt	JOSM places a new node or re-uses an existing one as usual, but the connection between the last node and the newly placed one forms the beginning of a new way. Use this if you are drawing a continuous line which consists of multiple ways.
Ctrl	The new node is placed independently from existing data; JOSM won't re-use an existing node or insert the new node into an already existing way. Use this if you have to place a node near another node or way but do not want them connected.

Properties (Tags)

After drawing a new way, it's a good idea to assign the proper tags right away. JOSM has a number of tagging presets that cover the most frequently used tag combinations. Simply call up the "Presets" menu (see figure 10-11), and if, for example, you have been mapping a primary road, you can choose "Highways", then "Streets", and then "Primary". A small dialog then appears, giving you the opportunity to enter a street name, a road number, and other details. Once you close this dialog, the highway and name tags are automatically assigned to the way.

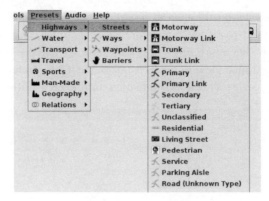

Figure 10-11: Presets.

Using the presets to begin with will help you find out how things are usually tagged in OpenStreetMap. Most dialogs that open from the presets menu also have a "More information about this feature" link, which leads to an online help page for that setting.

All icons, drop-down selections, and pop-up dialogs are defined in XML files. If you find that you regularly use certain tag combinations, you can add your own tagging presets by writing appropriate XML files, or even replacing the default presets altogether. The JOSM wiki at http://josm.openstreetmap.de/wiki/TaggingPresets has a description of the XML format used, and information on how to create and use your own presets.

Once you are familiar with certain tags, you don't need to use the presets at all – just set or change all tags for an object directly in the "Properties/Memberships" dialog (figure 10-12) that displays in the right-hand column of JOSM. It shows all tags defined for the currently selected object, and allows you to modify or delete them or add new ones.

Figure 10-12: The properties dialog.

If multiple objects are selected, then the dialog shows a value only where all the objects share the same value; where a tag is present for only some of the selected objects, or has different values, the value in the dialog is listed as "<different>".

The lower part of the properties dialog tells you if the selected object(s) are part of any relations, and if so, in which role. You can't modify relation membership directly in this dialog, but double-clicking on a relation opens the relation editor (see section 10.7).

How an object is displayed on the map in JOSM depends on its tags. Important roads are drawn thicker, residential roads are narrower, areas are filled, and points of interest are represented by symbols (see figure 10-13 and color plate 8). Use the "View" menu to switch from the default themed map view to a *wireframe mode* if you prefer a more basic look; in wireframe mode, all ways are shown as single lines and nodes as little squares.

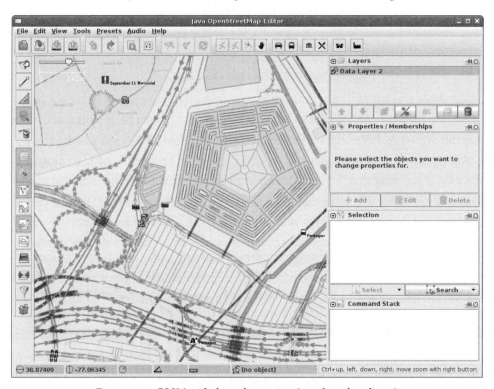

Figure 10-13: JOSM with themed map view (see also color plate 8).

Selecting and Modifying Objects

To inspect or modify an object, you first need to select it. To do this, enter selection mode by clicking on the appropriate button (see figure 10-4) or pressing the "S" shortcut key, and then either click on the object directly, or draw a selection rectangle around a number of objects. Holding down the Shift key while selecting objects adds them to the current selection (instead of changing the selection), and holding down the Ctrl key while selecting objects removes them from the current selection.

The selection dialog in the right-hand column (see figure 10-14) lists the currently selected objects ordered by type (ways, relations, nodes) and then name. Objects without a defined name are listed under a generic name (e. g. "way 4 nodes").

The dialog keeps a list of previous selections; you can reactivate any of these using the "Select" button at the bottom.

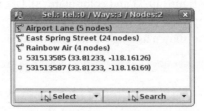

Figure 10-14: The selection dialog.

You can move selected objects with your mouse or, if you only want to move something a little bit, use the Shift+Arrow keys to nudge it by one pixel. If you press Shift and Ctrl, you can use the mouse to rotate the selected objects around their center.

Editable ways (those on the current layer) are shown with a little "+" midway between any two nodes. If you drag that "+" with the mouse, a new node will be created at that location. This is very useful for refining the geometry of a way that has only been roughly done.

Use the "Copy" and "Paste" options in the "Edit" menu to copy selected objects to the clipboard and insert them again from there. On pasting, the object will be slightly displaced so as not to hide the original object. The "Paste Tags" option applies the tags of whatever is in the clipboard to all currently selected objects. You can delete selected objects either by using the "Delete" option in the "Edit" menu or by pressing the "Delete" key on the keyboard, but beware that if you delete a way using either of these methods, all nodes that were used by the way and aren't used or tagged otherwise will also be removed.

To have greater control over what gets deleted, switch to the dedicated delete mode (the trash button in the left toolbar, see figure 10-4). In this mode, every object you click on will be deleted, but the following modifier keys control the process:

Modifier	Function of left mouse key
Alt	Removes the way that was clicked on, but doesn't remove the nodes it was using.
Shift	Removes the way segment that was clicked on, meaning the bit of way between the two nearest nodes. This splits the way in two.
Ctrl	Normally, JOSM removes a deleted node from any way that was using it but leaves the way in place; the same happens, after a confirmation dialog, for objects used by a relation. If you hold Ctrl while deleting, JOSM will remove all ways or relations that reference the object you clicked on instead of simply dropping the object from them.

JOSM records all changes, and lists them in the command stack dialog. You can undo them step by step right back to the start of the session as long as they haven't been uploaded.

Rectangles and Rectangular Areas

There are two ways to draw rectangles in JOSM. The first is to draw them freehand and then use the "Orthogonalize shape" option in the "Tools" menu. If you select one or more ways that are close to rectangular, this function will try to make every angle into a right angle without distorting the shape too much. If, in addition to ways, you also select exactly two nodes, then the orientation of the resulting shapes will be aligned to a (hypothetical) line through these two nodes.

You can use this to align skewed houses along a road, for example. The figure below illustrates the process. We selected the two houses and the two nodes marked with arrows before applying the "Orthogonalize shape" function.

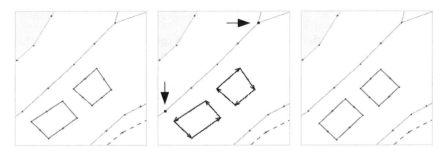

Figure 10-15: Two skewed buildings being made rectangular.

The second way of drawing rectangles is to use the "Create areas" mode (shortcut key "X", for extrude). Activate it by clicking on the set square icon in the left toolbar (see figure 10-4). With this tool you can extrude lines into rectangular areas, as illustrated in figure 10-16:

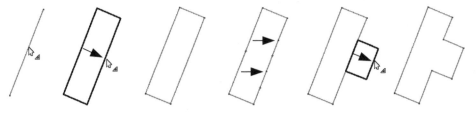

Figure 10-16: Using the "Create areas" function.

First, you draw a simple way. Then you extrude it into a rectangle by dragging it with the mouse. Place two additional nodes on one side of the rectangle (marked with horizontal arrows), and then extrude the rectangle again between these two nodes. With a little practice, this tool will help you draw complex rectangular buildings or areas quickly.

Other Advanced Editing Tools

JOSM has many more tools to help with everyday editing tasks. From the "Tools" menu, you can:

- Arrange nodes in a circle or a straight line, or distribute nodes equally between two end points.
- Combine or split ways.
- Join nodes to another node or a nearby way, or *unglue* (disconnect) a node from a way without removing it.
- Create individual nodes by entering a pair of coordinates.
- Create a group of nodes forming a circle.

We won't cover these all in this book, but the JOSM wiki has documentation for them at `http://josm.openstreetmap.de/wiki/Help/Menu/Tools`.

Searching

The "Edit" menu has a search function that lets you select or deselect all objects that match certain criteria.

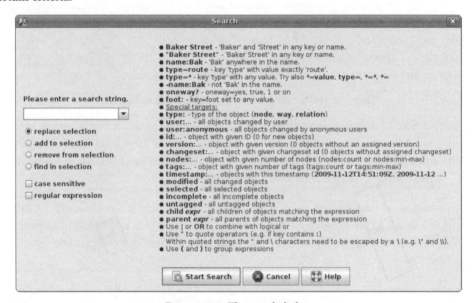

Figure 10-17: The search dialog.

If you simply search for some text, then all objects are found that contain this text in one of their tags: "Mill Street" will find the street of that name, but also an object named "Upper Mill Street Pharmacy". A search for "residential" will select all roads that are tagged high-way=residential but also areas with landuse=residential.

A colon has a special role when used in the search string; it works as a delimiter between a tag key and value. Searching for "railway:rail", for example, yields all ways tagged `railway=rail`. Using a minus sign negates the search term or in other words selects only those objects that do not have a specific tag.

Search term	Finds
carl benz	All objects where the strings "carl" and "benz" occur in any of the tags.
"carl benz"	All objects where "carl benz" occurs as a phrase in any of the tags.
name:benz	All objects with a name tag containing the string "benz".
type:way	All ways (similarly, type:node and type:relation).
id:12345	Objects with the ID 12345.
type:node -name:benz	All nodes that don't have the string "benz" in their names.
type:way -name:	All ways without names.
type:way selected	All ways that are currently selected (this effectively deselects all nodes and relations).
parent selected	All objects that contain at least one of the currently selected objects (for example, if a node is selected, it finds all ways that use this node).

In the search dialog you can choose whether the list of results is added to the current selection, removed from it, or whether it is to replace the current selection. If you tick the "regular expression" check box, you can use placeholders like ".*" (for any number of characters) and special expressions like "$" (end of text) in the search box. In regular expression mode, searching for "name:.*close$" will, for example, find everything with a name ending in "close".

The selection dialog saves the result to a list of recently performed searches. The "Search" button at the bottom of the dialog (figure 10-14) lets you get back to earlier search results.

10.5 Uploading Changes to the OSM Server

Use the upload button (figure 10-2) to send all changes you have made in the current session to the server. If you have a long editing session, it is a good idea to upload your intermediate results every now and then to reduce the danger of conflicts with other edits in the same area.

When you upload for the first time, JOSM will ask you to enter your OSM username and password. Changes are only accepted from authenticated users. We covered how to register with OSM in section 3.1.

Before every upload, JOSM displays a confirmation dialog (figure 10-5) with a run-down of the changes it is going to upload, grouped into object creation, object modification, and object deletion. This forms the basis of the changeset (see section 6.1), and JOSM lets you supply a short description of what you did in this editing session, which will be added as a comment tag to the changeset.

> ☞ *Some operations, for example joining two ways, lead to the deletion of ob-*
> *jects without the user explicitly deleting anything. Do read the upload*
> *message carefully, but don't be overly concerned if some objects you have*
> *worked on are listed for deletion. If you are unsure, cancel uploading and*
> *investigate the situation before restarting the upload.*

After you have confirmed the upload dialog, JOSM sends your changes to the server. They are visible immediately for anyone accessing the database, but not every web map (for example the map on the OpenStreetMap web page) will be updated straight away.

Working with Changesets

The upload dialog has a number of options that control how JOSM creates changesets.

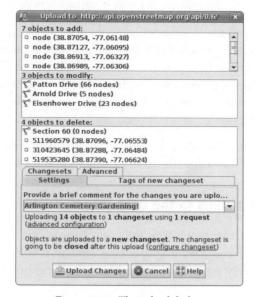

Figure 10-18: The upload dialog.

By default setting, JOSM combines all your changes into one changeset, adds the comment you have entered, uploads everything in one go, and then closes the changeset again. But you can also set JOSM to leave the changeset open so that you can add more changes later – provided you do so within one hour, after which the server will close the changeset automatically.

On the tab "Tags of new changeset" you can add any number of tags to the changeset in addition to the already specified comment and an automatic editor signature. You could use this for example to add a source tag to the changeset as a whole instead of adding it to lots of individual objects.

Uploading a changeset in one go is transactional. This means that if one of your changes is rejected by the server, the whole changeset is rejected. This is usually desirable; if anything goes wrong, you can detect and repair the conflict and then try again. For cases where a stubborn problem blocks your upload, you can also instruct JOSM (on the "Advanced" tab of the upload dialog) to upload all changes as individual requests. They will still belong to the same changeset, but each change will be uploaded separately so that one or two problems don't stop the whole upload.

If you have performed more changes than fit into one changeset (the current limit is 50,000), JOSM prompts you to create multiple changesets.

Users can review all changesets affecting a given area. Various tools help you do this, one of which is inbuilt in JOSM: The "Changesets" dialog which, can be activated by clicking on the lowermost button on the left toolbar (see figure 10-4).

Problems on Upload

Apart from network or server problems, the most common problems when uploading data are the integrity errors (message "precondition failed") and version conflicts.

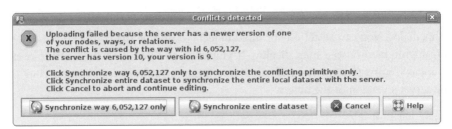

Figure 10-19: Conflict message during upload.

These messages appear if you try to upload an invalid change. Typical reasons for this are the following:

- You are uploading a way that uses a node that has been deleted by someone else in the mean time.
- You have deleted a node that is still used by a way (JOSM won't normally let you do that, but JOSM might not have known that there was a way using that node because someone else only just created it).
- You are uploading a relation that has one or more deleted objects as members, or you are trying to delete something used by another relation.

- You are uploading a new version of an object, but the object has been modified by someone else in the mean time.[4]

Problems like that can never be avoided altogether because the OSM database doesn't offer exclusive access – you can't "block" a certain area because you are working on it. But the chance of running into problems can be greatly reduced by always working with freshly downloaded data.

If JOSM detects a conflict when uploading data, you are offered the option to immediately synchronize your data with that on the server (figure 10-19) so that a subsequent upload would succeed. Such synchronization usually means that JOSM will document the conflicts it has detected and ask you to resolve them. The next section explains how to do that.

Conflicts During Download

You can download data from the OSM server at any time, even when your changes haven't been uploaded yet. JOSM never overwrites your changes. If there is a conflict between data downloaded from the server and what you have locally, JOSM will displays a conflict dialog showing the objects that don't match (figure 10-20).

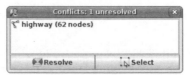

Figure 10-20: The conflict dialog.

From this dialog, you can select one or more objects to resolve the conflict. Objects selected here are highlighted on the map display. If you click on "Resolve", the conflict resolution dialog opens (figure 10-21) with a detailed description of differences between your version and the server's version of the object.

The dialog has four tabs:
- "Properties" shows possible differences in node location (where a node has been moved by you and by someone else on the server) and compares the deletion status. A conflict in deletion status occurs if you modify an object but someone else deleted it.
- "Tags" (active in figure 10-21) shows tag differences.
- "Nodes" displays the list of nodes if it is different for a way on the server and your local copy, for example because a way for which you have only changed tags has undergone a change in its node list on the server.
- "Members" has a similar display for differences in relation members.

---

4 This type of problem couldn't be detected with API 0.5; only with API 0.6 did it become possible to avoid accidental overwriting of someone else's changes.

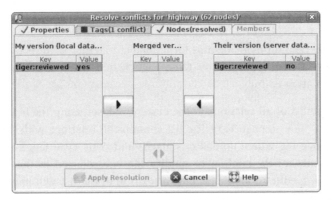

Figure 10-21: Resolving conflicts.

On any of these tabs, you can use the arrow buttons in the dialog box to decide whether you want to resolve the conflict by using your version of the data (shown on the left-hand side), or the server's version (shown on the right-hand side). Once you have finished resolving the conflict, click on "Apply Resolution" to accept your changes.

10.6 Saving Changes to a File

If you tell JOSM to save your data to a file, only data from the current layer will be saved. JOSM saves the data in the XML format commonly used within OSM, but there are two minor differences:

All objects that have been changed will receive an `action` attribute. The value of this attribute can be one of `insert`, `delete`, or `modify`. When the file is loaded into JOSM again later, JOSM uses these attributes to determine which objects have to be uploaded to the server and which not (because they are unchanged). This means that deleted objects are still present in the file saved by JOSM. If you process that OSM file with software that is ignorant of JOSM's `action` attribute, deleted objects will become visible again.

The second difference is that newly created objects receive negative IDs. Normally it is the OpenStreetMap server's job to assign fresh object IDs to newly uploaded objects: JOSM uploads the object, and a new ID is returned. But where no upload has taken place yet, JOSM has to issue its own numbers to ensure referential integrity. For example, way #-1 may use nodes #-5, #-13, and #-14. If you load the file into JOSM again later and then upload it to the server, these negative IDs will be replaced by those assigned by the server.

Never merge multiple files you have saved in JOSM – this would lead to collisions in the negative ID range!

10.7   Creating and Modifying Relations

JOSM displays the relation memberships for an object together with its tags in the "Properties/Memberships" dialog (see figure 10-12 on page 122). There is also a list of all relations, and a universal relation editor.

You can access the list of all relations in the current dataset using the button with the gear symbol (see figure 10-4 on page 113). The list contains all relations with their name (or the contents of the note tag where no name is given) and their type tag. Below the list there are buttons to create a new relation or modify the one selected in the list; both buttons bring up the relation editor. Double clicking a relation in the list will make it the currently selected object in JOSM.

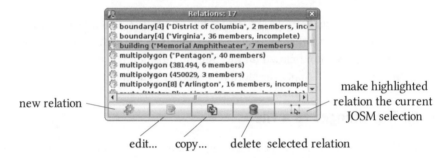

Figure 10-22: List of relations.

The Relation Editor

JOSM's relation editor is a very powerful tool but requires a bit of practice to get used to. Figure 10-23 shows how a multipolygon relation is modified in the editor. The most important tab, "Tags and Members", contains all tags in the upper half and all relation members in the lower half. The tags can be changed by simply entering new values into the table; but changing the member list is more complicated.

Under "Members" there is a list of all current members of this relation together with their role. The third column in that table has an icon that tells you whether two consecutive way members are connected, so that the last node of the first way is the first node of the second way. In this example the icons even form a ring, indicating that all ways together form a ring on the map – just as you would expect for a boundary. You can change the order of members with the buttons on the left-hand side. The role can just be changed in the table. If you want to set the role for many members at once, select them in the table, enter the role into the "Apply role" input field and press the button next to it.

Sometimes objects in the member list for a relation are described as "incomplete". This means that while the object is a member of a relation that has been downloaded, the object itself was outside the downloaded area. You can still edit the relation, but you don't have detailed information about those members that are incomplete. The relation editor has an option for downloading those objects to make the "incomplete" flag go away.

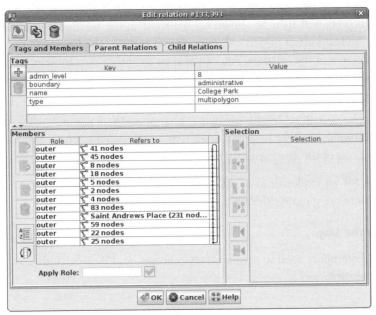

Figure 10-23: The relation editor.

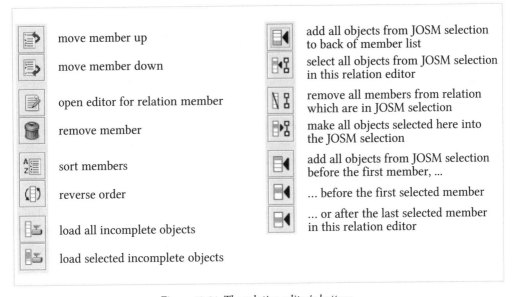

Figure 10-24: The relation editor's buttons.

To make relation members visible on the map display, or to add new elements to the selection, the relation editor makes use of JOSM's normal object selection mechanism. Those objects that form the current selection in JOSM are shown in the block on the right, titled "Selection". To add one or more objects to the relation, select them on the map using the mouse.[5] The objects will then be shown on the right in the relation editor, and with one click on the topmost button in that column you can transfer the objects to the left, making them into members of the relation. You can also go the other way by selecting an object in the relation editor and then transferring it to the JOSM selection so that it gets highlighted on the map.

Relations may be nested, which means that a relation can be a member of another relation. There are additional tabs that help you work with such nested relations by showing parent and child relations of the one currently being edited.

See chapter 8 for an explanation of different relation types. For some types, such as turn restrictions, there are plugins offering a specialized relation editor.

Relations on the Map

Relations are commonly used to map abstract concepts, and thus can't always be drawn on the map in a sensible way.

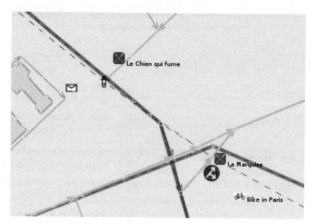

Figure 10-25: Representation of a turn restriction in JOSM.

If you select such an object that is part of a relation, the "Properties/Memberships" dialog will have information on the relations that have this object as their member. Multipolygon relations, as explained in chapter 8, are shown as proper areas (with holes where needed).

---

5 The relation editor window isn't "modal", which means that you can have it open and still use other JOSM functionality at the same time.

Turn restrictions are symbolized with little blue traffic signs (figure 10-25). In wireframe mode, JOSM will draw a halo around objects that are members of a relation to make them stand out.

10.8 JOSM Plugins

Many plugins are available to extend the functionality of JOSM. We present a few in this section; more are documented in detail on the JOSM/Plugins wiki page.

From time to time plugins that are widely used and very stable are merged into the JOSM core; if you should find that one of the plugins discussed here isn't available any longer, then that is probably what has happened.

Unfortunately, not all plugins support the full range of languages that JOSM does, but most are at least available in English.

To get a list of all currently available plugins, open the preferences dialog, choose the plugins screen (fifth icon from the top in the lefthand column), and click the "Download list" button (figure 9-26). Clicking the "Update plugins" button checks for new versions of already installed plugins, downloading them right away. When you close the dialog, JOSM downloads and installs any new plugins that you have selected from the available list.

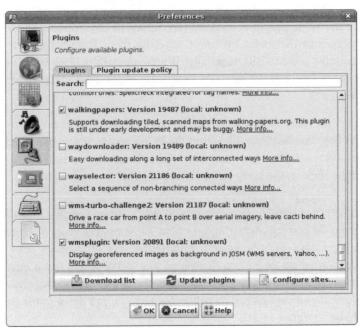

Figure 10-26: Plugin selection.

RemoteControl

The RemoteControl plugin (JOSM/Plugins/RemoteControl) enables other applications running on your computer to control JOSM. They can ask an already running instance of
JOSM to download a specific area from the OSM server and zoom there, or download data
from an arbitrary URL and optionally also select an object. This plugin is for example used
by the OSM Inspector (see section 12.2) to let you edit an object you have identified on the
Inspector.

Surveyor and LiveGPS

The Surveyor and LiveGPS plugins, together with a GPS receiver connected to the computer and the gpsd software, make realtime mapping possible. They create a self-updating
GPS layer and let you define a number of hot keys for mapping with minimal user input.

WMS Plugin

The Web Map Service (WMS) plugin lets you download aerial imagery or raster maps from
any WMS server and display it as a background image in JOSM. WMS is a widely used GIS
standard, allowing a client to request map images or aerial photography from a server.

JOSM comes with some predefined WMS sources, among them the free NASA Landsat imagery. These are directly selectable from the "WMS" menu, which will be added to the
menu bar once the WMS plugin is installed (see figure 10-27). You can add any number of
other WMS sources to the menu by either selecting them from a list in the preferences
dialog, or by entering a WMS URL manually. When manually adding WMS servers, always
check the license before you derive OSM data from them; read more about the licensing
situation in chapter 13.

When you select an entry from the "WMS" menu, the WMS plugin creates a new WMS
layer and starts downloading map tiles from the WMS server. If you pan the map, new tiles
will be loaded automatically. You can disable this behavior in the context menu of the
WMS layer (right-click on the layer in the layer dialog to access this menu).

> ☞ *Just because something comes from a WMS server does not mean it must
> always be correct. Aerial images tend to be imperfect in their georefer-
> encing – they may be up to a hundred meters off or even more. Don't
> blindly trust an image you download. The WMS plugin has a method for
> letting you move images loaded from the server if you have reason to
> believe they aren't placed correctly (the sixth button down in the left hand
> column in figure 10-27).*

The map tiles are always loaded at the resolution that was in use when the plugin created the WMS layer. If you zoom in or out later, choose "Change resolution" from the WMS layer's context menu to request the reloading of images at a different resolution.

Yahoo has explicitly allowed their aerial imagery to be used for tracing in OpenStreetMap. Since there is no WMS server that directly serves Yahoo imagery, the WMS plugin has a built-in mechanism to download Yahoo images through a helper program. Read more about this on the JOSM/Plugins/WMSPlugin wiki page.

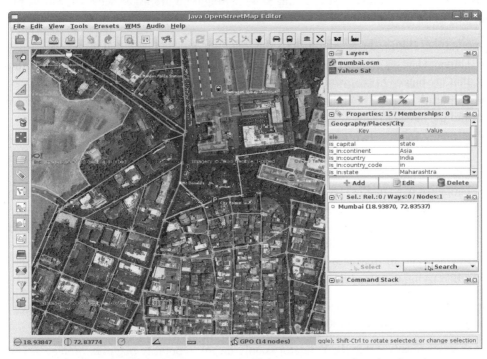

Figure 10-27: The WMS plugin in action (Yahoo imagery, see also color plate 9).

The WMS plugin is very helpful in areas where the Yahoo imagery has a good resolution (as in figure 10-27), allowing you to trace much detail. Unfortunately high-resolution coverage is limited, and in other places the images are often no better than those from Landsat.

You can even use your own images as a background in JOSM. But first the images need to be calibrated so that they display at the right scale and location – in GIS speak, they need to be orthorectified and georeferenced. Map Warper (`warper.geothings.net`) and Metacarta's Map Rectifier (`labs.metacarta.com/rectifier/`) can help you do this: Both show your uploaded image next to a map and ask you to identify identical points *(control points)* on each side. Once sufficient points have been defined, the software moves, rotates, or scales the image to fit the map, and returns a WMS URL for use with the WMS plugin.

Validator

The Validator plugin helps you to find and fix errors. You can have it check selected (or all) objects for errors or potential problems at any time. The Validator then shows a dialog listing the issues it has found, and they can be marked on the map. Some types of problems can also be repaired automatically.

In addition to that, the Validator hooks into the upload process and checks your data before it is uploaded. If it finds anything that looks wrong, you are asked whether you want to proceed or fix the problems first.

Among other things, the Validator finds the following kinds of potential problems:

- Unnamed ways – streets that would be expected to have a name (for example those that are tagged `highway=residential`), but don't have a name tag.
- Duplicate nodes – multiple nodes at the exact same location. Often this is an accident, and the mapper really wanted to use a common node.
- Crossing roads – two roads crossing each other without a node. If this is an intersection, a node has to be placed; if not, then one of the two roads is probably a bridge or tunnel and should be tagged accordingly (see section 7.1 on page 67).
- Untagged ways/nodes – ways or unconnected nodes without any tags are generally not useful (if they don't represent anything then they shouldn't have been mapped). It is possible, however, that someone else had just created the nodes at the time you downloaded the data earlier, planning to use them to construct ways, and hasn't quite finished yet. In that case if you were to delete them, they would run into a conflict when trying to upload their new way.

The Validator is work in progress; new tests are added constantly, and old ones refined. It has a "Preferences" dialog of its own where you can enable or disable each test.

Let us stress however that the Validator is only meant to point to potential problems. There may be cases where the Validator highlights a problem that upon closer inspection turns out to be fully correct. You, the mapper, always have the last word – it's your decision what to upload to the server, not the Validator's.

Further Plugins of Interest

The OpenStreetBugs plugin displays problems reported through the OpenStreetBugs platform and lets you close the reports after repairing the problem. The EditGPX plugin can be used to modify GPX tracks before you upload them to the server. Various plugins exist to help you map buildings or trace from WMS images. The WalkingPapers plugin shows maps uploaded to the Walking Papers service (see page 48). And if all that is too serious for you, get the WMS Racer plugin and drive a race car over the WMS map.

11 Other Editors

The Potlatch and JOSM editors that we have described in the previous two chapters are the oldest and by far the most commonly used editors in OpenStreetMap. But there are a number of alternatives. For Desktop use, consider the well-established "Merkaartor" and the recently released "Mapzen" editors, with Merkaartor being in some ways similar to JOSM and Mapzen being more like Potlatch. There are also a number of editors intended primarily for mobile use: "Vespucci" is an Android editor, on the iPhone you can use the "Mapzen POI Collector", and "Osm2go" runs on several platforms. We will briefly discuss these five editors in this chapter.

11.1 Merkaartor

Merkaartor (wiki page: Merkaartor) arrived a bit later than JOSM and Potlatch but is now being used by a growing number of mappers. It is available for Linux, Mac OS X, and Windows. As with JOSM, this editor downloads data for you to work on offline, and you upload your changes once you have finished your edits.

Installation

You can download the current software version from www.merkaartor.org. The page has source code if you want to compile Merkaartor by yourself, but also executables for different operating systems. For Windows, an installer is available that you can run by double-clicking it after download. Several Linux distributions already include a version of Merkaartor in their standard repositories.

Merkaartor was developed in English but has been translated into a number of different languages. If you want to use a language other than English, make your selection in "Tools" menu under "Properties", then "Locale".

User Interface

The Merkaartor user interface is divided into three areas (see figure 11-1 and color plate 11). The middle area contains the map (or an empty grid if nothing is loaded yet).[1] On the left and right there are areas for the layer setup, for tags and further information about the currently selected object, and other information. These areas can be changed with the mouse to configure the user interface.

Loading Data from the Server

In order to start working on an area, select the "Download" option from the "File" menu, or click the download icon. There are several possible ways to tell Merkaartor which area you want to download. For starters, it is easiest if you choose "from the map below" and then select an area with the mouse.

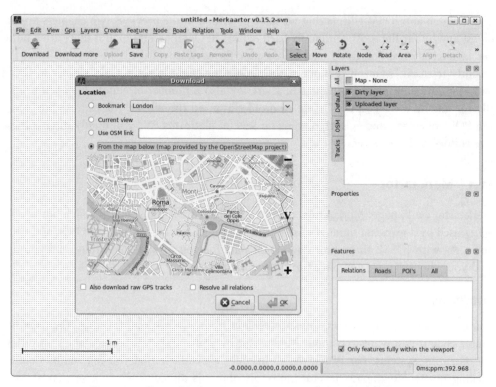

Figure 11-1: Empty Merkaartor working area with download dialog.

Merkaartor now loads the data and displays it in the main window. The newly downloaded layer is added to the layer list. Every time you download data, a new layer is added. If you

---

1 Later, the grid will only be visible outside of the downloaded area.

want to add data to the current layer, you can use the "Download more" option from the menu instead.

GPS Tracks

Merkaartor can load GPS tracks from GPX files (select "Open" from the "File" menu to create a new edit session, or "Import" to load a GPX file into the current session). For every track segment, which Merkaartor calls a *trail*, a new layer is created, as well as for the waypoints. These layers can be converted to OSM objects on demand. Merkaartor can also retrieve position information directly from a connected GPS device and center the map on the current location. You can activate these features from the "Gps" menu.

Editing

If you move the mouse across the map, Merkaartor will always highlight the object the mouse is over, and show details about it in an "Info" dialog on the right hand side of the screen. If you then click on the object, it remains selected, and the "Properties" dialog shows the object's tags and allows you to change them.

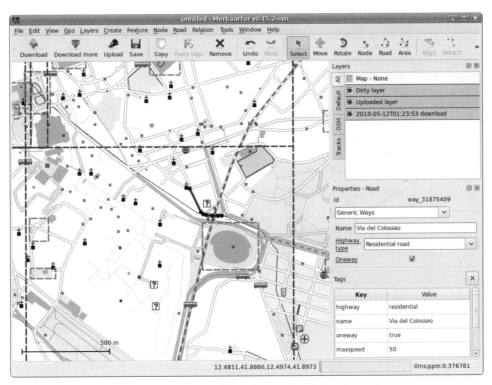

Figure 11-2: The tags of the selected object being changed.

Normally, the mouse only serves to pan the map (by holding down the right button and dragging) and to select objects. If you want to move an object, you first have to activate the "move" mode from the button bar. There is another mode (which you can activate by clicking on the "remove" icon the top button bar) for deleting objects.

To create a new object, first select the appropriate option from the "Create" menu, or press "Ctrl"+"N" for a new node or "Ctrl"+"R" for a new way. Then for a new node just click at the desired position, or for a new way, every click places a new node and continues the way, until you press the "ESC" key. If you move the mouse over an existing object while drawing, it is highlighted. Clicking now connects the new way being drawn with the highlighted object.

Figure 11-2 shows how Merkaartor draws rectangles encompassing all members of a relation (if you don't like this feature, you can switch it off in the "View" menu). Clicking on the outline of such a rectangle will select the relation. You can create a new relation by selecting all objects that are to be members and then selecting "Relation" from the "Create" menu. After that you can set the roles of the members in the "Members" dialog. There is also a "Relation" menu that lets you add and remove members.

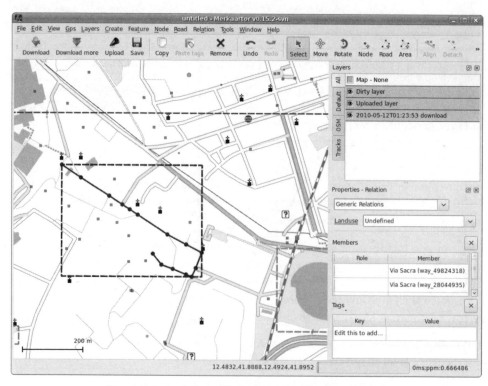

Figure 11-3: A relation with three members has been created.

The "Road" menu has commands for splitting or connecting ways. Each command is only available if a matching set of objects is selected:

Command	Selection required	Action
Split	A node that is part of a way.	Splits the way in two parts at the selected node. If the node is part of more than one way, the way to be split has to be selected also.
Break Apart	Two ways sharing a node.	Creates a duplicate of the node, so that each way uses its own version of the node and can be moved independently.
Join	Two ways ending in the same node.	Connects both ways to form one.
Reverse	One way.	Turns the direction of the way around.

Saving and Uploading Changes

You can save your Merkaartor session at any time as a Merkaartor Document (file extension .mdc). Such a file isn't just a list of OSM objects, but contains the full state of your session including the edit history and all layers. When you load the file later, you can continue working at the exact same place where you left off.

If all you need is a simple XML file with OSM objects, choose the "Export" option from the "File" menu and let Merkaartor export your session as an OSM XML file.

To upload your changes to the OSM server, choose "Upload" from the "File" menu.

The Layer Concept in Merkaartor

Merkaartor stores data on various layers. The lowermost layer is usually the "Map" layer which can be used to show a background image (see next section). Above that you can have any number of GPS track layers, and then one or more layers with data downloaded from OSM. On top of that, Merkaartor automatically adds a working layer (called the "Dirty layer") and a layer to store uploaded objects.

Whenever you modify an object in any way, the original object is removed from the OSM layer it was in, and the modified version is placed on the Dirty layer. If you now hide the OSM layer (click on the "eye" button next to it in the layer dialog), only the modified objects from the Dirty layer are visible – these are the ones that will be transferred to the server if you instruct Merkaartor to upload your changes.

Objects that have been modified and successfully uploaded to the server will be moved from the Dirty layer to the layer containing uploaded objects.

You can arrange the layers in any order you like, and also control their transparency. For example, this lets you create a display where unmodified objects are faint, but modified objects are displayed in strong colors.

Showing Background Images

The base layer named "Map", which Merkaartor always creates, is empty by default (the layer list will list it as "Map – None"). You can, however, have Merkaartor display one of a number of background maps loaded from the web in that layer (see figure 11-4). A right mouse click on the layer in the layer dialog shows the various *adapters* you can use to download maps: WMS for WMS servers, TMS for tiled map servers like the OSM tile servers, and a special adapter for Yahoo aerial imagery.

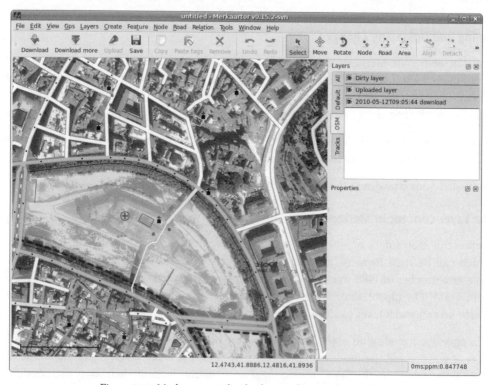

Figure 11-4: Merkaartor with a background image from Yahoo.

Different Map Styles

Merkaartor has a number of different map styles built in. In addition to the standard style used for the examples in this book (see also color plate 11), there is also a style that closely resembles the Mapnik rendering known from the OpenStreetMap website, or another one showing all ways in gray only. You can even create your own styles, or modify existing ones, by selecting "Style" from the "Tools" menu and then "Edit". In the dialog window that pops up, you can change any or all the settings for the style currently in use.

11.2 Mapzen

Mapzen (wiki: Mapzen) is a simple Flash based editor published by CloudMade under an Open Source license. Although the source code is freely available, the only instance publicly used is that operated by CloudMade themselves (mapzen.cloudmade.com). To use this editor, you need a CloudMade login in addition to your OpenStreetMap account. The website guides you through the sign-up process. This CloudMade login can be used to form a social network of mappers, where contributing to the map can be merged with participation in services like Facebook and Twitter.

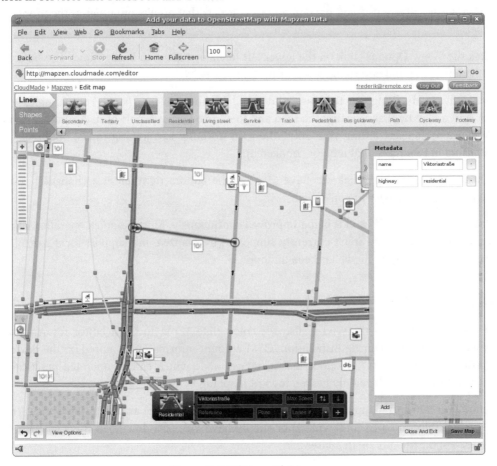

Figure 11-5: Editing with Mapzen.

Just like Potlatch, Mapzen requires that you first select an area to edit, and then the Flash application starts.

Using Mapzen is very simple (see figure 11-1). You use the mouse as normal for moving the map, or for selecting and moving objects. The "Delete" key deletes objects. A specialty of Mapzen is the large list of illustrated presets above the map, which makes it easier to create new objects. Select a road type or a POI from this list and then double-click in the map – it's that simple to create a new object of the chosen type. Depending on the kind of object selected, the black property panel at the bottom of the map shows certain attribute fields that you can fill out (roads, for example, have a maximum speed field and a check box for the one-way property).

A detailed tag panel, "Metadata", shown on the right in figure 11-1, is hidden by default and you can activate it if you have to add or edit tags that aren't contained in the property panel.

Click the "View Options" link on the lower left to change the map background. The buttons to the left of that link are for undoing or re-doing edits.

Some advanced editing functions are made available through *hint boxes*. For example, you can split a way by first selecting the road and then a node that is part of it. A hint box with two buttons appears, letting you "split" the road (forming two joining roads) or "break" it (resulting in two roads that are not connected).

When you are finished, click on "Save Map" in the bottom right, enter a changeset comment, and your changes are uploaded.

Mapzen is still in "beta" and is being improved continuously. More complex operations, like working with relations, aren't currently supported by Mapzen, but support for a specialist turn restriction editing mode has been announced.

11.3 Vespucci

Vespucci (Vespucci on the wiki – also see color plate 32) is an OSM editor for Android based smart phones. During installation, OSM account information is stored on the device. Starting with version 0.7, Vespucci has a novice mode which can be operated practically without training and is mainly geared toward mapping POIs.

Before you can start mapping, you have to load OSM data for the area onto the device. You can either select an area to download or simply have Vespucci download the local area or the area in the vicinity of an address.

With the GPS device activated, Vespucci can also render the downloaded data in a kind of "moving map" display.

For mapping, the GPS position can be "frozen", so that you can place an accurate POI while in a moving vehicle. POIs are usually selected from preset menus; the novice mode doesn't expect the user to enter tags manually.

The advanced edit mode also allows for editing ways and setting arbitrary tag values. To create a way, press the menu button and select "New", then click on the map to place the start node. Another click on the map creates a second node and joins them both with a new way. If you click on an existing node, the way will be linked to that.

To edit the tags of any object, press the menu button and select "Edit tags", then click on the node or way for which you want to change the tags. A panel shows all tags on the object and allows you to edit them. It is often sufficient to enter a few letters for a tag as Vespucci will auto-complete the name.

Modifications are uploaded to the OSM server automatically in the background.

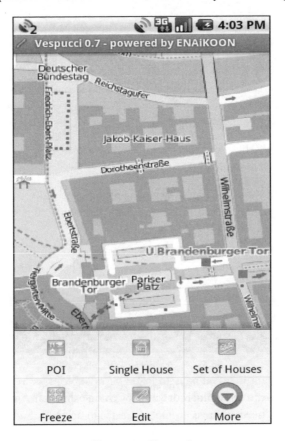

Figure 11-6: Vespucci.

11.4 Mapzen POI Collector

Mapzen POI Collector is an application for Apple's iPhone mainly aimed at creating or correcting POIs. It retrieves the current location from the device's GPS receiver and displays the map area around it (see figure 11-7). POIs are shown as editable symbols on the map.

You can create new POIs from an illustrated menu and delete or move existing POIs, but editing ways isn't possible. When using Mapzen POI Collector, remember that some points of interest are really mapped as closed ways (areas) in OpenStreetMap – for example a church building. Such POIs are visible on the map in Mapzen POI Collector, but they are not editable.

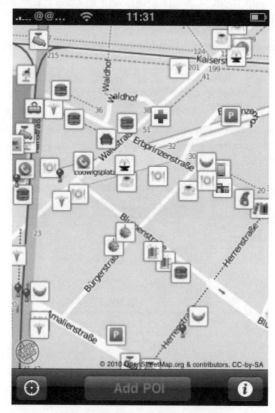

Figure 11-7: Mapzen POI Collector.

Mapzen POI Collector can be downloaded free of charge through Apple's AppStore. To use the POI Collector you need to have an OpenStreetMap account, and allow Mapzen to use that via OAuth authorization key. A CloudMade registration is not required.

A version for the Android operating system has been announced.

11.5 Osm2go

Osm2go (wiki: Osm2go; also see color plate 31) is a mobile OpenStreetMap editor originally developed for the Nokia Maemo platform (maemo.org), but it also runs on a standard Linux computer. Its functionality is restricted compared to Potlatch or JOSM because it is optimized for a small display and pen operation, but this makes it much more suitable for mobile use.

The software is available in pre-compiled form for the Nokia Internet Tablet and can be installed easily. Using it on other platforms might require compiling it specifically.

To use Osm2go, you first have to create a project. Specify a name and description, and instruct Osm2go to download the area of interest. You can move the map with the pen or mouse, and zooming works using zoom buttons or the scroll wheel. In contrast to other editors which often present all data at any zoom level, Osm2go adds more detail as you zoom in further (see figure 11-8).

The most common editing functions can be activated through buttons directly on the main screen, but everything else is hidden away in menus. You can access the main menu through the hardware "menu" key. Select "Style" from the "Map" menu to switch to another display style. There are several options differing in colors and symbols used.

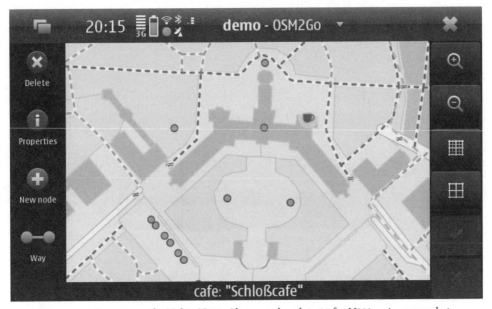

Figure 11-8: Osm2go on the Nokia N900. Also see color plate 31 for N800 series screenshots.

If you click on a node or way, it is highlighted in yellow. A selected way will also have highlighted nodes, and arrows to indicate its direction. Below the map display, some tags of the selected object are shown. Click the "Properties" button (or use the hardware button in the center of the cursor keys) to see all tags and further details for the object and to modify them. You can set arbitrary tags, or select them from a preset menu. Osm2go uses the same presets that JOSM uses (see section 10.4). There are further buttons to delete selected objects, create new nodes or ways, add nodes into a way, split a way, or change a way's direction. Osm2go even has a small relation editor. When you are finished with your edits, choose "Upload" from the "OSM" menu to save your edits on the OSM server.

If you use Osm2go on the Nokia Internet Tablet or have the computer it is running on connected an external GPS device, it can also record GPX traces and display your current position.

There is also a WMS menu that lets you configure Osm2go to display aerial imagery in the background.

12 Tools for Mappers

Members of the OpenStreetMap community have developed a number of tools designed to help mappers do their work. Some of these tools help you get the right picture when mapping complex situations by providing specialist map views. Others can find potential errors or inconsistencies in the data and point to areas where corrections might be needed. Most of these tools have been developed by individuals from the OSM community, and they can be accessed through the web, so you won't have to install anything on your computer in order to use them.

We present a selection of these mappers' tools here. You can find further information in the OpenStreetMap wiki, under Quality Assurance.

12.1 Data Layer and Data Browser

You can activate a data layer on www.openstreetmap.org by selecting "Data" from the layer switcher (behind the "+" symbol in the upper right corner of the map, see figure 2-1). That opens a dialog to the left of the map showing (if you are zoomed in far enough) a list of all nodes and ways that are currently visible on the map. The list is not shown if you aren't zoomed in far enough, as it would be too long. On the map, nodes are shown as green circles, and ways as gray lines (see figure 12-1). Areas receive a red border and are filled semi-transparently.

If you click on an object on the map, it is highlighted, and its tags displayed in the window on the left. Click on "Details" to switch over to the *data browser*, which tells you more about the selected object, including when and by whom it was last modified, plus all its tags. The data browser also shows references to other objects. For nodes, this is a list of ways using this node; for ways, the list of nodes it uses. If you select a relation, all its members are shown; if you select a relation member, the browser shows a link back to the relation that contains it.

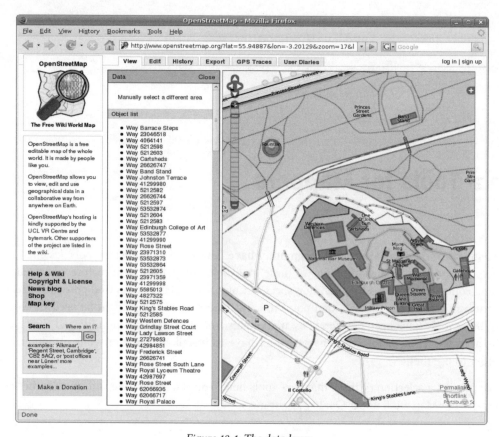

Figure 12-1: The data layer.

The "Show History" link (available in the data view as well as in the data browser) retrieves and displays a list of all previous changes to the selected object, together with the date and editor. The most recent version is listed at the top.

Using a URL of the form `http://www.openstreetmap.org/browse/type/id` you can call up the data browser for any object; replace "type" by "node", "way" or "relation", and "id" by the object id.

12.2 OSM Inspector

The OSM Inspector (`http://tools.geofabrik.de/osmi/`) shows different views of the OSM data, which helps to find bugs or to analyze complex situations. Each view is dedicated to a topic. The "address view", for example, shows address information with house numbers, postal codes, and so on. The "tagging view" pinpoints potential typing errors in tags and similar problems; a "geometry" view helps you find geometry problems such as self-intersecting ways, and so on. Color plate 26 has an illustration of the "address view" with house numbers and matching streets.

OSM Inspector synchronizes with the OSM database on a daily basis.

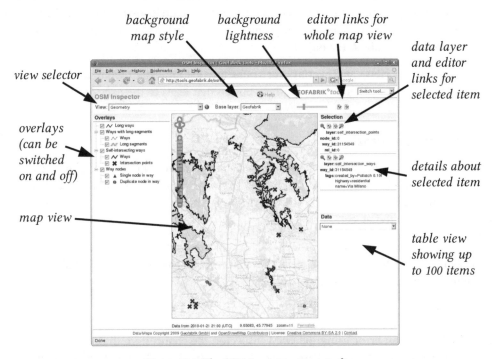

Figure 12-2: The OSM Inspector user interface.

Using the OSM Inspector

When you access the OSM Inspector website (Figure 12-2), the map view is in the middle of the screen. You can pan and zoom the map as usual, and the well-known OpenStreetMap tiles are shown in the background. In the foreground, the Inspector adds various overlays with special information depending on the selected view. You can choose the type of background map in the "Base layer" menu, and you can choose a view in the upper left area of the screen. A list of overlays is then displayed on the left-hand side. Some overlays are only available for certain zoom levels and will appear grayed out if the current zoom level is outside that range. If the overlay is listed in black, it is available for display.

Each overlay can be switched on and off using the attached check box. Some overlays are arranged in a tree structure. You can also select an overlay for exclusive display by clicking on its name. This temporarily hides all other overlays; the overlay thus selected appears in red. Click the name again to revert to the normal display.

When you hover the mouse pointer over an overlay name, a yellow pop-up box explains the overlay. In addition to the layer name and description, there is information about the data provenance (mostly OSM but the OSM Inspector also uses some other data sources for reference), the zoom levels for which this layer is available, whether or not this layer has written labels on the map (and in which zoom levels these are shown), and whether or not this layer is queryable. A queryable layer allows you to click on something you see on the map and view details about the object.

Try out the various views and overlays for yourself to get an idea of what data is available. To the right of the view menu there is a help button that leads to the page on the OSM wiki with details about that view.

Selection and Data Areas

Two further areas to the right of the map can display data in textual form. The "Selection" area shows details of an object that you have selected with the mouse from a layer that was marked as queryable. If you click on the magnifying glass icon, the map is centered on and zoomed to the selected object.

Below the "Selection" area there is the "Data" area. Here, you can select one of the overlays from a drop-down box and then view the elements on that overlay in tabular form; a maximum of 100 objects can be shown at once.

Links to Editors

If you have found an error using the OSM Inspector, the chances are that you want to correct it immediately. Therefore, the Inspector provides links to the Potlatch editor on www.openstreetmap.org (see chapter 9) and to JOSM (see chapter 10). The little "P" and "J" icons take you directly to the respective editors: The ones above the map bring up an editor for the same area of the map you are viewing, while the icons in the "Selection" area bring up an editor that shows the area containing the selected object.

In order to use the JOSM link, JOSM has to be running already, and the "Remote Control" plugin must be installed (see section 10.8).

12.3 ITO OSM Mapper

The "OSM Mapper" provided by ITO World (at http://www.itoworld.com/static/openstreetmap.html) is a web tool to help you analyze existing data and monitor changes (see also color plate 27).

Before you can use the OSM Mapper, you have to create an account on the ITO website. This account is separate from your OSM account, and only used for this tool. After creating an account and logging in, hover the mouse use over the white arrow next to the "Area" drop-down and select "Create a new area" from the menu. You can now set up an area that you are interested in and save it under a name of your choice. All later operations always refer to one of the areas you have created in this manner.

After you have created an area, select it in the "Area" drop-down. OSM Mapper creates a basic map, and you can now make further adjustments. At the top, under "Area", you can select one of the areas you have created. Under "View" you can select which feature is to determine the map color – you can select coloring by tags, users, or sessions. Any of these choices brings up a table to the right of the map, from which you can fine tune your choice (e. g. select only a single user, or a single tag). Behind the "+" button (opened in figure 12-3, thus showing as "–"), there is also an option to switch from a fixed one-color-per-feature coloring to a time-based color gradient. Don't worry if the tool looks a bit overwhelming at first – after a while you will be able to bring up meaningful maps quickly.

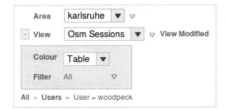

Figure 12-3: Interface detail for the OSM Mapper.

A powerful feature in OSM Mapper is the filter. If you have selected a specific tag or user, you can add that selection to the filter using the hover menu next to the "Filter" label. Until you remove it again, all maps generated will only show data that matches the filter.

The "OSM Sessions" selection tries to group edits made by the same person in a small time period. It isn't the same as OSM changesets – the same user can create a lot of changesets for the same location and timespan, but OSM Mapper will still combine them into one session. This is a good way of following who is editing what in an area that is of interest to you. If you want to follow edits in a certain area, you can even request an RSS Feed of all edits for it from OSM Mapper and thus be notified of all changes via your RSS reader.

12.4 Further Tools

Tagwatch and OSMDoc

The "Tagwatch" (wiki: Tagwatch) and "OSMDoc" (wiki: OSMDoc) utilities create statistics about the occurrence of tags and relations in OSM. They can tell you how often a certain key or a key/value combination are used worldwide or in a specific country, or which keys tend to be used in conjunction with other keys, helping you to select well-established tags for mapping. With Tagwatch, statistical entries are directly linked to the OSM wiki, and the wiki entries for most tags also link to Tagwatch. OSMDoc is the newer of the two, featuring more interactive features like the generation of detailed statistics for tags selected by the user.

Coastline Error Checker

The "Coastline Error Checker" (wiki: Coastline error checker) brings up problems with coastline continuity (which sometimes lead to "flooded" terrain when rendering images). It highlights holes and tagging problems in the coastline.

Relation Analyzer, Restriction Analyser

The "Relation Analyzer" (`http://betaplace.emaitie.de/webapps.relation-analyzer/`) shows details about relations and their members and is excellent for finding missing pieces and other problems in route or multipolygon relations. The "Restriction Analyser" (`http://osm.virtuelle-loipe.de/restrictions/`) draws a map with turn restrictions.

Keep Right

Similar to the OSM Inspector, Keep Right (wiki: Keep Right) shows possible problems on the map – among them for example *almost junctions,* where a way ends very close to another but isn't actually connected. A special feature of Keep Right is that such problems can be marked as "false positives" (stating that they aren't problems but indeed correct) or as "repaired", and this will make them disappear from the map at once. With other tools it often takes a while until they update their map after a correction.

OsmOse

The OsmOse (Open Street Map Oversight Search Engine) tool (see wiki under Osmose) is a flexible framework using pluggable backend scripts to do checks. It is used mainly by the French OSM community at `osmose.openstreetmap.fr`.

NoName Layer

The main OSM page offers a NoName layer in its map highlighting roads without names. Click on the "+" icon on the upper right and choose NoName to activate it. There are also NoName Garmin maps available. See the wiki at NoName for more information.

OpenStreetBugs

For the sake of completeness, OpenStreetBugs also features among the prominent error reporting tools; we discussed it earlier in section 2.2.

13 License Issues when Mapping

An important driving force behind the OpenStreetMap project has always been the desire to create a set of geodata that was free for everyone to use. If you contribute to OpenStreetMap, you therefore have to agree that this data can be passed on to others. OSM uses the "Creative Commons Attribution-Share Alike" license (CC-BY-SA) as a basis for contributions. If you haven't surveyed something yourself but retrieved it from another source, then you aren't the rights owner of that data, and you need authorization from the rights owner to use the data for OpenStreetMap. In this chapter we discuss which kinds of data sources can be used without problems, and which kinds of data sources require caution.

More on the CC-BY-SA license and on possible future changes can be found in chapter 20. Additional information and the full license text are on the Creative Commons web page, `http://creativecommons.org/licenses/by-sa/2.0/`.

> ☞ *Please note: The authors of this book are not lawyers. This chapter docu-*
> *ments community practice, or the authors' reasoning. When in doubt, you*
> *should consult a lawyer.*

The mode of operation that gets you into least trouble, intellectual property-wise, is of course surveying things yourself. Driving around, measuring locations and distances, making notes about street signs and so on are certainly not an infringement of anyone's copyright. Of course, you might be in a country that restricts free movement, or you might be trespassing on private ground, but that isn't a question of data licensing and copyright.

13.1 What Data can be Used?

You can only contribute data to OpenStreetMap that is suitable for distribution under the CC-BY-SA license. This is usually the case if any of the following is true:

1. You are the rights owner – then licensing is fully at your discretion.

2. The rights owner has placed their data under CC-BY-SA or a license compatible with it, declared it to be in the public domain,[1] or explicitly agreed that the data may be added to OpenStreetMap. **Caution**: A "free license" doesn't automatically mean it is CC-BY-SA compatible!

3. The data in question doesn't have copyright protection. In many countries this is true for acts of law and official publications of a legally binding character. In some countries, notably the US, any data created by the federal government resides in the public domain (with very few exceptions). **Caution**: Even if your country has such a provision, information obtained under a Freedom of Information Act", or similar, isn't necessarily in the public domain. These acts usually require that information be provided to those who ask, but permission to publish doesn't necessarily come with it.

4. Copyright protection for the data has expired because of its age.

Copyright provisions vary in different jurisdictions, and the differences (and insecurities) are even greater when it comes to geodata, as this is usually not a creative work but a representation of facts. If you want to find out more about the legal situation in your country, check Wikipedia – they want to steer clear of copyright violations themselves, so have compiled good copyright guides for many jurisdictions.

13.2 Copying from Other Maps

Copying something from someone else's map doesn't make you the author of the data so copied. You are not allowed to take data from an online or paper map and add it to OpenStreetMap without explicit permission from the author of that map. Even if you obtained the map for free on the Internet, that does not equate to permission for copying data from it. This holds true for the road geometry as well as the street name or other additional features.

Of course there is a gray area here. If I buy a printed map of my home town and in the course of many years memorize all the street names from it, then nobody can tell me I must not add what has now become my knowledge to OpenStreetMap. If, on the other hand, I buy a map of a foreign city with the purpose of adding street names to my GPS tracks then this would be considered copying from the map. But what if I were surveying an unknown

---

1 In many countries there is no real "public domain" because authors can't give away the rights they have to their work, but there are legal constructs that have the same effect as public domain for all intents and purposes.

city, asked a local for the name of a street, and they pulled out an A-Z and read the name to me – is this original research (allowed), or is it copying from A-Z (forbidden)?

There have been court cases where only the artistic aspect of map creation was judged to be protected by copyright; the facts contained in the map were not. Copying a road geometry or street name would be allowed by this yardstick. But there have also been cases that ended the other way, especially when large amounts of data were copied. The semi-governmental mapping agency of the UK, the Ordnance Survey, were notorious for zealously watching over their intellectual property, sending letters to anyone who even slightly transgressed the bounds of the license granted.[2] It is common practice in the geodata world to add defects to your maps or datasets on purpose, for example by depicting a non-existent street (these are sometimes called Easter eggs). This allows the originator to detect when someone else copies information from the map.

In the face of all these uncertainties, the OpenStreetMap project prefers to err on the side of caution. A legal battle could do a lot of damage to a project like OpenStreetMap, even if the project is without fault. The OSM rule of thumb is: Don't map anything that you haven't surveyed yourself – no roads that you haven't traveled, and no street names unless you have seen the sign.

Using map sources whose copyright has expired is something that carries no legal risks (if you can be reasonably sure that copyright really has expired). Be careful however if you aren't using the original old map but a reproduction in paper or electronic form; depending on your jurisdiction, the person creating the reproduction might have acquired additional rights in the work. When in doubt, check with whoever created the reproduction, or get your hands on the original.

13.3 Satellite and Aerial Imagery

You should regard satellite and other aerial imagery in the same way as third-party maps. Even though many people are of the opinion that tracing the geometry of roads, rivers, woodland, and other features from aerial imagery is probably allowed, no matter what the license of those images, OpenStreetMap again chooses the cautious approach. Surely it can't be illegal to freshen your memory by looking at available images while processing the GPS traces from last weekend, but a systematic use of such images, even if it only serves to "find blank spots", is generally not accepted in OpenStreetMap. Some project members even advise caution when copying from third-party "public domain" sources if there is a danger that this data might have been created by copying from Google or other such services.

---

2 This attitude was one of the reasons why OpenStreetMap was conceived. Meanwhile though, Ordnance Survey have released a sizable part of their data to the public at no charge and under a free-to-use license.

Using imagery that has been released as public domain, for example NASA Landsat imagery, is allowed. Landsat images are usually good enough to trace woodland, lakes, or major roads from them. Also, Yahoo has said that a selection of their images (but not their maps!) may be traced for OpenStreetMap. Several national or regional image providers have also been convinced to allow their images to be used as an OpenStreetMap data source. Sometimes, orthophotos (non-distorted and true-to-scale images) have been made available to OpenStreetMap by local authorities.

13.4 Importing Data

When directly importing data from other sources, there is usually no gray area – either the license of the other source allows the import or it doesn't. Sources that are in the public domain can be imported without problems. As we said earlier, this is the case with most publications of the US federal government. Some other governments offer data for unrestricted use, but require attribution. In these cases, you need to determine whether OpenStreetMap meets the conditions of that attribution: For example, you could use a special account when importing the data and document the source on the wiki, but OpenStreetMap can't make sure that the attribution is visible whenever the data is used.

Sometimes, OpenStreetMap is offered data which is "free for noncommercial use". While OpenStreetMap itself is certainly a noncommercial project, the data made available by OpenStreetMap comes without such a "noncommercial" restriction and thus any data incorporated into OSM can ultimately be used commercially. This means that "free for noncommercial use" data can't be imported.

Unfortunately, many "free licenses" aren't compatible with each other. You may not, for example, import data that comes under the GNU FDL (GNU Free Documentation license). This license allows free use of the data, but demands that derived products must again be under the GNU FDL (only) – which collides with the CC-BY-SA stipulation that derived works must be under CC-BY-SA. In cases like this, it is often worthwhile to talk to the rights owner and ask them whether they would consider *dual licensing,* i. e. releasing data under both licenses. If that happens, the data can be imported without problems.

13.5 A Change in the License?

It is planned for OSM to switch from CC-BY-SA to another license, the Open Database License. You can read more on this in chapter 20. If this switch happens, it doesn't change things written in this chapter, except that you would have to replace any occurrence of "CC-BY-SA compatible" by "ODbL compatible". If you are planning a large data import, it is advisable to check the license transition status, and make sure that the import is compatible with both the old and new license.

Part III

Making and Using Maps

In this part we show you how to make use of OSM data for creating your own maps. We start by looking at showing importing maps on web pages using the major tile servers (Mapnik and Tiles@Home), and then take an in-depth look at the main rendering engines. These chapters will guide you through the coding so you are able to start making maps using your own styles. Then we move on to how to use OSM data for route navigation, and how to load it on mobile devices. The final chapter in this section covers the licensing issues related to publishing maps and services derived from OSM data.

Part III

Using Cascading Style Sheets on Web Pages

Creating and Verifying Maps

14 Using OpenStreetMap on Web Pages

The intuitive and easy-to-use maps pioneered by Google have revolutionized the web. Even first-time users quickly grasp how to pan the map with the mouse, and how to zoom in and out using the mouse wheel or the on-screen controls. Maps à la Google are now a quasi-standard on the web. In OpenStreetMap jargon, this kind of zoomable and pannable map is often called a slippy map. OpenStreetMap has a web map like that on its main website, `www.openstreetmap.org`, and the free JavaScript library OpenLayers enables everyone to create a similar offering.

This chapter explains the tile structure of a web map, discusses the Tiles@Home and Mapnik tile servers, which are the two servers most commonly used for retrieving tiles, and then talks you through the code for inserting an interactive OSM map into your web page.

14.1 Anatomy of a Web Map

It would be great if there could be maps of every corner of the globe, in any projection, any map style, and at any resolution. This is theoretically possible with OpenStreetMap data, because it is available in vector format, i. e. an idealized, geometric description of features. In practice, however, the rendering process – the conversion of raw data into something that looks good – takes a lot of computing power.[1] Therefore, web maps on OpenStreet-Map, Google, et al. are usually produced to a fixed specification in advance, and presented as *raster images,* i. e. pixellated bitmaps designed to display the data at a certain resolution.

The most commonly used method, which is also employed by OSM, splits up the world into a grid of square *map tiles* which are saved as individual images then combined into a full map display by the web browser or other client software.

---

1 Not a huge amount – a few seconds for a decent-sized map – but enough to make it impossible to offer the service to thousands of users at the same time.

The map tiles currently used by OpenStreetMap are produced in a spherical Mercator projection and cover the Earth between 85° North and 85° South. This results in a perfectly square world map. The projection severely distorts the map in the vicinity of the poles, but that is a small price to pay for the ease of use that comes with the square form.

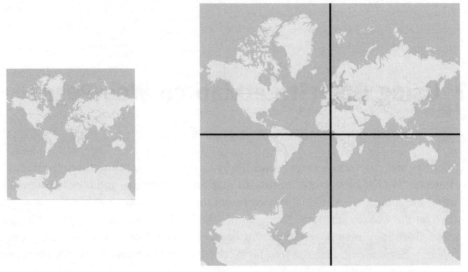

Figure 14-1: A world map covering one tile at zoom level 0, and four tiles at zoom level 1.

The web map uses tiles with dimensions of 256 x 256 pixels. On zoom level 0, the whole world fits onto one tile. With every increase in zoom level, each tile is split up into four tiles, as shown in the figure above. Thus, the world has 512 x 512 pixels in four tiles at zoom level 1. At level 2, there are 1024 x 1024 pixels in 16 tiles and so on. The highest zoom level is usually 17 or 18, depending on the level of detail the map is supposed to cover.

Tile coordinates start with 0,0 in the top left corner and increase when going right or down. The following figure shows how the tile coordinates for a specific area of the web map change as you zoom in a level:

(2x, 2y)	(2x+1, 2y)
Zoom z+1	Zoom z+1
(2x, 2y+1)	(2x+1, 2y+1)
Zoom z+1	Zoom z+1

(x, y)

Zoom z

Figure 14-2: Calculating tile coordinates when zooming into a web map.

The following table shows how much storage space is required to store tiles covering the whole planet, and how big the physical area covered by each tile is.

The given tile width has been computed for tiles at the equator; moving away from the equator will reduce the width of the area covered by the tile (due to the projection). The storage requirement was estimated using an average value of 2 KB per tile. This is a figure determined from experience. Single-colored tiles, e. g. those of sea, require almost no storage space, and innercity tiles will be much larger.

The scale number is just an approximation; digital maps can't have a precise scale because the print (or display) resolution isn't fixed, but if you are used to thinking in scale values then this gives you an idea at least.

Zoom level (z)	Tiles (4^z)	Tiles cumulative	Storage	Storage cumulative	Tile width	Pixel width	Scale approx.
0	1	1	2 KB	2 KB	40,075 km	157 km	1:500 million
1	4	5	8 KB	10 KB	20,038 km	78 km	1:250 million
2	16	21	32 KB	42 KB	10,019 km	39 km	1:150 million
3	64	85	128 KB	170 KB	5,009 km	20 km	1:70 million
4	256	341	512 KB	682 KB	2,505 km	10 km	1:35 million
5	1024	1365	2 MB	3 MB	1,252 km	5 km	1:15 million
6	4096	5641	8 MB	11 MB	626 km	2 km	1:10 million
7	16384	21845	32 MB	43 MB	313 km	1,222 m	1:4 million
8	65536	87381	128 MB	171 MB	157 km	611 m	1:2 million
9	262144	349525	512 MB	683 MB	78 km	305 m	1:1 million
10	1 million	1 million	2 GB	3 GB	39 km	152 m	1:500,000
11	4 million	6 million	8 GB	11 GB	20 km	76 m	1:250,000
12	17 million	22 million	32 GB	43 GB	10 km	38 m	1:150,000
13	67 million	89 million	128 GB	171 GB	5 km	19 m	1:70,000
14	268 million	358 million	512 GB	683 GB	2 km	9 m	1:35,000
15	1 billion	1 billion	2 TB	3 TB	1 km	4 m	1:15,000
16	4 billion	6 billion	8 TB	11 TB	611 m	2 m	1:8,000
17	17 billion	23 billion	32 TB	43 TB	305 m	1 m	1:4,000
18	69 billion	92 billion	128 TB	171 TB	152 m	0.5 m	1:2,000

If you need to compute tile coordinates (x, y) for a given geographic position (lat, lon) and a given zoom level (z), for example because you want to find out which tile contains the position reported by a GPS receiver, you can use the following equations:

$$\varphi = \frac{\pi}{180} lat$$

$$x = \text{round}\left(2^z \frac{(lon + 180) \bmod 180}{360}\right) \qquad p = \ln\left(\tan\varphi + \frac{1}{\cos\varphi}\right)$$

$$y = \text{round}\left(2^{z-1}\left(\frac{\pi - p}{\pi}\right)\right)$$

To get the geographic position for the center of a tile given as x, y on zoom level z, use:

$$lon = 360 \frac{x + 0.5}{2^z} - 180 \qquad lat = \arctan\left(\sinh\left(\pi - \frac{\pi(y + 0.5)}{2^{z-1}}\right)\right)\frac{180}{\pi}$$

The wiki page Slippy map tilenames has example code for this computation in a number of programming languages.

Three different programs have to work together to display a web map. A renderer is required to create bitmap tiles from OSM vector data. A tile server makes these tiles available for download on the web, and JavaScript code running in the web browser downloads and combines these tiles into a coherent map display.

There are various rendering engines that can be used with OpenStreetMap. The most important ones are Osmarender and Mapnik; we cover them in chapters 16 and 17 respectively. OpenStreetMap data has also been successfully rendered with Open Source packages UMN Mapserver and Geoserver, as well as with various commercial tools, but we focus on the first two, as they are the ones that produce the maps on the main website.

If you want to create your own map style for a web map, you have to run your own tile server, using one of the renderers to produce the tiles you want. But if you are happy with one of the map styles offered by existing tile servers, then just use one of these servers. That saves you a lot of work, storage space, and time.[2]

The following two sections discuss the two most important tile servers for OpenStreetMap: The Mapnik tile server and the Tiles@Home project (using Osmarender).

14.2 The Mapnik Tile Server

The Mapnik tile server is based on a PostGIS database that is continually updated with the latest OpenStreetMap data. The Mapnik rendering package uses data from the database, plus some external resources, to draw the map tiles. Tiles from this server are used in the default map view on www.openstreetmap.org.

The server generating the Mapnik tiles is called tile.openstreetmap.org. A client can request the URL http://tile.openstreetmap.org/z/x/y.png to download the tile with the

---

2 The project allows everybody to use these tiles but if you are planning to make heavy use of them, for example in a commercial application, you are asked to use your own tile source.

coordinates x, y at zoom level z. Other tile servers using the same technology have a similar URL scheme, and many of them can easily be added to a web map.

It takes several days to render tiles for the whole world from OSM data. It is generally not a good idea to prepare a full set of tiles for the whole world because relatively few tiles are actually looked at by users; most servers only generate a full-coverage tile set for zoom levels 0 to 8 or 0 to 10 or similar, and compute any further tiles on demand. The Mapnik tile server uses the `mod_tile` Apache module and a program called `renderd` to ensure that any tiles that don't already exist are created the moment they are requested.

Different tile servers employ different strategies for updating tiles. The best strategy for each server depends on how often tiles are requested, how often data gets updated, and also on the zoom level. It is possible to analyze the change files loaded from the OSM server (see section 15.2) to determine which tiles have to be regenerated because data on them has changed. The `osm2pgsql` utility (see section 17.2) can also generate lists of changed tiles. Some servers are also configured to update tiles on a regular basis, regardless of whether the data has changed or not.

In section 27.3 we describe the set-up and operation of a `mod_tile` based tile server.

In addition to steadily updated OpenStreetMap data, the Mapnik tile server also uses a pre-processed set of coastline data that is extracted from OpenStreetMap about once every one or two weeks. The preprocessing step, which forms closed water areas from individual stretches of coastline, requires a lot of computing power and thus the coastline cannot be updated continually. Therefore, in contrast to other kinds of edits, changes to the coastline take considerably longer to appear on the map.

Tiles can also be accessed using arbitrary subdomains (`a.tile.openstreetmap.org`, `b.tile.openstreetmap.org` and so on). This is a trick employed with most tile servers (including the Tiles@Home server discussed in the next section). It generally speeds up the loading of map tiles by web browsers, because browsers can make multiple parallel requests for embedded images but will often restrict the number of parallel connections to the same server. By inventing various names for the same server, this limitation can be circumvented.

Requesting Tile Status and Rendering

Tile servers based on the `mod_tile` module can be told to re-render an existing tile by adding `/dirty` to the tile URL:

```
http://tile.openstreetmap.org/z/x/y.png/dirty
```

You can also ask for the current status of a tile by adding `/status`. The server then tells you whether the tile is "clean", meaning it has been updated since the last full data import (and will give the details of when that was), or "dirty", meaning the tile is still awaiting re-rendering based on the most recent full data import.

14.3 The Tiles@Home Project

The second important tile server within OpenStreetMap is the Tiles@Home tile server (tah.openstreetmap.org). Tiles@Home serves tiles from this central location, but tiles aren't computed centrally; instead, tiles are created on the computers of hundreds of contributors. Tiles for Tiles@Home are rendered using the Osmarender software which has been developed specially for OSM. (For more on Osmarender see chapter 16.)

Tiles can be downloaded from http://tah.openstreetmap.org/Tiles/tile/z/x/y.png, where z is the zoom level and x and y are the tile coordinates. As with the Mapnik server, this server also uses the names on a.tah.openstreetmap.org, b.tah.openstreetmap.org, and so on.

In addition to the map tiles, the server also maintains a request queue that receives requests for rendering individual tiles. Tiles@Home contributors run a client software on their computers that regularly queries the server for new rendering jobs. If there is something in the queue, the server hands out the request to the client, and the client retrieves the data from one of the read-only OSM mirrors. It then runs Osmarender for every zoom level to create an SVG file ("Scalable Vector Graphics", an XML based vector graphics format). An SVG rendering engine then creates bitmaps from the SVG files. The resulting PNG files are split into tiles and uploaded to the Tiles@Home server.

For a long time, this procedure did in fact provide the shortest turnaround time (usually less than one hour) from making a change to the OSM database to being able to view the updated map; even though Mapnik has always rendered tiles much faster (by about two orders of magnitude), it originally worked based on weekly data imports with a turnaround time of up to two weeks. But today Tiles@Home no longer has this advantage, since the Mapnik tile server is updated continually and offers a turnaround time usually of only minutes (as it normally works on 1 minute change files).

Tiles@Home rendering is based on *tilesets*. A tileset encompasses one tile at zoom level 12 and all tiles of higher zoom levels covered by that. In the past, when Tiles@Home used to load data directly from the OSM API, a tile at zoom level 12 was just inside the allowed maximum download size. Today's read-only mirrors are more generous in handing out data, but the tilesets remain. The standard Osmarender tiles are computed for zoom levels 12 to 17, so that a full tileset has up to 1365 individual tiles: 1 on zoom level 12, 4 on level 13, 16 on level 14 and so on up to 1024 on level 17.

Tiles on zoom levels 0 to 11 are rendered using a different process covered later.

The Tiles@Home client can apply any number of preprocessing and rendering styles to every dataset downloaded from the server, and this enables it to compute a number of different map layers in one go (provided that the server is configured to accept uploaded tiles for these layers). There will usually be one Osmarender style sheet for every layer and every zoom level, and one SVG file is created per layer and zoom level.

The following layers are currently created in the standard Tiles@Home setup:

Layer	Zoom levels	Usage
tile	0-17	The normal map rendering.
captionless	12	Map rendering with captions omitted, suitable for downscaling.
caption	6-11	Labels only, rendered on a transparent background. (Caption tiles for level 1-5 exist as well but are not created by clients.)

Handling of Oceans and Coastline

When creating tiles for Tiles@Home, areas will usually be filled properly because the renderer requests a slightly larger region than it will draw, and in addition the server returns complete ways even if they lie only partly within the area requested. This doesn't work for oceans however; we explained earlier that they can't be created as areas because they would become too large.

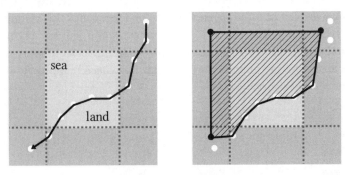

Figure 14-3: Automatic area creation.

The program close-areas.pl (wiki: Tiles@home/Dev/Interim Coastline Support) is used by Tiles@Home to fill water areas. It throws away all nodes that aren't needed to draw the coastline, and connects the remaining bits of coastline to form a fillable area (figure 14-3). To achieve this, the program looks at the direction of the coastline ways and makes the assumption that water is always on the right-hand side.

The illustration on the left shows the coastline, and the illustration on the right has the area that was created from it. The unconnected nodes have been discarded because they were outside of the visible area (light gray), and the black nodes have been added to form a closed polygon.

Tiles without any coastline on them are either fully on land, or fully on water. To choose the right color for them, Tiles@Home uses an index file that has land/water information for each level-12 tile on the planet.

Every now and again parts of the Tiles@Home map are "under water" (i. e. drawn with a blue background). This happens if either the coastline is broken (when it has holes or runs in the wrong direction), or if the tile index is wrong for that specific tile. The tile index can be modified with the png2tileinfo.pl script.

Zoom Levels 0 to 11 in Tiles@Home

Because Tiles@Home only ever renders a level-12 tileset at a time, the tiles for smaller zoom levels must be created by other means. In Tiles@Home, this is called the "Lowzoom Process".

This process runs on the server and uses the "captionless" tiles that have been uploaded by the clients, scaling them down to the desired size, and overlaying them with caption tiles. Just scaling down normal tiles in size wouldn't be any use as the labels would look like bird droppings, hence the rather complicated overlaying process.

On lower zoom levels, this process makes the Tiles@Home map quite attractive for OSM project members because it gives a good visual indication of the density of data. Figure 14-4 compares the map display of a European tile at zoom level 4 on Tiles@Home and on Mapnik: The Tiles@Home map tells you at a glance whether you will see anything interesting when you zoom in, whereas the standard Mapnik rendering looks roughly the same across the whole land area, whether only the largest roads have been mapped, or every individual residential home has been surveyed.

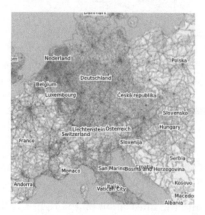

Figure 14-4: The same section of the map on Tiles@Home (left) and Mapnik (right).

Requesting Tile Status and Rendering

The Tiles@Home server maintains comprehensive statistics about the size and contents of its render queue and the current rendering speed. This information is available from tah.openstreetmap.org. To find out about the status of a specific tile, use the following URL: http://server.tah.openstreetmap.org/Browse/details/tile/z/x/y/

Replace x, y, and z by coordinates and zoom level of the tile you are interested in. The resulting web page will show the tile and tell you when, and by whom, it was last updated. There is also a button that allows you to mark the tile "dirty" and thereby put it in the rendering queue. The web map on www.informationfreeway.org (which, historically, was the first site to make good use of the Tiles@Home tiles) also has a built-in feature to request such re-rendering.

14.4 Using OSM with Google Maps

Google Maps (maps.google.com) not only offers maps for viewing on their site – you can also embed these maps directly into your own web pages. This only requires a little bit of HTML and JavaScript on your page. The Google API also allows you to use map tiles from sources other than Google, which works perfectly with OpenStreetMap tiles as these use the same coordinate system as Google. If you have already used the Google Maps API, then this is the easiest way for you to work with OpenStreetMap tiles.

> ☞ *To be able to interact with Google you need an API key. Read the terms of use at* http://www.google.com/apis/maps/signup.html *and then apply for a free API key. This key can be used in the following examples.*

In the first example, we will build a very simple page that nonetheless contains a full-featured Google map, with standard Google map tiles, and including the various zoom and pan buttons and an overview map in the corner. The user can also choose from the layers "Map", "Satellite", and "Terrain". This is the HTML source code for the first example (the ↙ arrow is a line continuation symbol – do not start a new line here, it has only been done for printing):

```
<html>
    <head>
        <title>Google Maps Example 1</title>
        <script type="text/javascript"
            src="http://maps.google.com/maps?file=api&amp;v=2&amp; ↙
                key=YOUR API KEY"></script>
        <script type="text/javascript">
function init() {
    var lon = 13.38;
    var lat = 52.52;
```

```
        var zoom = 13;
        map = new GMap2(document.getElementById('map'));
        map.addControl(new GLargeMapControl());
        map.addControl(new GMapTypeControl());
        map.addControl(new GOverviewMapControl());
        map.setCenter(new GLatLng(lat, lon), zoom);
    }
        </script>
    </head>
    <body onload="init()" onunload="GUnload()">
        <h1>Google Maps Example 1</h1>
        <div id="map" style="width: 100%; height: 700px"></div>
    </body>
</html>
```

The web page has an empty <div> element with an ID of map, which will be used by the Google code to place the map into. It can be sized and positioned through the usual CSS styling methods.

A <script> element at the beginning loads the Google Maps API. This is where you have to specify your API key details. The onload attribute of the <body> element makes sure that the init routine is called after the page has loaded. Then, a few calls are made to initialize the map, to configure the user interface controls, and to set a particular map center and zoom level for the initial map display – this example uses Berlin, Germany.

In our second example, we want to add an OpenStreetMap layer to this map. The init method is expanded to add the attribution required by OpenStreetMap's license:

```
var copyright = new GCopyright(1,
    new GLatLngBounds(new GLatLng(-90,-180), new GLatLng(90,180)), 0,
    '(<a rel="license" ✓
    href="http://creativecommons.org/licenses/by-sa/2.0/">CC-BY-SA</a>)');
var copyrightCollection =
    new GcopyrightCollection('Map Data &copy; 2010 ✓
    <a href="http://www.openstreetmap.org/">OpenStreetMap</a> ✓
    Contributors');
copyrightCollection.addCopyright(copyright);
```

Then, we create two additional layers named "Mapnik" and "Tiles@Home" that will load their tiles from the appropriate tile servers. In this example the "Mapnik" layer becomes the default layer:

```
var tilelayers_mapnik = new Array();
tilelayers_mapnik[0] = new GTileLayer(copyrightCollection, 0, 18);
tilelayers_mapnik[0].getTileUrl = GetTileUrl_Mapnik;
tilelayers_mapnik[0].isPng = function () { return true; };
tilelayers_mapnik[0].getOpacity = function () { return 1.0; };
var mapnik_map = new GMapType(tilelayers_mapnik,
    new GMercatorProjection(19), "Mapnik",
    { urlArg: 'mapnik', linkColor: '#000000' });
```

```
map.addMapType(mapnik_map);
map.setMapType(mapnik_map);

var tilelayers_tah = new Array();
tilelayers_tah[0] = new GTileLayer(copyrightCollection, 0, 17);
tilelayers_tah[0].getTileUrl = GetTileUrl_TaH;
tilelayers_tah[0].isPng = function () { return true; };
tilelayers_tah[0].getOpacity = function () { return 1.0; };
var tah_map = new GMapType(tilelayers_tah,
    new GMercatorProjection(19), "T@H",
    { urlArg: 'tah', linkColor: '#000000' });
map.addMapType(tah_map);
```

Finally, we need to tell the Google API how to get hold of the tiles for the new layers. We do this by creating, for each layer, a function that constructs a tile URL from a given zoom level and coordinate pair. The names of these functions have already been specified during the tile setup above:

```
function GetTileUrl_Mapnik(a, z) {
  return "http://tile.openstreetmap.org/"+z+"/"+a.x+"/"+a.y+".png";
}
function GetTileUrl_TaH(a, z) {
  return "http://tah.openstreetmap.org/Tiles/tile/"+z+"/"+a.x+"/"+a.y+".png";
}
```

The website accompanying this book (www.openstreetmap.info) has these examples available for download. If you want to continue playing with the Google API, you can find the full documentation at http://code.google.com/apis/maps/index.html. A wiki with lots of additional information about Google Maps is at mapki.com.

14.5 Using OSM with OpenLayers

OpenLayers (www.openlayers.org) is an Open Source JavaScript library that can be used to deliver an interactive web map by loading map data and map images from a variety of sources. For many data sources, like Google, Yahoo, or Bing maps, and also for WMS servers (which are popular in professional GIS circles), there are ready-made source modules available. Of course you can also display OpenStreetMap data with OpenLayers – indeed OpenLayers is the tool of choice for most web developers for displaying any kind of OSM map.

If you want to embed OpenLayers in your web page, you should first download the JavaScript library from http://www.openlayers.org/download/, including icons and CSS files. A link to the most recent version is always given on the OpenLayers website.[3] Create

---

3 Alternatively you can use the developer version from the Subversion repository, which you can access at http://svn.openlayers.org/trunk/openlayers/. The examples in this book and on the website use version 2.8.

a directory named ol on your web space. Unpack the tar file and copy the OpenLayers.js file as well as the complete img and theme subdirectories to that directory.

Now, create your map HTML file:

```html
<html>
    <head>
        <title>OSM OpenLayers Test</title>
        <script type="text/javascript" src="/ol/OpenLayers.js"></script>
        <script type="text/javascript"
        src="http://openstreetmap.org/openlayers/OpenStreetMap.js"></script>
        <script type="text/javascript">
...
        </script>
    </head>
    <body onload="init()">
        <div id="map" style="width: 100%; height: 700px;"></div>
    </body>
</html>
```

The first <script> element loads the OpenLayers library that you have just installed. The second <script> element embeds OpenStreetMap.js from the OpenStreetMap server, which creates OSM-specific layer objects that can be used later. The third <script> element is still empty – we will add more JavaScript content here later. The only HTML element on the page is the empty <div>, which will contain the map display.

We will now fill the missing JavaScript section. Just like in the Google example, an init routine serves to initialize the map after the page has loaded. It starts with a few definitions for the initial map display (again, Berlin in this example). After that, the map object is created using the required parameters. They are a list of user interface controls (Controls), the geographic size of the map (maxExtent), the maximum available detail (numZoomLevels), and a few settings for the map projection.

```javascript
function init() {
    var proj4326 = new OpenLayers.Projection("EPSG:4326");
    var projmerc = new OpenLayers.Projection("EPSG:900913");
    var lonlat = new OpenLayers.LonLat(13.38, 52.52);
    var zoom = 13;

    var map = new OpenLayers.Map("map", {
        controls: [
            new OpenLayers.Control.KeyboardDefaults(),
            new OpenLayers.Control.Navigation(),
            new OpenLayers.Control.LayerSwitcher(),
            new OpenLayers.Control.PanZoomBar(),
            new OpenLayers.Control.MousePosition()],
        maxExtent:
            new OpenLayers.Bounds(-20037508.34,-20037508.34,
                                   20037508.34, 20037508.34),
        numZoomLevels: 18,
```

```
                maxResolution: 156543,
                units: 'm',
                projection: projmerc,
                displayProjection: proj4326 } );
```

After that, we define two layers and place them on the map. The objects required for this have been defined by `OpenStreetMap.js`, which we have already included:

```
        var mapnik_layer = new OpenLayers.Layer.OSM.Mapnik("Mapnik");
        var tah_layer = new OpenLayers.Layer.OSM.Osmarender("Tiles@Home");
        map.addLayers([mapnik_layer, tah_layer]);
```

Finally we have to project the map center from geographic coordinates into the Mercator projection used by the map, and make the map display that area:

```
        lonlat.transform(proj4326, projmerc);
        map.setCenter(lonlat, zoom);
}
```

The complete code for this example can be downloaded from openstreetmap.info. There are also two other helpful examples there: The first doesn't use `OpenStreetMap.js` – this is useful if you want to create layers that access other tile servers than the ones maintained by OpenStreetMap; the second demonstrates how to set a marker at a given position.

Please remember that using OpenStreetMap data publicly requires that you add proper attribution (see section 20.1). Using the ready-made `OpenStreetMap.js` takes care of this for you.

OpenLayers is a powerful library, under constant development, and it has many other useful features. For example, it allows you to add vector data to the map (drawing points, lines, and areas) and even to have basic editing functionality. These methods are in fact used to create the Data Layer on `www.openstreetmap.org` (see section 12.1). OpenLayers can also access a WMS server, display KML files, and do many other interesting things. We can't cover all these features here, but a good starting point for using OpenLayers is the OpenLayers wiki page.

14.6 CloudMade Maps

The US-based company CloudMade has a JavaScript Framework of its own called "Web Maps Lite", and also offers a number of other services for use with OpenStreetMap data. Just as with Google Maps, you need an API key to use their framework. Using CloudMade services is currently free for personal use (but do check their web pages for pricing and policies).

Services offered at `developers.cloudmade.com` include a number of libraries for various mobile devices and programming languages, a routing engine, and a style editor. The style editor can be used to define your personal map style (based on a number of predefined CloudMade styles), and then instantly access the world map drawn in that style.

The CloudMade style editor doesn't offer the same degrees of freedom as writing your own style definition for a full-blown renderer like Mapnik (which is also the engine behind the CloudMade offering) or Osmarender, but on the other hand you don't have to set up your own tile server to produce map tiles in your style – all that is done for you by CloudMade.

Unfortunately there is currently no way to export a CloudMade style for use in your own rendering installation, and you can only edit certain of the style features.

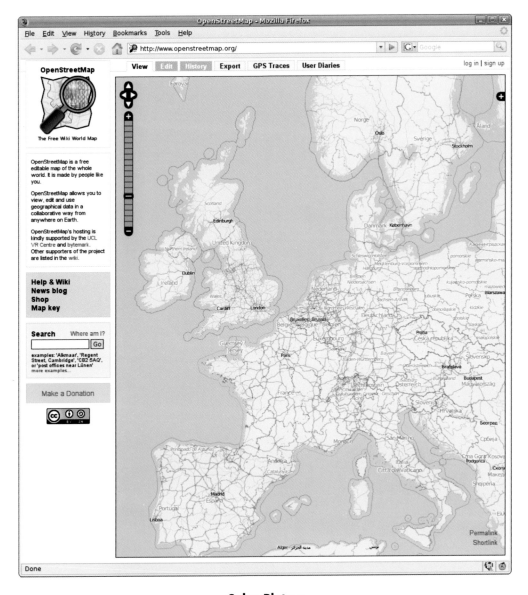

Color Plate 1

The main OpenStreetMap website (www.openstreetmap.org) lets you browse the map data that has been collected so far. The map is interactive, and can be zoomed and panned. The "+" button in the top right corner can be used to switch between different renderings (shown above is the Mapnik variant).

The gray "Edit" tab becomes active once you are zoomed in further. Once you have created an account with OpenStreetMap you can click this tab to start editing the data with the Flash editor Potlatch (see chapter 9 and color plate 10).

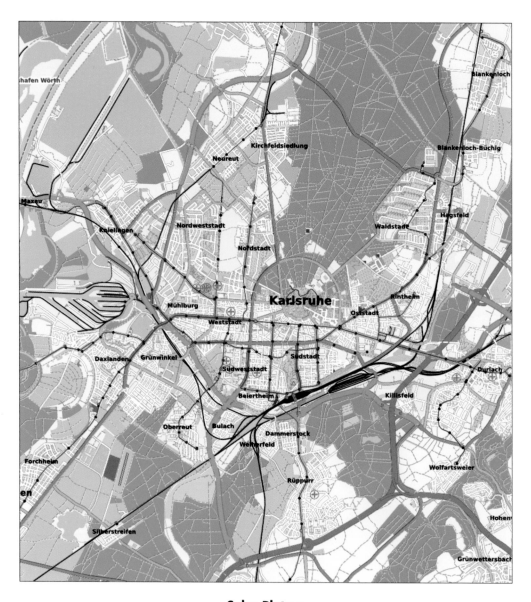

Color Plate 2

In the summer of 2007, Karlsruhe, Germany, was one of the first cities to be "fully mapped" in terms of roads and paths. The high level of detail, especially concerning footpaths and forest paths, was and still is a big advantage over many other maps. Of course the Karlsruhe map is far from perfect – for example, it still lacks many buildings and house numbers.

This Karlsruhe map has been created using Osmarender, one of two widely used renderers in OpenStreetMap. More about Osmarender, and how to render your own maps with it, can be found in chapter 16.

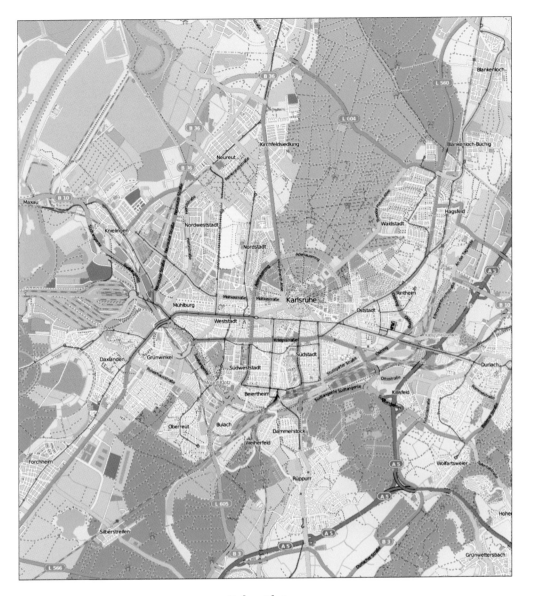

Color Plate 3

The same Karlsruhe dataset, this time rendered using the standard Mapnik style. As you can see, both renderings use a UK color scheme, where freeways are drawn in blue, other large roads in green, and smaller roads in red or orange.

Read more about Mapnik in chapter 17.

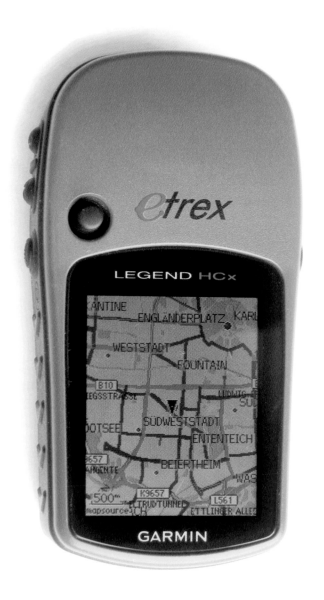

Color Plate 4

Data acquired with GPS devices (like this Garmin eTrex Legend HCx) are an important basis for the OpenStreetMap project.

The map you can see on the display of this device has been created from OpenStreetMap data. Section 19.3 explains how you can create maps for Garmin devices and transfer them to the GPS.

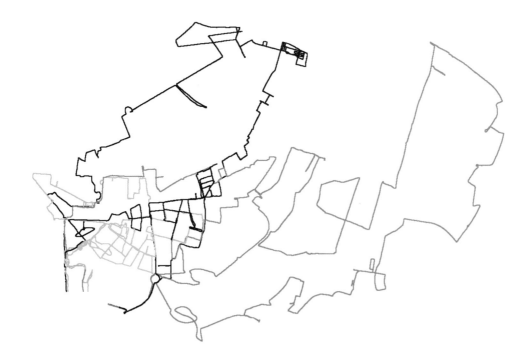

Color Plate 5

A collection of several GPS tracks recorded in the eastern half of Karlsruhe. Compare this with the maps on color plates 2 and 3 and you can see how they are already beginning to resemble the map.

GPS tracks form the source from which much OpenStreetMap data is compiled. The GPS device is set to record its current position at regular intervals, for example once per second. The recording can later be viewed in an editor and used as the basis for adding roads to OpenStreetMap.

Read more about GPS and GPS tracks in chapter 4.

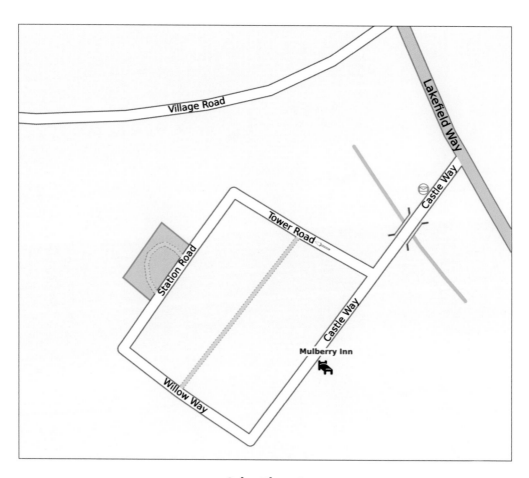

Color Plate 6

In chapter 5 we accompany mapper Max on his short mapping sortie. He starts at the Mulberry Inn, from where he surveys a small part of a fictitious neighborhood for OpenStreetMap. He records a few streets and footpaths and a small park. This is the result of his work.

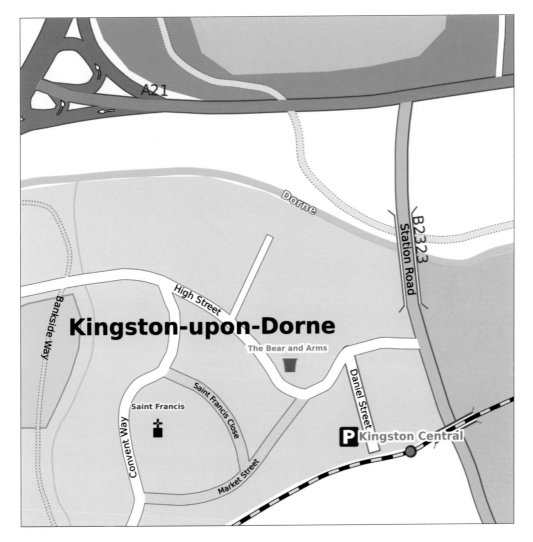

Color Plate 7

Using the example of the fictitious village of Kingston-upon-Dorne, we show how the world is recorded as map data, and how that data is rendered into a map by Osmarender. You can easily distinguish the various land use areas, road types, and points of interest such as the Saint Francis church and the Bear and Arms pub.

The various objects (Map Features) are explained in chapter 7.

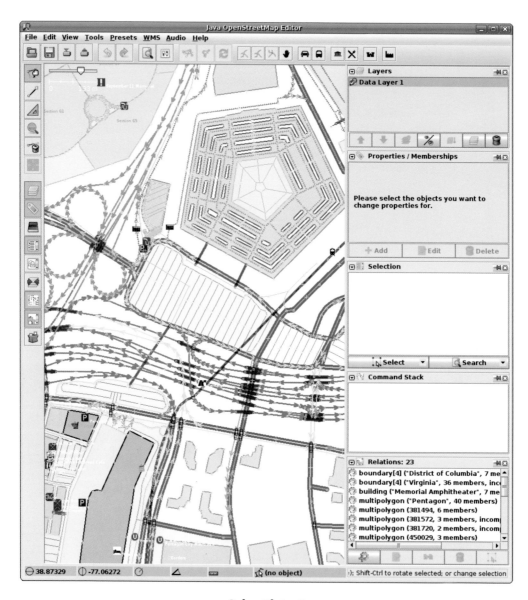

Color Plate 8

This is a screen shot of the JOSM Java editor described in chapter 10.

Newly drawn objects will initially be points and lines of standard color and thickness, but when tags are assigned to them, their representation in the map view changes.

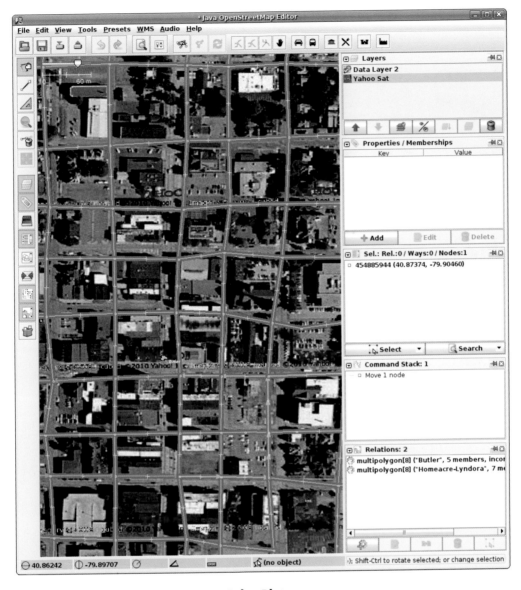

Color Plate 9

This is the JOSM editor again, this time with a background image from Yahoo via the WMS plugin (see section 10.8, page 136). The image demonstrates how OpenStreetMap data imported from TIGER (see page 325) is often out of sync with aerial imagery, and why people in the project check and correct where necessary.

Aerial imagery can be useful to trace roads, but it is most valuable for tracing woodland, lakes, coastlines, or building outlines – features that can be quite difficult to map for a GPS-equipped mapper.

Color Plate 10

The Flash editor Potlatch (see chapter 9) is an easy-to-use alternative to JOSM. One click on the "Edit" tab on the OpenStreetMap website, and you can start editing.

Potlatch supports a number of pre-defined background image sources, among them Yahoo imagery and the highly detailed NearMap images for selected areas of Australia (shown above).

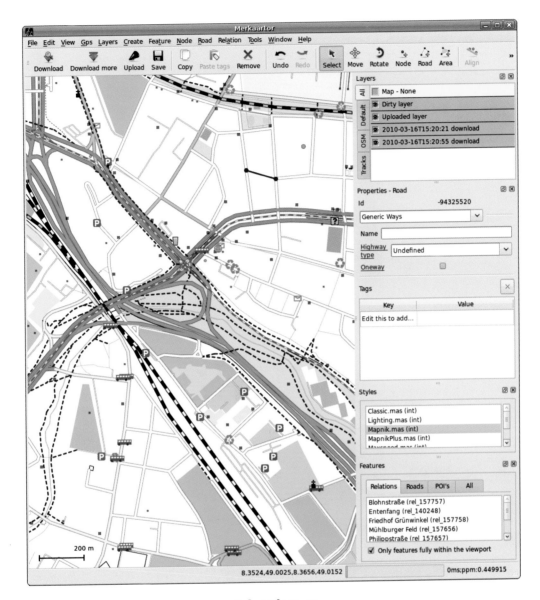

Color Plate 11

This screen shot shows the Merkaartor editor, which works in a similar way to JOSM in that you download an area to edit, make changes, then upload them again. Merkaartor is a word-play on the widely used Mercator projection and the Flemish word "kaart", meaning "map". Since the software is written in C++, it is a bit faster and less memory-hungry than JOSM. Merkaartor also has some innovative features that other editors lack; it can for example automatically draw parallel ways.

More on Merkaartor in section 11.1.

Color Plate 12

The "OpenStreetBrowser" (www.openstreetbrowser.org; showing a portion of Paris) uses a different rendering style than the main OpenStreetMap website, and many layers can be switched on or off individually. It also supports routing and hill shading. OpenStreetBrowser only covers Europe at the time of writing, but the code is freely available to anyone who wants to set it up for other regions.

Details of OpenStreetBrowser are on the wiki under OpenStreetBrowser.

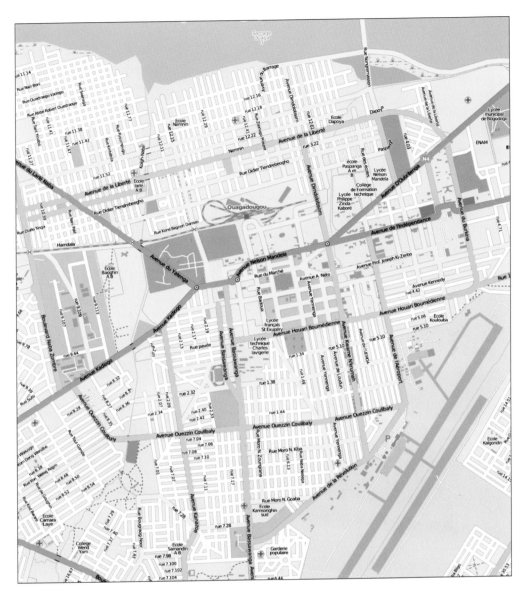

Color Plate 13

OpenStreetMap is of course not limited to Europe and North America. OpenStreetMap data for many developing countries is better than anything available locally.

This image shows the OpenStreetMap data for the center of Ouagadougou, the capital of Burkina Faso in Africa.

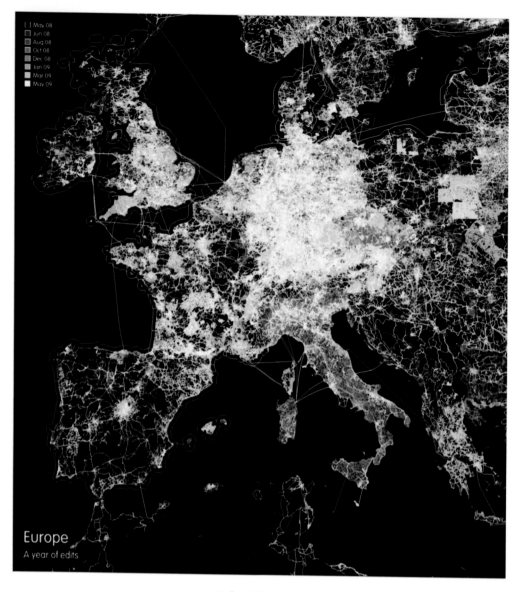

May 08
Jun 08
Aug 08
Oct 08
Dec 08
Jan 09
Mar 09
May 09

Europe
A year of edits

Color Plate 14

This image visualizes OpenStreetMap edits in Europe between May 2008 and May 2009. More recent changes are shown in a lighter color. It is easy to determine the hot spots of editing activity of England, Germany, the Netherlands, the Czech Republic, and Austria.

UK-based ITO World Ltd, who have prepared this image, make similar images and also animations available from time to time, for various regions of the world. You usually find these published on the web platforms "flickr" or "vimeo" (search for the ITO tag). The company homepage is www.itoworld.com.

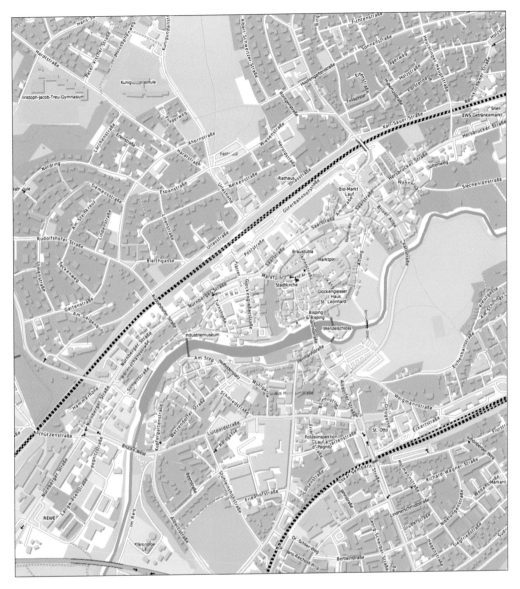

Color Plate 15

This OpenStreetMap rendering of the German town Lauf an der Pegnitz was created using the popular UMN map server (mapserver.org). UMN map server has been around much longer than OpenStreetMap and is widely used for GIS applications.

This rendering is taken from the online version of discOSM. At the website http://www.lingner.eu/discosm/ you can also download CD images with OpenStreetMap data for various countries and the software needed to create such images yourself.

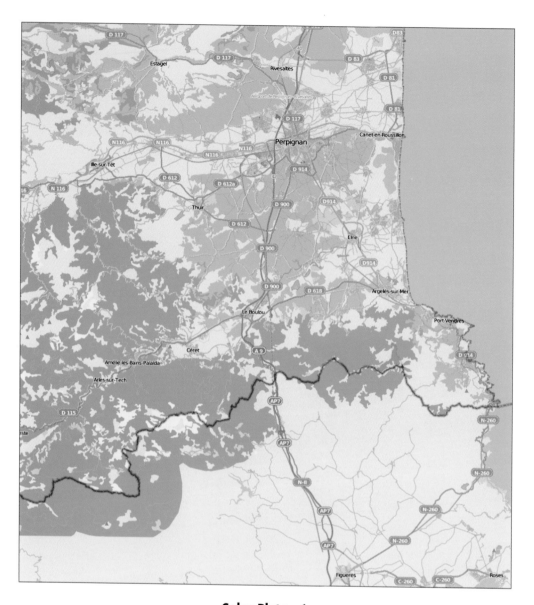

Color Plate 16

In 2009, data from the Corine Land Cover dataset was imported in several European countries (see page 318). The impact of that import becomes visible here at the border between France and Spain: The import has only been made in France, not in Spain.

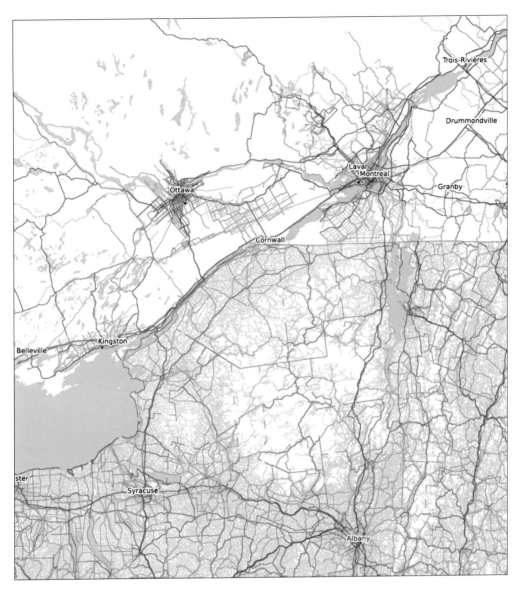

Color Plate 17

In the US, OpenStreetMap has wide coverage thanks to the import of TIGER data release by the federal government. TIGER data isn't as detailed or even as correct as data properly surveyed, and much work needs to be done to bring that basic dataset up to speed.

This image shows the US-Canadian border shortly after the TIGER import was completed. Imported data stops precisely at the border. Meanwhile Canada is catching up, not least due to the availability of Geobase data for import into OpenStreetMap.

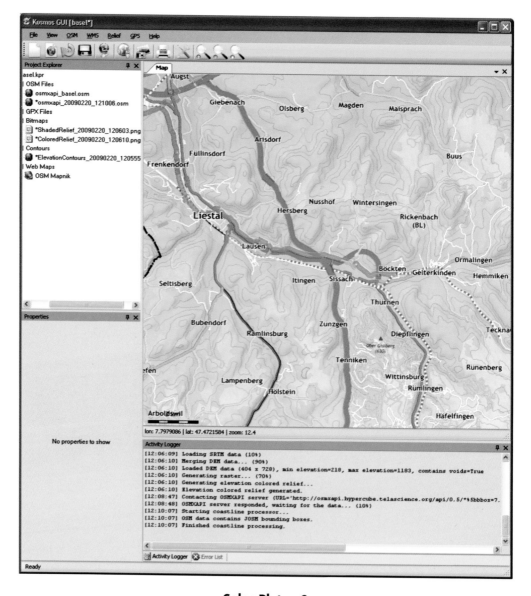

Color Plate 18

The Windows renderer Kosmos can load map styles from the OpenStreetMap wiki, and supports height contours and hill shading. It uses a free NASA dataset with height information called SRTM (Shuttle Radar Topography Mission), which is available for many parts of the world.

More about Kosmos and its successor, Maperitive, in chapter 18.

Color Plate 19

Of course OpenStreetMap data can also be used as the basis for printed maps. This photo shows a folded hiking map for the area of Gutau in Austria that was created from OpenStreetMap data.

Such printouts often require a great deal of work in preparing for print – not only the making of the map itself, but also the integration of additional information like a legend, information for tourists, or the cover.

More information about this specific project can be found at
http://ancalime.de/gutau.html.

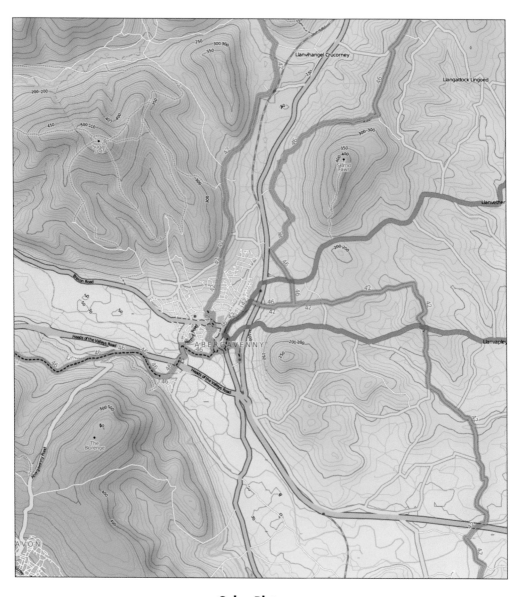

Color Plate 20

The cycle map at www.opencyclemap.org is a good demonstration of how you can do much more with OpenStreetMap than with other map websites. This cyclists' map is made from specially rendered tiles that, in addition to the usual data, have cycle routes and other information relevant for cyclists (including contours and hill shading). Large roads are drawn much less prominently than on a map aimed at motorists.

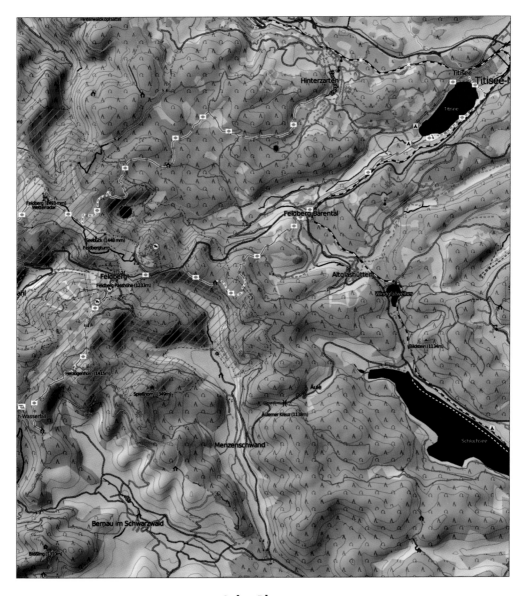

Color Plate 21

Another example of what can be done with OpenStreetMap. This riding and hiking map from topo.openstreetmap.de depicts part of the Black Forest in Germany. Hiking trails are highlighted and even drawn with their signpost symbol.

The contour lines and hill shading give a good impression of what the terrain is like. Altitude information comes not from OpenStreetMap, but from CGIAR, a refined version of the NASA SRTM dataset.

This mapping only covers parts of Europe.

Color Plate 22

The www.öpnvkarte.de (trans. "public transport map") site highlights railway lines, streetcars, subway lines and bus lines, all mapped in OpenStreetMap. This image shows the center of Cologne in Germany.

The mapping only covers Europe. If you have trouble with the "ö" in the URL, try www.openbusmap.org, an alias set up by a UK project member to avoid this problem.

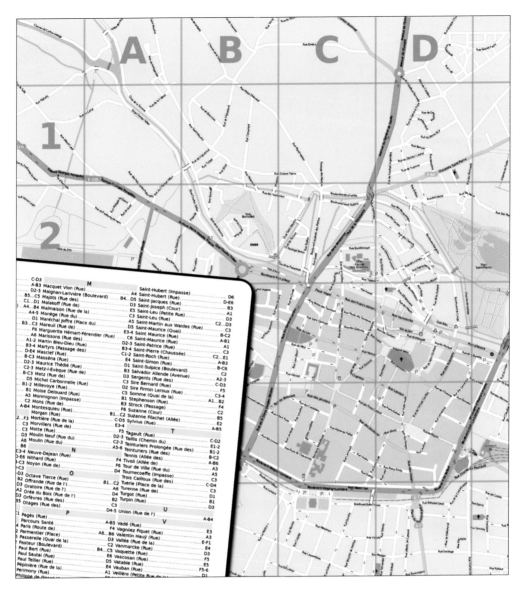

Color Plate 23

MapOSMatic (www.maposmatic.org) is a project to deliver free city maps from OpenStreetMap data. Uniquely, MapOSMatic creates fully indexed maps as shown in this montage.

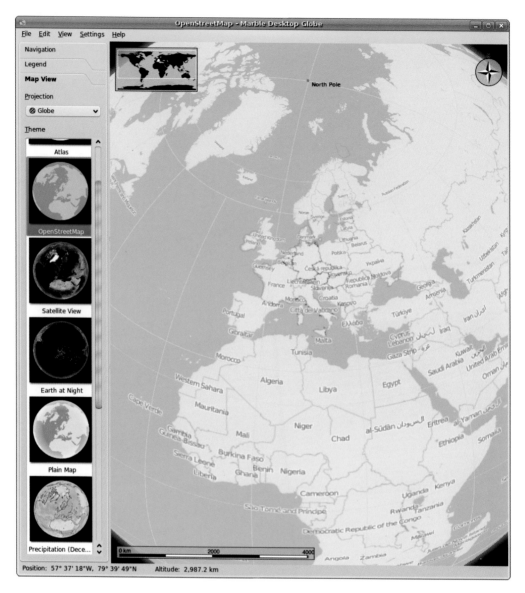

Color Plate 24

The KDE program Marble shows different views of our globe, either as flat maps or, as in this image, projected onto a sphere.

The standard OpenStreetMap tiles as well as the OSM-based OpenCycleMap (www.opencyclemap.org) can be selected as a map source in Marble. Marble is available via the standard software installation procedures in most Linux distributions.

Color Plate 25

The osmexport utility can convert OpenStreetMap data to KML, which can then be overlaid on a 3D aerial view in Google Earth. This image shows the German town of Mittenwald, just north of the Alps, looking South, with important roads and points of interest from OpenStreetMap.

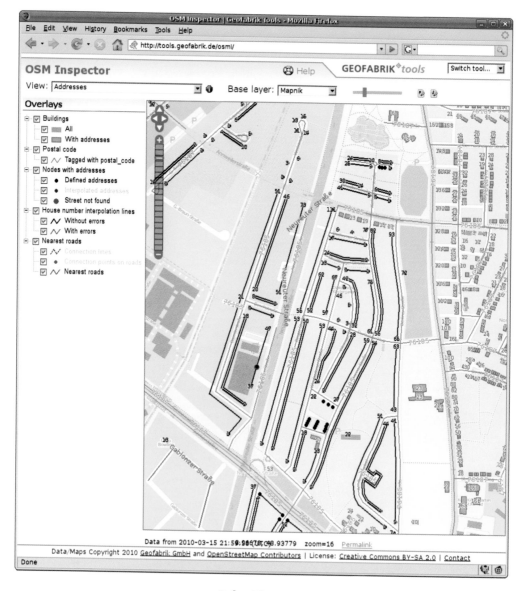

Color Plate 26

The OSM Inspector (http://tools.geofabrik.de/osmi/) helps mappers find bugs or problems with the map. This picture shows the "address view", which highlights addresses, house numbers, and other related information.

The OSM Inspector is discussed in section 12.2.

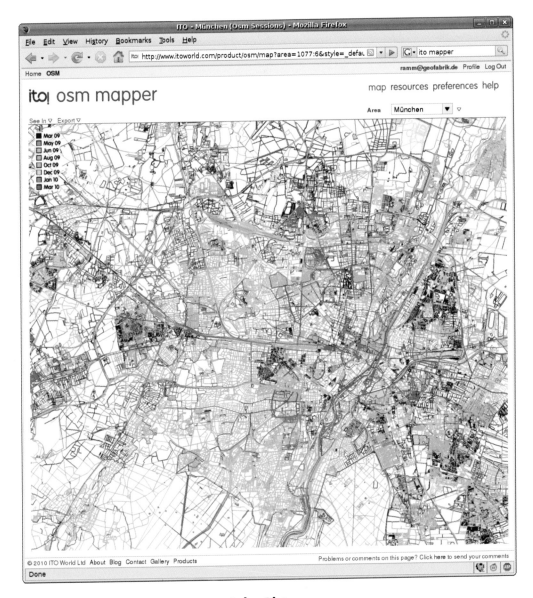

Color Plate 27

ITO World's "OSM Mapper" is another widely used debugging tool. It can color a map dynamically by tags, editing user, or time last edited. Various filters can be used to check and investigate details.

This image shows Munich, Germany.

Old data is colored blue, and recently modified data is red.

Read more about OSM Mapper in section 12.3.

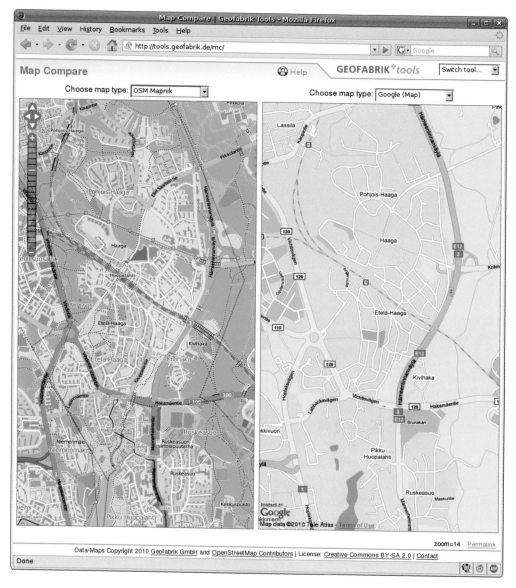

Color Plate 28

At `http://tools.geofabrik.de/mc/` you can view two maps from different providers side-by-side. This image has an OpenStreetMap map on the left, and the corresponding Google map on the right. Zoom or pan one of the maps, and the other will follow suit.

This tool can be used to compare maps from different providers, or different map styles. But remember that you must not copy data from other maps without permission. More about data licensing in chapter 13.

Color Plate 29

For use with GIS software, OpenStreetMap data can be exported to shapefiles (see section 26.3).

In this example we have exported data for Munich, Germany to a shapefile and displayed it using the Open Source GIS software Quantum GIS.

You can find regularly updated shapefiles for various countries at download.geofabrik.de.

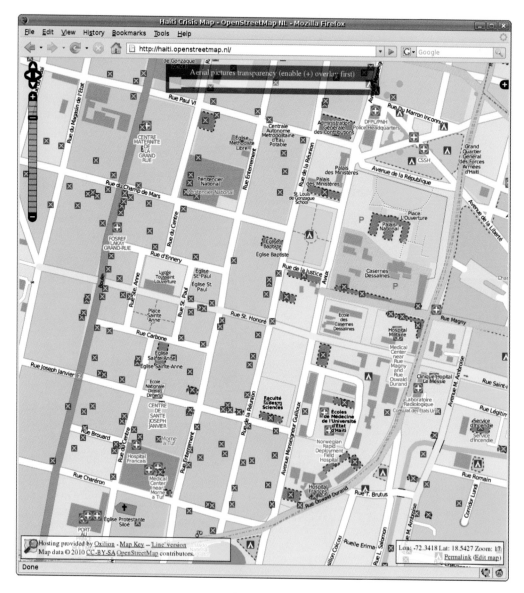

Color Plate 30

On 12th January 2010, a strength 7.0 earthquake shook the Caribbean state of Haiti. Within a few days, hundreds of OpenStreetMap contributors were tracing the Haitian road network. As new aerial imagery was released, OpenStreetMap contributors were able to mark collapsed buildings and spontaneous camps for internally displaced persons. New online maps and download files for GPS units were created every five minutes so that aid workers in the field always had access to the most current data.

Read more about this project on the wiki under WikiProject Haiti.

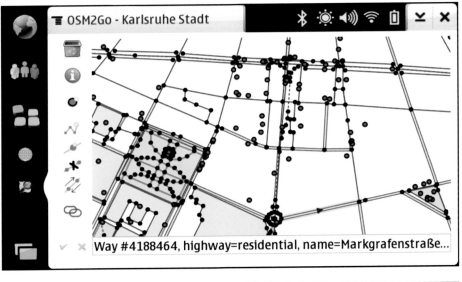

Color Plate 31

Osm2Go lets you view and even edit OSM maps on mobile devices. The editor might not offer all the features of a full-fledged desktop editor but it is optimized for being used while on the move.

There is more on Osm2Go in section 11.5.

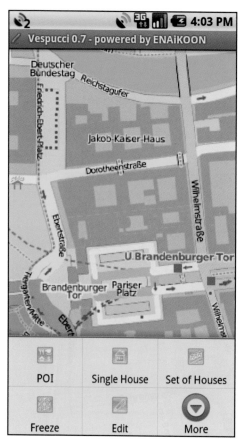
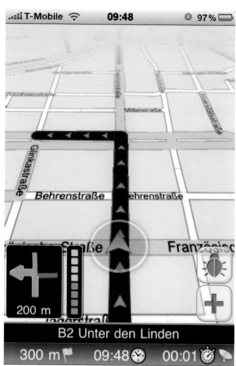

Color Plate 32

The mobile Android editor Vespucci (on the left, see page 146) displays a live OSM map and can be used to modify OpenStreetMap data while on the move. The picture shows Vespucci's beginner mode with buttons for placing POIs.

Skobbler (on the right, see page 231) does routing and navigation on OpenStreetMap data for the iPhone. Skobbler isn't an editor, but it has an option for quickly and easily reporting problems found in the data.

15 Accessing OSM Data

To do anything with OpenStreetMap data, for example produce your own map or set up a web service using that data, you have to download the data from somewhere. The OpenStreetMap project runs a central database server located in a computer room at University College London, but there are a number of ways to obtain the data (figure 15-1).

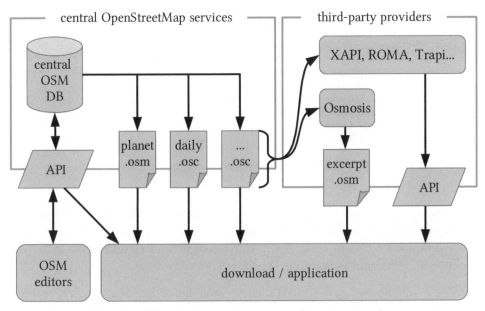

Figure 15-1: There are various ways to access OpenStreetMap data.

This chapter discusses downloading the current data for a geographic area directly from the OSM API, or using one of the regularly created data files, the *Planet Dumps,* and the associated *change files.* Both methods use the same XML file format (described in section 6.2), so the same tools can be used to process data retrieved by either method. There can however be subtle differences in the XML because it is generated by completely different software systems on the OSM servers. Another, more important difference is that the API always returns the latest data, but lets you only download a comparatively small amount of data at a time. If you need data for a larger area, you have to use the Planet Dump and possibly extract the area of interest from there.

Various third parties also download the OSM data in regular intervals to create filtered or regional excerpts of the data, or to feed them to a database of their own and offer a service using that database. You can read more about such services in chapter 23.

15.1 Downloading Data from the OSM API

If you wanted to download data from the API for the city of Reykjavik, Iceland, which sits inside a rectangular area, or *bounding box,* of 22.1 to 21.7 degrees of western longitude and 64.0 to 64.2 degrees of northern latitude, you would request this area from the server using the URL

http://www.openstreetmap.org/api/0.6/map?bbox=-22.1,64.0,-21.7,64.2

You would probably use a download program like `curl` or `wget` for this:

```
% wget -Oreykjavik.osm "http://www.openstreetmap.org/api/0.6/map? ↵
                              bbox=-22.1,64.0,-21.7,64.2"
--23:59:32--  http://www.openstreetmap.org/api/0.6/map?bbox=-22.1,64.0,-21.7,64.2
Resolving www.openstreetmap.org... 128.40.168.98
Connecting to www.openstreetmap.org|128.40.168.98|:80... connected.
HTTP request sent, awaiting response... 200 OK
Length: unspecified [text/xml]
Saving to: 'reykjavik.osm'
    [                        <=>              ] 11,012,235  26.0K/s   in 1m 58s
2010-04-23 00:03:35 (91.1 KB/s) - 'reykjavik.osm' saved [11012235]

%
```

Alternatively you can use the "Export" tab on the main website for this, or even the JOSM editor discussed in chapter 10: Fill in the desired coordinates in the download dialog and save the downloaded data to a file. Apart from minor formatting differences in the XML, the result will be the same as that from the above direct download.

The API can only be used to download a limited amount of data at a time. Currently, the server will return an area with a maximum size of 0.25 degrees squared, in other words (max_longitude-min_longitude) * (max_latitude-min_latitude) < 0.25. At the equator this corresponds to an area of approximately 50 km x 50 km, and roughly half that at far Northern or Southern latitudes. In addition to that restriction, the server won't return any data if the requested area contains more than 50,000 nodes, so if you request data from a densely mapped area, you may need to select an even smaller bounding box. (There are programs that can split a download request into several smaller requests and then combine the answers, effectively circumventing the API restriction. Using these programs is, however, frowned upon, and you should only do it if there is really no other way to achieve the desired result.)

The API has much more to offer than just a data download facility – you'll find a comprehensive list of API features in chapter 22.

15.2 Downloading Data Using Planet Dumps

Once a week, the main OSM database is dumped out to a file, called the *Planet Dump* or *Planet File.* You can download the file directly from planet.openstreetmap.org or from one of the mirrors listed on the Planet.osm wiki page.

As the name implies, the Planet Dump has current data for the whole world. The XML file in its uncompressed form has a size of about 200 GB, but it usually comes compressed with gzip (file extension .gz) or bzip2 (file extension .bz2). You need the matching decompression tools to unpack it.

In addition to nodes, ways and relations, the Planet Dump also has a concise list of all changesets ever applied to the database.

There are several websites that offer regional extracts of OpenStreetMap data, generated from the Planet Dump. This means that if you are interested in one country only, you don't have to work with the whole Planet Dump. For example, download.geofabrik.de has current extracts for most continents, countries, and even some sub-country administrative units such as UK counties, German Länder, or French régions. Files for individual US states are available from downloads.cloudmade.com. Additional download pages are listed on the Planet.osm wiki page.

A relatively new development is the *Full History Planet,* or *History Dump,* a less frequently generated version of the Planet Dump that contains the full history of every object instead of only the most recent version.

Finally, there are plans to make a regular dump of all GPS tracks uploaded to OSM and publish that under the name *GPX Planet.*

Change Files

In addition to the Planet Dump, the download server also offers daily, hourly, and even minutely change files (with the file extension .osc for OsmChange, see section 6.2). These files, sometimes also called *daily, hourly,* or *minutely diffs,* are generated on the server using the Osmosis program (see chapter 24), and contain all changes committed to the database between two consecutive days, hours, or minutes respectively.[1] You can use these files to update a Planet Dump downloaded earlier. This is done with the Osmosis program which we discuss in chapter 24.

Daily updates are about 0.5 % of the size of a Planet Dump, hourly updates are usually smaller than 0.1 %. Using these updates is especially attractive if you keep OpenStreetMap data in your own local mirror database, as updates can be applied much more quickly than re-importing a whole Planet Dump, which may take several hours or even days. Chapter 27 has more information on running your own OSM database.

---

1 Initially OSM used change files that only contained the newest version of a changed object – so if the object had changed twice during the change period, only the second version was included. Today, most change files are *replication diffs* that also contain all interim changes.

16 Making Maps with Osmarender

Osmarender is a rendering engine originally developed by Etienne Cherdlu (username 80n) that converts OSM data into vector graphics output (in SVG format). The resulting files can be viewed, edited, postprocessed, printed, or converted to bitmaps using SVG editors like the free Inkscape. Osmarender is well suited to rendering your own small-scale maps from OSM data as it is well maintained and widely used, and at the same time does not have as many prerequisites as, for example, Mapnik. The user can define how the map data is to be represented, for example by defining colors, line widths, symbols and other aspects of the map design. Osmarender is also used for creating tiles in the Tiles@Home project (see section 14.3). If you want to render your own tiles, however, we recommend using Mapnik (see chapter 17); Osmarender is better suited for making individual maps and maybe fine tuning them, and too slow to be used in a mass-production environment.

The map projection used by Osmarender is Mercator – or more precisely a slightly simplified version of the Mercator projection, but the difference is hardly noticeable at the usual zoom levels.

Osmarender and its accessory files are available from the OpenStreetMap Subversion repository, under `applications/rendering/osmarender`.

16.1 Scalable Vector Graphics

Scalable Vector Graphics (SVG) is a powerful, XML based data format for vector graphics that has been standardized by the W3C (World Wide Web Consortium). Many drawing programs can read SVG. As distinct from bitmap (or raster) images, vector graphics can be scaled easily, which makes them very useful for printing. Even when enlarged, vector graphics don't look jagged or pixelated like bitmap images would. SVG drawings are also relatively easy to modify in an editor; if you don't like the output of the renderer, you can remove unwanted detail or displace labels by hand, for instance.

Vector graphics consist of geometric objects that can be colored and filled. SVG also supports more complex objects like gradient fills. What you later see on the map is a large number of individual objects drawn one after the other. Figure 16-1 shows how a typical road rendering is created: A thinner white line (the *core* or *fill*, in rendering jargon) is superimposed onto a wider black line *(casing)*. The resulting image is a white road with a black border. On top of that, one-way arrows or street names are drawn.

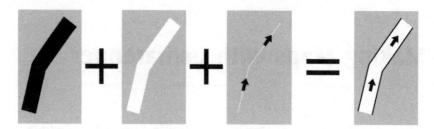

Figure 16-1: Several SVG objects are combined to make up a road.

After Osmarender has created an SVG file, SVG renderers like Inkscape, Batik, or the Firefox SVG engine can be used to process it, but each program has its own little bugs and idiosyncracies, leading to slightly different results. This means that it isn't always easy to find the right combination of SVG object types and drawing styles to make a good-looking map. Different SVG rendering engines all have their little bugs or idiosyncrasies, leading to slightly different results. That is why Osmarender maps sometimes look a bit odd when you closely inspect an intersection, a bridge, or a tunnel exit.

There is a good introduction to SVG in Wikipedia, and you can find more information at the W3C website, `http://www.w3.org/Graphics/SVG/`.

16.2 Osmarender and XSLT

XSLT (Extensible Stylesheet Language – Transformation) is a language for transforming one kind of XML file into another kind of XML or text file. As both the OSM and SVG files are XML files, XSLT can be used to transform one into the other.

XSLT commands are saved in style sheets with the file extension `.xsl`. An XSLT processor reads the style sheet and the input file(s), processes the input data using the transformation rules given in the style sheet, and writes the result to the output file.

Osmarender, then, is the XSLT style file that details the process of making a map from geodata. It also needs a rules file to how to draw the map features. The whole rendering process is shown in figure 16-1.

XSLT processors usually work by reading the full input file into memory and building a DOM (Digital Object Model) tree, in which the input file is represented by a hierarchical tree of objects. This tree is then transformed into an output tree and written to the output file. This process requires a considerable amount of memory, because it is not possible to process the input file in smaller chunks.

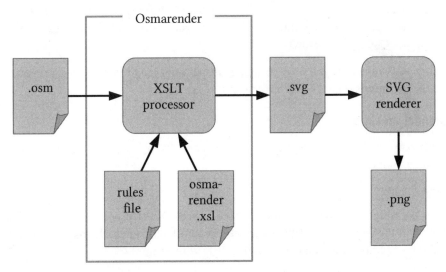

Figure 16-2: Map rendering with Osmarender and an SVG rendering engine.

Osmarender is a very complex XSLT style and thus extremely performance hungry. If you want to produce a map covering more than a small town with Osmarender, you need a fast computer with a lot of RAM. We recommend that you choose a small (or a sparsely mapped) area when you start experimenting with Osmarender.

Osmarender in Perl: or/p

While the XSLT version of Osmarender has the advantage of being runnable on every platform that has an XSLT processor, there is an alternative implementation created in Perl that achieves higher execution speeds. The program is called "or/p", and it replaces the combination of XSLT processor and osmarender.xsl, but everything else is the same – in particular, or/p processes exactly the same rule files as the original Osmarender, and produces near identical SVG output.

While we have documented the XSLT version of Osmarender in this chapter, the Perl version can be used in the same way. You can find or/p in a subdirectory of the Osmarender directory on the OpenStreetMap Subversion repository. The program requires a Perl interpreter to run.

16.3 Running Osmarender

The way you run Osmarender depends on which operating system and XSLT processor you are using. You can use any XSLT processor as they are more or less compatible; they do, however, differ in the way parameters are passed to them. Commonly used XSLT processors include Xsltproc, Xalan, and Xmlstarlet. Windows users have the option to use Microsoft's MSXML. Many web browsers (for example Firefox) also have a built-in XSLT processor. This section demonstrates some ways to run Osmarender, more are available on the wiki under Osmarender/Howto.

All examples assume that you have installed Osmarender from the OSM Subversion repository at `applications/rendering/osmarender/`.

Osmarender on Linux

On Linux you can use the shell script `osmarender` from the `xslt` subdirectory to run Osmarender conveniently:

```
xslt/osmarender map.osm
```

This uses the script `xslttrans` to find out which suitable XSLT processor you have installed, and calls it in the correct way. If you want to use a different rules file than the default, you can add the `-r` option, and you can set a map title with `-t`:

```
xslt/osmarender -r stylesheets/example.xml -t "My Nice Map" map.osm
```

The resulting SVG file is created under the same base file name as the OSM file, with the suffix changed to `.svg`.

Osmarender in Firefox

The Firefox web browser has a built-in XSLT processor. This means it can run any XSLT transformation directly in the browser and then display the resulting SVG image; however this is only feasible for small maps because large files take a very long time to process.

If XSLT style file is called `osmarender.xsl`, and the data file is called `data.osm`, and both are located in the same directory as the rules file, you should just need to open the rules file in Firefox. The other files will then be loaded from that directory, and the map displays in the browser.

If the files reside elsewhere, or have different names, you will need to change some URLs. The rules file begins with the following line:

```
<?xml-stylesheet type="text/xsl" href="osmarender.xsl"?>
```

This is used by the browser to find the XSLT style file. By default the rules file expects it to be called `osmarender.xsl` and located in the same directory as the rules file. The rules file also has information about where to find the data (`data="data.osm"`) – again defaulting to expect a file called `data.osm` in the same directory. These references can be changed to match your file names and locations.

All transformation parameters have to be specified in the rules file as there is no other way of passing them to Firefox. If you specify `interactive="yes"` in the rules file, zoom and pan buttons are added to the map.

Osmarender on Windows

On Windows, you have to use the command line as with Linux. If you are using the Java version of the Xalan XSLT processor, you have to enter the following command:

```
java -cp c:\path\to\xalan.jar org.apache.xalan.xslt.Process
    -in osm-map-features-z17.xml -out map.svg
```

The XSLT processor retrieves information about the XSLT style file and the data file from the rule file (here: `osm-map-features-z17.xml`). Details on changing these values have been given in the previous section on Firefox.

Converting SVG Files to PNG

Osmarender always creates SVG files. If you want to convert them into a bitmap graphic, you need an SVG renderer like Inkscape (see figure 16-1). With Inkscape, you can create PNG files interactively (go to the "File" menu, then choose "Export Bitmap") or on the command line:

```
inkscape --export-png map.png map.svg
```

There is a command line flag for exporting part of the image only (`--export-area`), and the bitmap size can be set as desired (`--export-width/height`).

16.4 An Introduction to the Rules File

Osmarender needs a rules file to control how OSM data is displayed on the map. For example, the rules file contains the information that a residential road is to be drawn as a white line with a certain stroke width overlaid on a black line with a slightly wider stroke. The rules file contains symbols for points of interest as well as color and pattern specifications. It also specifies the order in which features are drawn.

It is quite difficult to write a new and workable rules file from scratch – it's much easier to take an existing file and modify it in several iterations. You can download a number of rules files (those for the Tiles@Home project) from the SVN repository, in the directory applications/rendering/osmarender/stylesheets. You will also need the symbols sub-folder which contains SVG symbols referenced from some of the rules files.

The core of the rules file is the set of drawing rules, which specify the translation of OSM data into SVG objects. A rule is structured like this:

```
<rule e="OBJECT_TYPE" k="KEY" v="VALUE">
    DRAWING_COMMAND
</rule>
```

Each rule first specifies an OSM object type (node or way) with certain tags attached to it. Inside the <rule> element, one or more drawing commands then give details of how the object is to be represented on the map.

Osmarender processes all rules from top to bottom and in processing a rule applies it to all relevant objects, so the rules have to be present in the right order. Usually this means starting with areas, then adding linear features such as roads, and finally labels and symbols.

Example: A Car Park

Let us examine the rules needed to draw a car park, or parking lot:

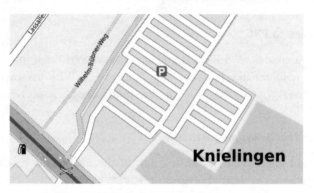

Figure 16-3: A car park as drawn by Osmarender.

The first thing we draw is the area of the car park:

```
<rule e="way" k="amenity" v="parking">
    <area class="amenity-parking"/>
</rule>
```

This rule applies to all way objects (e="way") which carry the amenity=parking tag. It draws an area (<area>) using the CSS class amenity-parking (see below).

The next thing to draw are service roads (the parking aisles are tagged as service roads). This needs two steps. The road casings are drawn first; road casings are usually thick dark lines that later show as the road outline:

```
<rule e="way" k="highway" v="service">
    <line class="highway-casing highway-service-casing"/>
</rule>
```

The roads, too, are of the "way" type, but they carry the highway=service tag. Osmarender is instructed to draw a line (<line>) using the two CSS classes highway-casing and highway-service-casing.

After the casings for all service roads have been drawn, the inner lines (cores) can be added:

```
<rule e="way" k="highway" v="service">
    <line class="highway-core highway-service-core"/>
</rule>
```

After that, a symbol for the car park is drawn if there is a matching node:

```
<rule e="node" k="amenity" v="parking">
    <symbol ref="parking"/>
</rule>
```

This rule specifies that nodes (e="node") tagged as amenity=parking should be symbolized by a car park icon (<symbol ref="parking"/>). The icon is defined further down in the rules file, or in an extra file.

Further down in the rules file, we have a section with CSS style information:

```
.amenity-parking {      /* car park area */
    fill: #f7efb7;      /* yellow fill */
    stroke: #e9dd72;    /* outline in darker tone of yellow */
    stroke-width: 0.2px; /* outline width */
}
.highway-casing { /* common settings for all road casings */
    stroke-linecap: square;
    stroke-linejoin: round;
    fill: none;
}
.highway-service-casing { /* road casings specifically for service roads */
    stroke-width: 1.2px;   /* line width */
    stroke: #777777;       /* gray */
}
.highway-core { /* common settings for all road cores */
    stroke-linecap: square;
    stroke-linejoin: round;
    fill: none;
}
.highway-service-core {  /* road cores specifically for service roads */
    stroke-width: 1px;    /* line width */
    stroke: white;        /* white */
}
```

All required symbols can either be defined in the rules file itself, or included from another file. For rules files from SVN repository, the symbols are located in `stylesheets/symbols`, each in a separate file. The car park icon is defined like this:

```
<svg ... width="20" height="20">
    <rect fill="#0087ff" width="20" height="20" x="0" y="-10"
              rx="4" ry="4" />   /* blue rectangle with rounded corners */
    <path fill="white" d="..."/> /* white "P" (details left out for brevity) */
</svg>
```

16.5   The Rules File in Detail

Osmarender has many options to influence the style of the produced map. This section documents the nuts and bolts of rules files, and the next section has some practical examples how to create your own map designs.

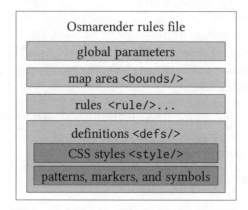

Figure 16-4: Structure of the Osmarender rules file.

Figure 16-4 illustrates the structure of an Osmarender rules file. In XML, it looks roughly like this:

```
<?xml-stylesheet type="text/xsl" href="osmarender.xsl"?>
<rules xmlns:xlink="http://www.w3.org/1999/xlink"
    xmlns:svg="http://www.w3.org/2000/svg" data="data.osm" ....>
    <bounds .../>
    <rule ...>....</rule> ...
    <defs>
        <style type="text/css" xmlns="http://www.w3.org/2000/svg">
        ...
        </style>
        <svg:pattern.../>...
        <svg:marker.../>...
        <svg:symbol.../>...
    </defs>
</rules>
```

Global Parameters

Global parameters are given as XML attributes to the <rules> element. Most of them can alternatively be specified as a parameter to the XSLT engine, overriding the value given in the file.

Parameter or attribute	Description
data	Name of the OSM file to be read. (When given as a parameter, the name isn't data but osmfile.)
interactive	Should the SVG file be furnished with buttons and JavaScript code for zooming and panning in web browsers (yes/no)? (This is not available as a parameter, only as an attribute.)
minimumMapHeight minimumMapWidth	Minimum height and width of the resulting map (in kilometers). Overrides a possible bounds specification.
scale	Controls the size of objects on the map in relation to the total map size. The default is 1; values larger than 1 leads to (relatively) thinner roads and smaller symbols, and values smaller than 1 leads to enlarged objects.
showBorder	Should a border be drawn around the map (yes/no)?
showGrid	Should 1km grid lines be shown on the map (yes/no)?
showLicense	Should the license be displayed beneath the map (yes/no)? Remember that when publishing a map, you must show the license somewhere; if this is set to "no" then other measures must be taken to inform the end user of the license.
showScale	Should a map scale be shown beneath the map (yes/no)?
svgBaseProfile	The SVG profile to use. The default value is "full", but for mobile devices with reduced SVG support the values "basic" or "tiny" may be more suitable. This setting only controls what is declared in the SVG file; it doesn't actually change the way Osmarender creates the map.
symbolScale	Enlarge all symbols by this factor (default: 1).
symbolsDir	Directory containing symbols to be added.
textAttenuation	A multiplier used in calculating text lengths. Osmarender doesn't know about font metrics so it has to guess how much room a label will need. If you use a font that takes up more space, you should use a value larger than 1 here. The setting can be overridden by <text> elements (see page 192).
title	Title to be shown above the map.
withOSMLayers	OSM data can use multiple layers (see page 67). If this option is active, Osmarender will honor that layering. Because this is relatively expensive in terms of processing power, layer processing can be disabled for maps that don't require it. (yes/no).

Map Bounds

If only a portion of the OSM data file is to be rendered, the area can be specified in the rules file using latitude and longitude values:

```
<bounds minlat="47.97" minlon="7.76" maxlat="48.03" maxlon="7.88"/>
```

This is usually required, because when downloading something from the API or when cutting something out of a Planet File, the excerpt often fully includes those objects that begin inside the requested area but extend outwards. Without the <bounds> element, Osmarender will determine the size by looking at the data, and will likely create a "jagged" map accommodating all those objects that extended beyond the boundaries of the downloaded area.

The Rule Element

A rule element is constructed like this:

```
<rule e="OBJECT_TYPE" s="SELECTOR" k="KEY" v="VALUE" layer="LAYER">
    DRAWING_COMMAND
</rule>
```

You can add an optional else section after the <rule>, which will be evaluated for all objects of the same object type for which the rule was written, but where the tags do not match.

```
<else>
    DRAWING_COMMAND
</else>
```

Rules can be nested:

```
<rule e="node" k="amenity" v="place_of_worship">
    <rule e="node" k="religion" v="christian">
        <symbol .../>
    </rule>
</rule>
```

The rule element has the following XML attributes:

Attribute	Description
e	Object type (node, way, or node|way to match both).
k	Tag key (e. g. amenity or highway).
v	Tag value (e. g. parking or residential).
s	Selector (optional; see below).
layer	Forces rendering to a specific layer (optional; takes values from -5 to 5).

The key and value attributes can have multiple alternatives listed, separated by a vertical line (|):

```
<rule e="way" k="highway" v="residential|unclassified">
```

A rule like this will match if any one of the mentioned alternatives matches.

The values "*" and "~" have special meaning:

Attribute	Value	Description
k / v	*	Any value.
k	~	Objects that have no tag at all.
v	~	Objects that have no tag with the given key.

The following rule will, for example, match any waterway:

```
<rule e="way" k="waterway" v="*">
```

For all nodes that don't have a name:

```
<rule e="node" k="name" v="~">
```

For all ways that are completely untagged:

```
<rule e="way" k="~">
```

The Selector Attribute

Sometimes the simple per-object rules aren't sufficient to select the desired set of objects. In these cases, the selector attribute ("s") can often help. It evaluates the relationship between objects, and is best explained with an example:

```
<rule e="node" s="way" k="railway" v="rail">
    <rule e="node" s="way" k="highway" v="*">
        <symbol ref="symbol-railway-crossing"/>
    </rule>
</rule>
```

This rule ensures that all nodes that are part of both a railway line and a road are drawn with a railway crossing symbol. Where a selector attribute is present, the "e" attribute still defines which object is to be evaluated for drawing, but the selector attribute defines which set of tags is compared – that of the object itself or that of a parent way or relation. Where no selector attribute is present, the "e" attribute serves both purposes.

Drawing Commands in the Rules File

The following commands for drawing shapes and symbols are supported in a rules file. (Commands for drawing text are discussed on the next page.)

Element	Object	Attributes	What will be drawn?
<area>	Way	class	A filled area.
<circle>	Node	class, r	A circle (r=radius).
<line>	Way	class, mask-class, smart-linecap	A line (mask-class is explained below, Smart Linecaps are explained on page 194).

Element	Object	Attributes	What will be drawn?
`<symbol>`	Node or Way	`xlink:href, width, height, position, transform`	A symbol (for ways, the symbol is placed at the center).
`<wayMarker>`	Node	`class`	A symbol that is drawn at a 90° angle to the first way passing through the node. The first way is the way with the lowest object ID.

The `class` attribute specifies the CSS class(es) used to draw an element. In the CSS section of the rules file, these classes are defined, using properties like line widths and colors.

Line elements can additionally carry a `mask-class` attribute referring to a CSS class that will be used to mask the line onto itself. In this context, the term "masking" means removing something. This is useful for tasks like drawing tunnels. Figure 16-5 illustrates the process: A line is drawn with a dashed stroke (a), then masked with the same line, filled and slightly thinner (b). The result is shown on the right (c).

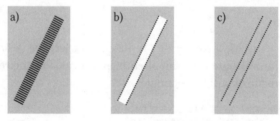

Figure 16-5: Masking a line.

For symbols, the `xlink:href` attribute can be used to link to a symbol definition inside the rules file, or `ref` to link to an external symbol file. The attributes `width` and `height` specify the width and height of the symbol, and the `transform` attribute can be used to move or rotate the symbol so that it is placed at the right position. The `position="center"` attribute centers an external symbol on the location.

Any SVG attribute attached to a drawing instruction will be copied verbatim to the SVG output. This means that you can add extra attributes from the SVG specification that Osmarender does not have to know about, and they will just be passed on the SVG renderer.

Text on the Map

There are three ways to add text to the map (see figure 16-6): Node labels are placed horizontally at the node location (a), line labels follow the line (b) and area labels are placed at the area center (c).

Node labels are created with the `<caption>` element:

```
<caption k="name" class="caption" dx="2px" dy="-2px"/>
```

This creates a label using the CSS class `caption` to the upper right of the node location. The value of the name tag is shown as the label.

Figure 16-6: Text on the map.

Line labels can be placed using `<pathText>`:

```
<pathText k="name" class="roadname" dy="-2.5px" startOffset="50%"/>
```

This creates a label using the CSS class `roadname`, placed in the middle of the line and displaced slightly upwards (`startOffset="50%"`, `dy="-2.5px"`). The value of the name tag is shown as the label.

You can also add the optional `textAttenuation` attribute (as a floating-point number) to specify a multiplier for guessing the width of the text, e. g. `textAttenuation="1.5"`. The exact letter width of the font used for labels is not known to Osmarender since it can't access the font information. Nevertheless it tries to guess the label widths, and selects smaller font sizes for labels that would otherwise be deemed too wide. Depending on which fonts you use, Osmarender's guesses might turn out too low or too high, and you can balance that with this setting. Increase it if you find that text often overflows a road, and decrease it if text is often unnecessarily printed in a smaller font size.

Area labels are again drawn using the `<caption>` element:

```
<caption k="name" class="parkname"/>
```

The range of possible attributes is the same as for node labels. The reference position is the area center point. Different Osmarender implementations may vary as to where they place the area center point.

The simple examples given here had Osmarender use the value of the tag specified by the "k" attribute. All types of labels also support a different way of placing text with tag substitution, where text given inside the `<caption>` element is copied verbatim, and any `<tag>` elements are substituted by the object's tag values:

```
<caption><tag k="name"/> (<tag k="ref"/>)</caption>
```

This comes in handy if you want to print more than just the contents of one tag, for example to add a unit or to give the contents of a second tag in parentheses, as above.

Smart Linecaps

SVG supports different types of line endings (see figure 16-7). Where two roads meet at an angle, flat ("butt") line endings lead to an ugly gap (a). Using round line endings makes the gap go away, but the road now has round endings as well (b). Osmarender's "Smart Linecaps" setting automatically draws round endings for joins and flat endings for true endings (c). This setting is on by default but may be disabled by adding the smart-linecap="no" attribute to a <line> drawing instruction.

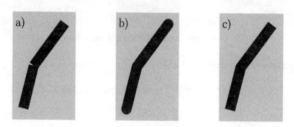

Figure 16-7: The Smart Linecaps setting.

CSS Styles

The CSS styles specify the look of features: The colors and pattern to use, the line widths, fonts, and so on. CSS styles are copied verbatim to the SVG output file, and processed by the SVG renderer. Drawing commands reference CSS classes through the class attribute.[1]

This is an example of CSS styles for highway=secondary:

```
.highway-secondary-bridge-casing  {stroke-width: 2.5px;}
.highway-secondary-bridge-core    {stroke-width: 2.2px;}
.highway-secondary-casing  {stroke-width: 1.7px; stroke: #777777;}
.highway-secondary-core    {stroke-width: 1.5px; stroke: #FDBF6F;}
.highway-secondary-name    {stroke-width: 0px; font-size: 1.5px;}
```

The format is always the same: The class name comes first, with a leading dot, and there-after follow the style elements enclosed by braces. In this example the color (stroke) and width (stroke-width) of the line are specified, as well as the font size for the street name.

You can find a detailed description of available styles in the SVG specification at the URL http://www.w3.org/TR/SVG/, or in related literature.

The following CSS styles are used by Osmarender to draw the map background, border, and so on: map-title, map-title-background, map-background, map-marginalia-back-ground, map-border-core, map-border-casing, map-scale-casing, map-scale-core,

---

1 If you have ever written HTML pages, you may have encountered CSS in that context already. CSS for SVG isn't much different from CSS for HTML.

map-scale-bookend, map-scale-caption, map-grid-line. They can be redefined as desired (see Osmarender/Options on the wiki).

Patterns, Markers, and Symbols

The last section of the rules file has SVG definitions for patterns, markers, and symbols, all of which are copied verbatim to the output file.

Patterns are typically used for filling areas (for example woodland or cemeteries).

Markers are meant to be used for arrows and other symbols at the ends of lines. In Osmarender, they are used for barriers, tunnel exits, and bridges.

Symbols are used for points of interest, like churches or post boxes.

Patterns, markers, and symbols may contain (almost) any SVG elements that describe how to draw them. All these elements have a unique ID that can be used to reference them from a style definition, using the syntax url(#ID):

```
.landuse-cemetery {              /* for cemeteries */
    fill: url(#cemetery-pattern); /* fill with this pattern */
    stroke: #eeeeee;              /* gray outline */
    stroke-width: 0.2px;          /* outline is 0.2 pixels wide */
}
```

16.6 Writing Your Own Map Styles

Now that you understand the structure of the rules file, you can start creating your own map styles. In this section we will guide you through some examples.

All rules files and example maps from this section can be downloaded from the book's website at www.openstreetmap.info.

First Example: Rail Network

You are interested in the local railway network and want to make a map that has all long distance, light rail, and tram lines. Here's how to create a suitable rules file for the task:

First, the standard prolog for the rules file with the usual global settings:

```
<?xml-stylesheet type="text/xsl" href="osmarender.xsl"?>

<rules
    xmlns:xlink="http://www.w3.org/1999/xlink"
    xmlns:svg="http://www.w3.org/2000/svg"
    data="data.osm"
    svgBaseProfile="full"
    scale="1"
    symbolScale="1"
```

```
                textAttenuation="14"
                minimumMapWidth="1"
                minimumMapHeight="1"
                withOSMLayers="yes"
                showScale="no"
                showGrid="yes"
                showBorder="yes"
                showLicense="yes"
                interactive="no">
```

We have specified a border around the map, a grid, and an embedded license display; everything else is the default.

Now we need a few drawing rules. As a backdrop for the railway network, we want to draw all roads (highway=...) but no footpaths, cycleways, or tracks. All roads will use the same drawing style. The rule is simple:

```
<rule e="way" k="highway" v="motorway|motorway_link|trunk|trunk_link| ↙
        primary|primary_link|secondary|tertiary|unclassified|residential| ↙
        pedestrian">
    <line class="highway"/>
</rule>
```

After that, we want to draw all railway lines (railway=*). Since we don't need to distinguish between different types here either,[2] this rule, too, is simple:

```
<rule e="way" k="railway" v="*">
    <line class="railway"/>
</rule>
```

Now we need to draw all stations and halts. We want the halts (railway=halt) to be represented by a filled circle with a radius of 2 and labeled with their name. The label needs to be shown to the right of the circle, something which we achieve (after a little experimentation) using the proper dx and dy settings. We also want to achieve a "halo" effect for better readability on the map where the text intersects with the linework (see figure 16-8). So we place the text twice, using two different CSS styles (halt-text-casing and halt-text-core).

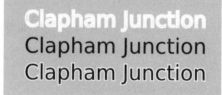

Figure 16-8: Text with halo.

---

2 For this example we accept that we might also draw some abandoned or disused railway lines.

The first is drawn a bit thicker, and in white; the second label thinner and in black. So the complete rule for halts is:

```
<rule e="node" k="railway" v="halt">
    <circle r="2" class="halt"/>
    <caption k="name" class="halt-text-casing" dx="3" dy="2.5"/>
    <caption k="name" class="halt-text-core" dx="3" dy="2.5"/>
</rule>
```

We do the same for stations, with a slightly larger circle and slightly different text displacement values:

```
<rule e="node" k="railway" v="station">
    <circle r="4" class="station"/>
    <caption k="name" class="station-text-casing" dx="5" dy="3"/>
    <caption k="name" class="station-text-core" dx="5" dy="3"/>
</rule>
```

This concludes the rules section; next section is the styles, which is opened by this prolog:

```
<defs>
    <style type="text/css" xmlns="http://www.w3.org/2000/svg">
```

Now we define the styles for roads and railways; we draw the roads as gray lines, and the railways as black lines, each with a width of 2 pixels[3]:

```
.highway {
    fill: none; stroke: #b0b0b0; stroke-width: 2px; stroke-linecap: round;
}

.railway {
    fill: none; stroke: #000000; stroke-width: 2px; stroke-linecap: round;
}
```

The circle for halts is filled in black and has no border; the circle for stations is filled in red and has a black border:

```
.halt    { fill: #000000; stroke: none; }
.station { fill: #ff0000; stroke: #000000; stroke-width: 2px; }
```

Next we define the label styles. As discussed above, the halo effect requires two different styles for each type of label. The names of halts are the same as the station labels, except that they are printed in a smaller size (font-size: 8) and have a smaller halo (stroke-width: 0.8px):

```
.station-text-casing {
    fill: black; stroke: white; stroke-width: 1px;
    font-size: 10; font-family: "DejaVu Sans",sans-serif;
}
```

---

3 SVG is a vector format. The "pixel" unit is simply used as a size unit and doesn't correspond in any way to a true pixel on output.

```
.station-text-core {
    fill: black; stroke:  none;
    font-size: 10; font-family: "DejaVu Sans",sans-serif;
}

.halt-text-casing {
    fill: black; stroke: white; stroke-width: 0.8px;
    font-size:  8; font-family: "DejaVu Sans",sans-serif;
}

.halt-text-core {
    fill: black; stroke:  none;
    font-size:  8; font-family: "DejaVu Sans",sans-serif;
}
```

Finally, we copy the styles for border and grid (not shown here) from the standard rules file, and conclude the file with:

```
        </style>
    </defs>
</rules>
```

A map generated using this rules file is shown in figure 16-9.

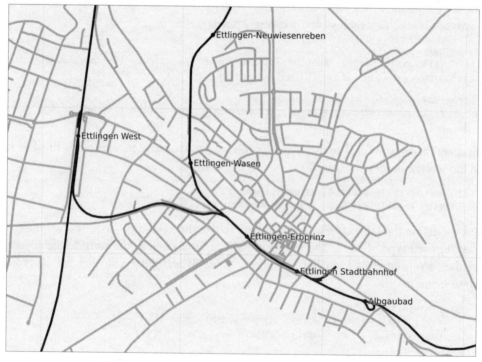

Figure 16-9: An Osmarender map highlighting railway lines.

Second Example: Post Box Density

In this example we want to visualize the distribution of post boxes and post offices. Each post box is to be shown with an approximate catchment area.

We start as in the previous example with the prolog and global settings. The first rule draws a filled circle of radius 50 around all post boxes and all post offices. With standard Osmarender settings, a 50 pixel radius corresponds to 300-400 meters; it isn't possible to specify the desired distance precisely in meters and you may have to experiment a little to achieve the result you want.

```
<rule e="node" k="amenity" v="post_box|post_office">
    <circle r="50" class="postbox-area"/>
</rule>
```

Over this we draw the road grid. We treat residential roads and pedestrian areas differently so that we can draw them with a different style:

```
<rule e="way" k="highway" v="motorway|motorway_link|trunk|trunk_link| ✓
                    primary|primary_link|secondary|tertiary|unclassified">
    <line class="highway-misc"/>
</rule>

<rule e="way" k="highway" v="residential|pedestrian">
    <line class="highway-residential"/>
</rule>
```

After that, every post box is symbolized by a small dot:

```
<rule e="node" k="amenity" v="post_box">
    <circle r="3" class="postbox-point"/>
</rule>
```

And finally we draw a dot plus a large circle for each post office:

```
<rule e="node" k="amenity" v="post_office">
    <circle r="3" class="postoffice-point"/>
    <circle r="100" class="postoffice-area"/>
</rule>
```

That concludes the rules section, and we add the styles. The large circle drawn around post offices is to be done in red and dashed, but not filled, and the post office dot is to be drawn in red too:

```
.postoffice-area {
    fill: none; stroke: #f00000; stroke-width: 2px; stroke-dasharray: 1 1;
}

.postoffice-point {
    fill: #f00000; stroke: none;
}
```

Post boxes are drawn as yellow areas and a black dot:

```
.postbox-area {  fill: #f0f000; stroke: none; }
.postbox-point { fill: #000000; stroke: none; }
```

Finally, the styles for the road network are specified. The residential areas receive a slightly darker shade of gray to make it more obvious where post boxes will be in high demand. We could also have drawn areas where landuse=residential was tagged but such areas aren't necessarily present everywhere in the database.

```
.highway-residential {
    fill: none; stroke: #a0a0a0; stroke-width: 2px; stroke-linecap: round;
}

.highway-misc {
    fill: none; stroke: #d0d0d0; stroke-width: 2px; stroke-linecap: round;
}.
```

A map drawn with this rule is shown in figure 16-10.

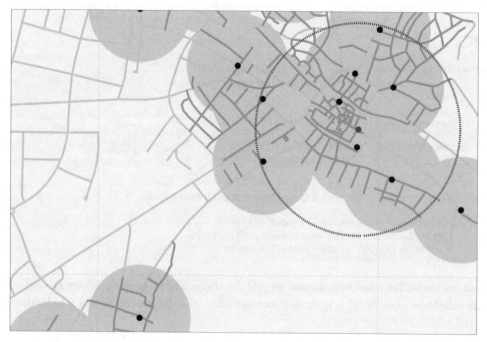

Figure 16-10: Post box and post office distribution.

Remember that Osmarender writes a path definition to the SVG file for every way present in the OSM file, regardless of whether it is used or not. Even if you only draw a tiny subset of OSM data, as we have done in these examples, the SVG file will contain the line geometries of all OSM ways that were present in the input file. Use the "Vacuum Defs" option from Inkscape's "File" menu to remove such unneeded information. This may take a while for large files.

16.7 Special Osmarender Tags

Sometimes the rendering result can be improved by asking Osmarender to draw some objects in an unusual way. You can achieve this by adding special tags to the objects. You should, however, be wary of uploading such tags to the OSM database – this should only be done as an exception.

The tags are processed in the standard rules files, and only supported by the XSLT implementation. You don't have to react to these tags in your own rules files unless you need them.

osmarender:render
Can be set to "no" to make Osmarender completely ignore the object.

osmarender:renderName
Can be set to "no" to make Osmarender not render a name for this object.

osmarender:renderRef
Can be set to "no" to make Osmarender not render the "ref" tag (for example a street number) for this object.

osmarender:nameDirection
Osmarender places road names along the road. It will normally write the name in the direction in which it is easiest to read. For roads with lots of bends, the automatic detection of the best direction sometimes fails. If you set this tag to "1" or "-1", you can force Osmarender to place the text always in the direction of the way ("1") or in the opposite direction ("-1").

16.8 Drawing Bézier Curves

Because OpenStreetMap always maps streets as a sequence of small straight lines, curvy roads sometimes look a bit jagged on the map – see, for example, the U-shaped "Eversley Crescent" in the left picture of figure 16-11.

This can be fixed by converting curvy roads to Bézier curves in an SVG editor. The result of that process is shown in the picture to the right.

A helper program named `lines2curves.pl`, which was originally designed for use within the Tiles@Home project, automatically changes all suitable roads to Bézier curves in an Osmarender SVG file..

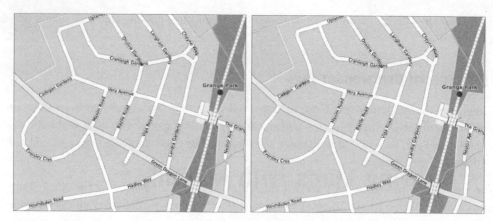

Figure 16-11: The same area drawn without (left) and with (right) Bézier curves.

You can download it from `applications/rendering/tilesAtHome` in the SVN repository. After you have created the SVG file with Osmarender, run the program from the command line:

```
perl lines2curves.pl <old-file.svg >new-file.svg
```

17 Drawing Maps with Mapnik

Mapnik (www.mapnik.org) is a program that renders geodata into map form. It has been developed by Artem Pavlenko independently of OpenStreetMap. Mapnik does have the ability to directly process OSM files, but the way in which it is commonly used involves converting OSM data to a PostGIS database and then processing it from there. In this, it is different from Osmarender, which always directly processes OSM files. Mapnik can also render data from shapefiles and other sources.

Mapnik is the most widely used renderer for OSM in production environments (tile servers etc.); it is fast and relatively robust, and has good support from the OSM community.

In order to render OSM data with Mapnik, a number of components have to be installed. Figure 17-1 has an overview.

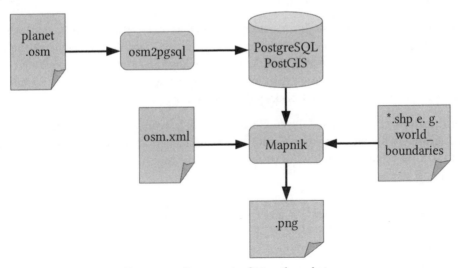

Figure 17-1: Components of Mapnik rendering.

Mapnik is typically used to create bitmap images in PNG format. Current versions of Mapnik also support SVG output via the Cairo graphics library but at the time of writing this isn't widely used because there are some issues with it, most notably lack of support for vector (SVG) icons. Cairo-generated SVG is a very complex patchwork of objects and nowhere near as suitable for postprocessing in an SVG editor as the SVG created by Osmarender.

Mapnik is written in C++ and hence is fast. Each map tile takes only fractions of a second to render, varying slightly depending on the zoom level and the amount of data displayed. Many of Mapnik's features are accessible through a Python API so that no C++ experience is required.

This chapter only describes the installation and configuration under Linux, but all components can also be run on Windows or OS X.

17.1 Installing PostgreSQL and PostGIS

Using Mapnik for OSM usually requires installing PostgreSQL and PostGIS. PostgreSQL (www.postgresql.org) is an Open Source SQL database. PostGIS (www.postgis.org) is a PostgreSQL extension that adds support for spatial operations and data types like points, lines, and polygons. This makes it possible to have the database compute the intersection point between two lines or to check whether a certain point lies within a polygon. This is complemented by spatial indexing of geodata, which makes the PostgreSQL and PostGIS combination into a very functional workhorse for many GIS applications, and a PostGIS database is also the preferred data source for Mapnik.[1] PostGIS can also convert geodata into (almost) any desired projection.

All major Linux distributions have packages available. For Debian/Ubuntu you need to install `postgresql-8.3` (server software), `postgresql-client-8.3` (various client programs), `postgresql-8.3-postgis`, and `postgis` (the PostGIS extension). Depending on the version of your Linux distribution, you might also be using a newer version of PostgreSQL than 8.3 which would mean your packages and directories are named differently.

After the packages are installed, PostGIS functionality is available, but it still has to be activated separately for each database. Create a database named "osm" and enable PostGIS features for it by typing the following (using an account that has PostgreSQL administrator privileges, e. g. postgres):

```
createdb osm              # create database "osm"
createlang plpgsql -d osm  # add programming language support
psql osm -f /usr/share/postgresql-8.3-postgis/lwpostgis.sql
```

---

1 Other data sources, like shapefiles, OSM files, or OGR drivers are supported as well.

```
psql osm -f /usr/share/postgresql-8.3-postgis/spatial_ref_sys.sql
psql osm --command 'GRANT SELECT ON spatial_ref_sys TO PUBLIC'
psql osm --command 'GRANT ALL ON geometry_columns TO PUBLIC'
psql osm -f 900913.sql
```

The files lwpostgis.sql and spatial_ref_sys.sql contain definitions required for Post-GIS operations. They are normally contained within the PostGIS package.[2] The path given here is the one used by Debian/Ubuntu package; other systems may have the file installed elsewhere.

The two GRANT statements ensure that the non-admin user "osm" has access to the system tables when creating tables with geometry columns. The last line adds knowledge about the spherical Mercator projection to PostGIS. The file 900913.sql can be found in the OSM Subversion repository, in applications/utils/export/osm2pgsql.

Further information about PostGIS and its setup can be found in the PostGIS package of your distribution, or online at http://www.postgis.org/docs/.

17.2 Importing OSM Data into the PostGIS Database

Reading OSM data directly into Mapnik is possible, but it doesn't offer the same speed and versatility as reading it from databases. So OSM data is generally first imported into a database before being used for rendering. This job is done by the osm2pgsql program. It can be run on any .osm file, for example the Planet Dump. If you are only interested in a small part of the world you can use an excerpt (see chapters 15 and 24).[3]

Some Linux distributions already contain the osm2pgsql package. But since the software evolves rapidly, your distribution may not have the latest version. If you want to compile Osm2pgsql yourself, you can find the source code in the Subversion repository under applications/utils/export/osm2pgsql. It is written in C/C++ and uses the autoconf build system, so to build it you have to type:

```
autoconf
./configure
make
```

If the compiler and the required libraries are present, this will only take a few seconds. The README.txt file can be helpful with troubleshooting if your system happens to lack some of the prerequisites.

---

2 On PostgreSQL 8.4, the PostGIS file is called postgis.sql, not lwpostgis.sql.
3 A database populated with osm2pgsql can also be read with other GIS software like the UMN Map Server (see color plate 15).

Once Osm2pgsql is installed successfully, you can call it and give the name of the OSM file on the command line. The -d option is used to specify the name of the PostgreSQL database created beforehand:

```
osm2pgsql -d osm file.osm
```

The program can also process compressed input files:

```
osm2pgsql -d osm file.osm.bz2
```

When trying this for the first time, use a small extract and not the full planet.osm. It may take a while to import large files, and may also use considerable amounts of memory (about 20 GB of RAM for importing the full planet, but see the discussion of the "slim mode" below).

By default the program connects to a PostgreSQL database on the local machine, and uses the current user's login to the database. The options --host and --username let you set different connection parameters. Run osm2pgsql --help to see a list of all options.

Osm2pgsql uses the default.style file to define which OSM tags are brought in to the database. Only these tags can be accessed by rendering rules later on; anything not listed in this file is discarded on import. You can override the default and use --style to specify your own list of tags, or modify default.style to allow access to other tags if you wish.

Osm2pgsql stores data in a schema that is more suitable for quick rendering than the original OSM data format. The database schema is covered in section 27.4.

17.3 Projections

By default, Osm2pgsql projects OSM data with a spherical Mercator projection as it is used for standard web tiles (see section 14.1). The advantage of this is that data doesn't have to be projected when rendering tiles. PostGIS refers to projections as *spatial reference systems* (SRS), and identifies them by a unique numeric ID. The spherical Mercator projection is known as SRS 900913.[4]

You can specify the option --latlong to have Osm2pgsql write un-projected coordinates to the database. Your database will then have geographic coordinates (also known as WGS84, EPSG:4326, or SRS 4326). Or use the --proj option to store your data in a projection other than these two.

The standard OSM map style file (see below) assumes that the spherical Mercator projection is used, but Mapnik can be made to re-project coordinates when rendering.

---

4   The standard SRS for this projection is now 3857. 900913 is an older ID that is being phased out.

17.4 Slim Mode and Updates

Running Osm2pgsql needs a lot of RAM because all nodes and ways have to be remembered until the import is complete (as they might still be referenced by something). If you can't afford to run Osm2pgsql in this mode, you can use the option --slim which causes Osm2pgsql to store intermediate information in database tables (planet_osm_nodes, planet_osm_ways, and planet_osm_rels) instead of in memory. This reduces memory usage, but needs more time during import and creates a larger database.

The option --cache can be used with --slim to allocate some RAM to a node cache so that Osm2pgsql doesn't have to go to the database for every single node required to process a way. This speeds up the import again but takes more RAM, albeit not as much RAM as a non-slim import would require. The cache size is specified in MB, and the ideal value can be computed by multiplying the highest node ID with 8 bytes. If the Planet Dump uses nodes Ids up to 800 million, then the ideal cache size is roughly 6500 MB.

The slim mode has another effect. If you use slim mode, Osm2pgsql can process the daily, hourly, or minutely updates made available by the OpenStreetMap server (see section 15.2) to keep the database current. If you want to use this feature however you have to activate the IntArray module in PostgreSQL before the initial import. As database administrator, enter the following:

```
psql osm -f /usr/share/postgresql/8.3/contrib/_int.sql
```

If you haven't installed that module, Osm2pgsql will issue the warning:

```
*** WARNING: intarray contrib module not installed
*** The resulting database will not be usable for applying diffs.
```

After the initial import, you can then add an update with the following command:

```
osm2pgsql -d osm --slim --append file.osc.gz
```

So for the price of a more time-consuming initial import, the --slim option opens the possibility of keeping the database current. If you use the replication facility offered by Osmosis (see section 24.4), downloading all required updates and applying them can be automated easily.

17.5 Installing Mapnik

Finally you need to install Mapnik itself. Many distributions come with a ready-to-use Mapnik package, but if you don't have it in yours, or want to compile the absolutely latest version, you can download the source code from www.mapnik.org or check it out of the project SVN at http://svn.mapnik.org/trunk.

In the source directory, you then have to run

```
python scons/scons.py
```

to compile Mapnik, and (as root)

```
python scons/scons.py install
```

to install everything in the right paths for your system.

Mapnik needs a few libraries to work: In particular boost, libpng, libtiff, libjpeg, libltdl, libpq, libfreetype, libfribidi, and zlib, as well as Python and the Python development libraries. The INSTALL file that comes with the software has details of all the dependencies.

17.6 Anatomy of a Map Style File

The map style file lists all data sources (databases, shapefiles, etc) from which Mapnik is to assemble the map. It also contains all rules and style definitions that tell Mapnik which data to select for drawing and how to draw it.

The map style file is an XML file and is structured like this:

```
<Map bgcolor="..." srs="...">
    <Style name="...">
    </Style>
    ....
    <Layer name="..." status="on" srs="...">
        <StyleName>...</StyleName>
        ....
        <Datasource>
            ...
        </Datasource>
    </Layer>
    ....
</Map>
```

The whole definition is enclosed by <Map> which requires attributes for the background color (bgcolor) and for the map projection (srs). Inside that, there are a number of <Style> elements and a number of <Layer> elements. Each layer has a sub-element <Datasource> for specifying the data source – for example, a shapefile, a database table, or a SQL SELECT statement that selects data from a table. The <Layer> element has an srs attribute to specify the map projection used by this data source. Each layer also has a list of one or more <StyleName> elements that link to the style definitions that are used to draw the data provided by this layer. The location of the <Style> elements in the file does not matter, but the file is easier to read if you try to keep the style definitions close to the layers that use them.

When designing a map style file, it is important to know the order in which things will be placed on the map. Mapnik processes all of the layers in the order in which they appear in the map style file. Inside a layer, it processes all of the styles in the order in which they are referenced by the layer. A style, finally, processes all objects in the order in which they come from the database (which might be random, or given by a SQL "order by" clause).

For lines and areas, whatever is painted first will get painted over by objects being processed later. This technique is sometimes referred to as the "painter model" or "painter's algorithm". On a standard map, you would for example create the "land use" layer first and add the roads later, so that they are displayed on top. While the same basically holds true for labels and icons, Mapnik does record the area used by these in order to make sure that they aren't overwritten by other labels and icons later. If there is no room left for an item, it is omitted. Thus, more important labels and icons should be drawn first to make sure they get space allocated to them on the map.

A style definition is constructed like this:

```
<Style name="...">
    <Rule>
        <MinScaleDenominator>....</MinScaleDenominator>
        <MaxScaleDenominator>....</MaxScaleDenominator>
        <Filter>...</Filter>

        <...Symbolizer>

            <CssParameter>...</CssParameter>
            ....
        </...Symbolizer>
    </Rule>
    ....
</Style>
```

A <Style> has to contain at least one <Rule> element. A rule specifies:

- For which map scales it is to be applied (defined by the <MinScaleDenominator> and <MaxScaleDenominator> elements – the zoom level table on page 165 gives you an idea of which zoom levels correspond to which scale denominators, but the standard OSM Mapnik style also comes with convenient shorthands in the form of XML entities that can be used for this).
- Which data from the data source is to be used for this style (<Filter>).
- How the data is to be drawn (<...Symbolizer>).

Mapnik has a number of symbolizers for various purposes. There is a <LineSymbolizer> for lines, a <PolygonSymbolizer> for areas, a <PointSymbolizer> that draws symbols at a point, a <TextSymbolizer> for drawing labels, and a <ShieldSymbolizer> used for drawing "road shields", small icons that carry the number of a road. The authoritative resource on these is http://trac.mapnik.org/wiki/XMLConfigReference in the Mapnik wiki.

Most symbolizers have a number of <CssParameter> sub-elements that define colors, line widths, and other styling details.

17.7 Your First Mapnik OSM Map

Let us write a new map style file that creates a very simple map of roads and waterways, similar to our railway example from the Osmarender chapter. Again you can download this example from the book's website, www.openstreetmap.info.

```
<Map bgcolor="#ffffff" srs="+init=epsg:3857">
```

This initializes the map to use a white background, and the spherical Mercator projection. For this to work, the projection 3857 must be known to the proj.4 library on your system, a library that Mapnik uses for coordinate projections. If that isn't the case, then you can write a longer init string that sets the projection parameters individually, as it is done in the standard OSM map style file:

```
<Map bgcolor="#ffffff" srs="+proj=merc +a=6378137 +b=6378137 +lat_ts=0.0
+lon_0=0.0 +x_0=0.0 +y_0=0 +k=1.0 +units=m +nadgrids=@null +no_defs +over">
```

We now create a style that can be used to draw all kinds of roads as thin gray lines (the stroke width is set to 0.4 pixels):

```
<Style name="roads">
  <Rule>
    <LineSymbolizer>
      <CssParameter name="stroke">#aaa</CssParameter>
      <CssParameter name="stroke-width">0.4</CssParameter>
    </LineSymbolizer>
  </Rule>
</Style>
```

Defining the style doesn't yet lead to anything being drawn; we also have to create a layer that retrieves data and uses the style to draw it:

```
<Layer name="roads" status="on" srs="+init=epsg:4326">
  <StyleName>roads</StyleName>
  <Datasource>
    <Parameter name="table">
    (select way from planet_osm_line where highway is not null) as road
    </Parameter>
    <Parameter name="type">postgis</Parameter>
    <Parameter name="port">5432</Parameter>
    <Parameter name="user">osm</Parameter>
    <Parameter name="dbname">osm</Parameter>
    <Parameter name="estimate_extent">false</Parameter>
    <Parameter name="extent">-180,-85,180,85</Parameter>
  </Datasource>
</Layer>
```

This assumes that there is a database called "osm" on the local PostGIS server, that the user "osm" has access to it, and that it has a table named `planet_osm_line`, populated with geometry data in the EPSG:4326 projection, from which we can load information about roads. This is exactly what Osm2pgsql produces when you run it with the `--latlong` option. (Note how we have defined a layer with a different projection than that of the map; Mapnik will automatically re-project the data loaded from this layer to match the map's projection.)

Since the SQL query only loads roads, and all of them are drawn, the style doesn't need to filter for anything. (It would be different if we were to, for example, only draw major roads, or use different styling for different road types.) The layer is called "roads" and relies on the style named "roads" that we have defined earlier to draw the data.

Now we add a second style for drawing waterways. This time, we distinguish between different types of waterways:

```
<Style name="waterways">

  <Rule>
  <Filter>[waterway] = 'river'</Filter>
  <LineSymbolizer>
    <CssParameter name="stroke">#55f</CssParameter>
    <CssParameter name="stroke-width">2</CssParameter>
  </LineSymbolizer>
  </Rule>

  <Rule>
  <Filter>[waterway] = 'canal' or [waterway] = 'stream'</Filter>
  <LineSymbolizer>
    <CssParameter name="stroke">#55f</CssParameter>
    <CssParameter name="stroke-width">1</CssParameter>
  </LineSymbolizer>
  </Rule>

</Style>
```

This style draws all rivers, canals, and streams in blue, but uses a wider line for rivers than for the other waterways. The layer must now make sure to supply the waterway attribute to the filter by selecting it from the database:

```
<Layer name="waterways" status="on" srs="+init=epsg:4326">
  <StyleName>waterways</StyleName>
  <Datasource>
    <Parameter name="table">
    (select way, waterway from planet_osm_line where waterway is not null)
    as waterway
    </Parameter>
    ... (more database access parameters, same as above) ...
  </Datasource>
</Layer>
```

Finally we introduce a text layer and matching style to label towns and cities, using a bold font for cities:

```
<Style name="places">
   <Rule>
     <Filter>[place] = 'town'</Filter>
     <TextSymbolizer name="name" face_name="DejaVu Sans Book" size="6"
                     fill="#000" halo_radius="1" wrap_width="20"/>
   </Rule>
   <Rule>
     <Filter>[place] = 'city'</Filter>
     <TextSymbolizer name="name" face_name="DejaVu Sans Bold" size="6"
                     fill="#000" halo_radius="1" wrap_width="20"/>
   </Rule>
</Style>

<Layer name="places" status="on" srs="+init=epsg:4326">
   <StyleName>places</StyleName>
   <Datasource>
     <Parameter name="table">
     (select way,place,name from planet_osm_point where place in ('city','town'))
     as placenames
     </Parameter>
     ... (more database access parameters, same as above) ...
   </Datasource>
</Layer>
```

Note the halo_radius attribute on the <TextSymbolizer> – this is Mapnik's way of doing the text halo that we have discussed in section 16.6 when we dealt with Osmarender.

We conclude the example with a closing:

```
</Map>
```

You can save this map style file as osm.xml, and then use the generate_image.py Python script to try it out. You have to set the bounding box for the area that is to be rendered by modifying the script. There is a block in the script that says:

```
#----------------------------------------------------
#  Change this to the bounding box you want
ll = (-6.5, 49.5, 2.1, 59)
#----------------------------------------------------
```

Put the desired bounding box there (minlon, minlat, maxlon, maxlat). Figure 17-2 shows a rendering created in this map style. Of course you can only use bounding boxes for data that you have imported.

For this simple example we haven't bothered to define different styles for different map scales; a map style file that supports a zoomable map will almost certainly have to define many different styles for various zoom levels because many details should only show up when the user zooms in.

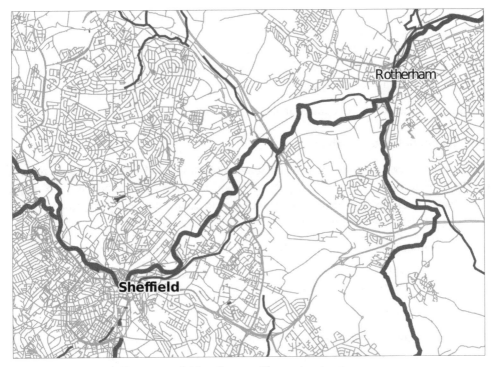

Figure 17-2: A Mapnik map with prominent waterways.

A more convenient way of playing around with style files and generating maps is the Nik2img utility (http://trac.mapnik.org/wiki/Nik2Img). It allows you to set image size, bounding box, style name, and output file format all on the command line.

The pre-defined map style file osm.xml, and the include files in the inc subdirectory linked from there, have a large number of styles covering many different map features. If you are writing your own map style file, you can learn much about how things are done by analyzing these files.

17.8 Making Standard OpenStreetMap Maps With Mapnik

You probably aren't interested in Mapnik as a general rendering engine – you just want to create maps like the standard Mapnik map on the OpenStreetMap website. For this, you need three things:

1. World boundary and coastline data.

2. Icon files.

3. The original map style file and assorted include files.

All of these are available from the OSM Subversion repository or other servers. Just as with the example map above, you can use `generate_image.py` or `Nik2Img` to generate single images. There is also a script called `generate_tiles.py` that generates map tiles. If you want to set up a system that serves tiles directly, you can use the Apache module `mod_tile`, which we describe in section 27.3.

So let's look at each of these required items:

World Boundaries and Coastlines

The coastlines and boundaries which the standard Mapnik map uses on the low zoom levels don't come directly from the OpenStreetMap database, but are added from preprocessed files. These files contain a generalization of the data to allow quick rendering even on small zoom levels where large parts of the world are visible at once.

To render boundaries you need to get the `world_boundaries` file and unpack it:

```
wget http://tile.openstreetmap.org/world_boundaries-spherical.tgz
tar xzf world_boundaries-spherical.tar.bz2
```

This gives you a directory named `world_boundaries` with a set of shapefiles.

The coastlines are computed from OSM data once every few weeks. Load these preprocessed files as well and unpack them:

```
wget http://tile.openstreetmap.org/processed_p.tar.bz2
wget http://tile.openstreetmap.rg/shoreline_300.tar.bz2
tar xjf processed_p.tar.bz2
tar xjf shoreline_300.tar.bz2
wget http://www.nacis.org/naturalearth/10m/cultural/10m-populated-places.zip
wget http://www.nacis.org/naturalearth/110m/cultural/110m-admin-0-boundary-
lines.zip
unzip 10m-populates-places.zip
unzip 110m-admin-0-boundary-lines.zip
mv processed_p.* world_boundaries/
mv shoreline_300.* world_boundaries/
mv 10m_* world_boundaries
mv 110m_* world_boundaries
```

The last four lines move the downloaded data into the `world_boundaries` directory that was created in the previous step, because Mapnik expects them to be there.

Icons

Download the set of icons from `applications/rendering/mapnik/symbols` in the project SVN repository, and save them to a `symbols` directory.

The OpenStreetMap Map Style File

You can find the current map style file used by OpenStreetMap in the SVN repository under `applications/rendering/mapnik`. Use this script to simplify the adaptation of the file to your setup, inserting the correct username, password, and database settings:

```
python generate_xml.py osm.xml my_osm.xml --host localhost \
   --port 5432 --user osm --password osm --dbname osm
```

The script uses the map style file template `osm.xml` and a lot of include files from the `inc` subdirectory to produce a map style file called `my_osm.xml` that you can use with Mapnik. The script supports some additional options; you can get a list of these by using `--help`.

Since many styles in the standard map style file are tailored to a specific zoom level or a range of zoom levels, most of them carry extra XML elements like this:

```
<Rule>
  <Filter>...</Filter>
  <MaxScaleDenominator>100000</MaxScaleDenominator>
  <MinScaleDenominator>25000</MinScaleDenominator>
  <LineSymbolizer>
    ...
  </LineSymbolizer>
</Rule>
```

To make it easier to work with this, suitable XML entities for scale denominators have been declared (in the file `inc/entities.xml.inc`). An XML entity is like a symbolic constant in programming – define it once, use it many times. The rule can therefore be written more simply as:

```
<Rule>
  <Filter>...</Filter>
  &maxscale_zoom13;
  &minscale_zoom14;
  <LineSymbolizer>
    ...
  </LineSymbolizer>
</Rule>
```

The same has been done for database access parameters that have to be repeated for every layer.

The standard map style file also uses another XML technique to give it better structure, and make editing simpler. Many thematic layers, with their styles and matching layer definitions, are defined in small files that are then referenced from the main map style file. These XML snippets are located in the `inc` subdirectory and are included in the main map style file by a line like this:

```
&layer-placenames;
```

Even with simplifications like these, the OSM map style file still has more than 8,000 lines and can be challenging to work with.

17.9 Performance Considerations in Map Style Files

When rendering a map for a given zoom level, Mapnik will determines which layers are visible, and then processes them in sequence as described above. To find out whether a layer is visible or not, Mapnik looks at all the rendering rules of all the styles associated with that layer, and if at least one of them is applicable to the current zoom level, then the layer is processed.

This may lead to too much data being processed if the same layer is used on very many zoom levels. Consider this hypothetical example:

```
<Style name="highway">
  <Rule>
    <Filter>[highway] = 'motorway'</Filter>
    &maxscale_zoom5;
    &minscale_zoom10;
    <LineSymbolizer>
      ...
    </LineSymbolizer>
  </Rule>
  <Rule>
    <Filter>[highway] = 'footway'</Filter>
    &maxscale_zoom16;
    &minscale_zoom18;
    <LineSymbolizer>
      ...
    </LineSymbolizer>
  </Rule>
</Style>

<Layer name="roads" status="on" srs="+init=epsg:4326">
  <StyleName>highway</StyleName>
  <Datasource>
    <Parameter name="table">
    (select way, highway from planet_osm_line where highway is not null) as road
    </Parameter>
    ...
  </Datasource>
</Layer>
```

The intention here is to draw freeways (highway=motorway) at the low zoom levels, and footpaths on the high zoom levels. (This is only an excerpt; almost certainly freeways would also be drawn, albeit differently, on high zoom levels.)

However, because both rules use data from the same layer, Mapnik will have to load all highway objects, including the smallest footpaths, even if a tile on zoom level 5 is rendered.

The example can be improved greatly by defining different data sources:

```
<Style name="motorways">
  <Rule>
    <Filter>[highway] = 'motorway'</Filter>
    &minscale_zoom10;
    &maxscale_zoom5;
    <LineSymbolizer>
      ...
    </LineSymbolizer>
  </Rule>
</Style>

<Style name="footpaths">
  <Rule>
    <Filter>[highway] = 'footway'</Filter>
    &minscale_zoom18;
    &maxscale_zoom16;
    <LineSymbolizer>
      ...
    </LineSymbolizer>
  </Rule>
</Style>

<Layer name="large_roads" status="on" srs="+init=epsg:4326">
  <StyleName>motorways</StyleName>
  <Datasource>
    <Parameter name="table">
    (select way, highway from planet_osm_line where highway='motorway') as road
    </Parameter>
    ...
  </Datasource>
</Layer>

<Layer name="small_roads" status="on" srs="+init=epsg:4326">
  <StyleName>footpaths</StyleName>
  <Datasource>
    <Parameter name="table">
    (select way, highway from planet_osm_line where highway is not null) as road
    </Parameter>
    ...
  </Datasource>
</Layer>
```

This way, the potentially expensive "small_roads" layer will only be used on high zoom levels where the rendering area tends to be small. For lower zoom levels the "large_roads" layer is used, which returns far less data.

Database Indexes

All database tables accessed by Mapnik should have a spatial index set up. A spatial index is an index that allows the database to quickly find objects in a given area – a basic query type when rendering. Osm2pgsql creates these indexes automatically. If you have a lot of queries that only use a small subset of objects in a table, partial indexes that use the same selection criterion as the layer's SELECT statement can also help because they save the database from having to examine every matching row. You should however only create such indexes if they really make a difference – for example after you have evaluated the PostgreSQL log file to see which queries take longest. The more indexes you create, the more work the database has to do when applying updates, so while read access may be faster, updates get slowed down.

Shapefile Indexes

Shapefiles consist of at least three individual files (.shp, .dbf, .shx) but you can also have an additional file with the extension .index which speeds up access by allowing Mapnik to quickly determine where the data for a given area is located in the shapefile. These index files can be generated with the shapeindex utility that is part of the Mapnik source code.

17.10 Cascadenik

There is a tool called Cascadenik (http://code.google.com/p/mapnik-utils/) that is used by many people to simplify working with Mapnik map style files. Cascadenik uses an extended but easier-to-use syntax for defining map styles that is modeled after the well-known CSS style sheets for web pages.

Because Mapnik doesn't understand Cascadenik styles out of the box, they have to be transformed into a Mapnik map style file before they can be used. Cascadenik comes with the right scripts to perform this transformation. The main OSM site doesn't use Cascadenik, but some other OSM projects do.

18 Making Maps With Kosmos

Kosmos, written by Igor Brejc, is a Windows renderer that is easy to install in comparison to Osmarender or Mapnik. Just like its better-known siblings it uses a set of rules to transform OSM data into a map; but unlike Osmarender and Mapnik, Kosmos retrieves its rendering style from the OpenStreetMap wiki, where anyone can look at it, or indeed make copies and modify it. Kosmos is the only rendering engine with a graphical user interface, and appeals to casual users making their first steps in OSM cartography or those who shy away from using the command line.

18.1 Installation

The Kosmos wiki page has a download link for the current Kosmos version. You have to download a zip file and unpack it to a destination of your choice. There will be a subdirectory named Gui, and an executable program called Kosmos.Gui.

Kosmos requires version 2.0 of the .NET-Framework. If you don't have that installed, there is another download link on the wiki page that you can follow to get it.

18.2 Starting Kosmos and Loading Data

When you run Kosmos, it will ask you what you want to do. One of the menu options is "Start with a new Kosmos project with a Web map and download OSM data for your favourite". Choose that, and the main window will show a world map that works much like the usual web maps. Zoom to the area you want to work with, and then select "Download OSM Data" from the "OSM" menu. Kosmos will now contact the XAPI server (see section 23.1) and download data for the currently visible section of the map. If you already have an OSM file, you can of course open that instead.

After having obtained the data, Kosmos uses its standard rendering rules to create a map image for the currently selected zoom level. The standard rules yield an image roughly matching the Mapnik style on the main OpenStreetMap website.

Initially Kosmos will show its own rendering on top of tiles loaded from OpenStreetMap. To see the Kosmos layer on its own, you have to disable the "OSM Mapnik" layer (click on the layer in the Project Explorer dialog on the left-hand side, and then select "False" in the "Visible" dropdown in the Properties dialog below) .

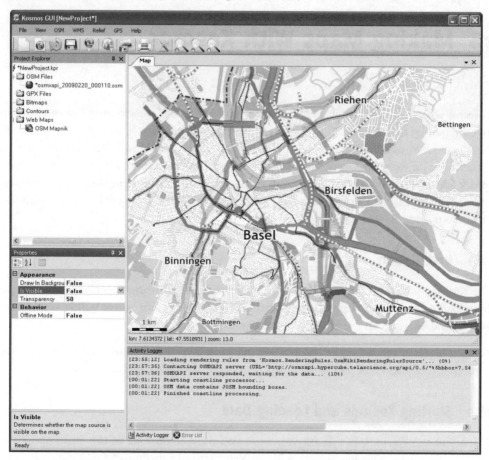

Figure 18-1: Kosmos has loaded data for a section of the map, and rendered it.

As you zoom in further, Kosmos re-renders the image with every step, and thus shows increasing levels of detail. In contrast to the pre-rendered OpenStreetMap tiles, Kosmos doesn't use discrete zoom levels; you can zoom in continuously.

18.3 Choosing a Map Style

Kosmos loads its rendering rules directly from the wiki. Every style has its own wiki page, which must be formatted in a special way. It doesn't matter where the page resides, it can be a user page or a standard article. Many of these rendering rules are collected on the page Category:Kosmos rules. To switch the map display to one of these styles, go to the "Project Explorer" dialog and click on the project file (in this example, "New Project.kpr"). You can now specify a rule URL under "Properties". For example, one of the styles linked from above category is called "Clean Style":

```
http://wiki.openstreetmap.org/wiki/Kosmos_clean_style
```

When you enter that URL as a rendering rule URL, Kosmos immediately re-renders the current data according to the new rules and presents you with a new map (figure 18-2).

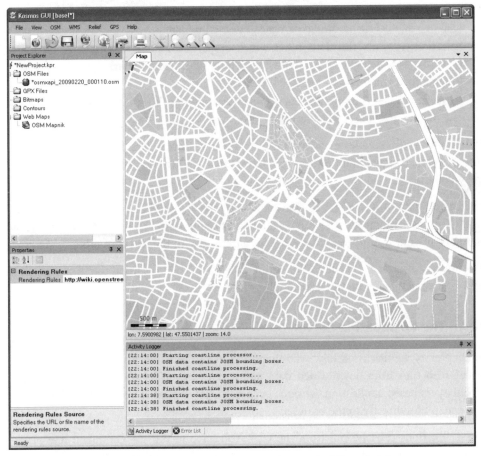

Figure 18-2: Rendering has been changed to use the "Clean Style".

18.4 Defining Your Own Map Styles

Kosmos doesn't use a special file format to store its render rules; instead it uses wiki pages. If you want to create your own map style, you have to create a wiki page for it.

The best way to get an understanding of this concept is to look at some of the existing map styles on the wiki. These pages always contain one or more rules tables, which are what Kosmos reads and processes. Everything that sits outside of the tables – explanations or pictures – is aimed at the person reading the page, and is ignored by Kosmos.

A row in a rules table consists of at least four columns:

- Rule name – a unique name for this rule.
- Target objects – this is where you specify what kinds of objects the rule should apply to; use {{IconNode}}, {{IconWay}}, {{IconArea}}, or {{IconRelation}} for nodes, ways, areas, and relations, respectively. The braces are part of the MediaWiki syntax and will lead to a symbol being displayed instead of the raw name.
- Selection criteria – this determines which properties the object must have for the rule to apply. For example, {{tag|highway}} selects all objects having a highway tag, and {{tag|highway|motorway}} selects all freeways.
- Rendering specification – this column defines how the object is to be drawn; it sets colors, line widths, labels and symbols.

Optionally, a fifth column may contain flags and a sixth may be added to comment on the rule. A detailed explanation of the table format is in the Kosmos Rendering Help article on the wiki.

The easiest way to start using Kosmos is to copy the standard rules, which are also on the wiki (Kosmos General Purpose Rules), and modify your copy. You can create the style in a sub-page of your user page so that it doesn't interfere with the works of others.

Kosmos can also read style definitions from a file on disk, but writing the files is much easier when done directly on the wiki.

18.5 The Kosmos Tile Server

In chapter 14 we discussed how web maps and map tiles work. Kosmos is able to create a set of map tiles from downloaded data and a rendering rule, ready for display with an OpenLayers-based application. Kosmos even has a small built-in web server that can serve these map tiles directly to the browser.

These functions can't be run from the GUI. You have to run the command line program `Kosmos.Console.exe` from the Console directory to access them. (You have to run the program "cmd" under Windows to get a command line window.)

You can start tile creation with the following generic command:

```
Kosmos.Console.exe tilegen proj.kpr bbox minzoom maxzoom -ts tiledir
```

The file name proj.kpr points to a project file that you have saved from the GUI (or created by hand); it contains references to the downloaded OSM data file and the map style to use. For bbox you have to give four values separated by spaces (minimum latitude, minimum longitude, maximum latitude, maximum longitude); Kosmos will create tiles for this area only. The minzoom and maxzoom specify the zoom range for which to create tiles, and -ts specifies the target directory. Kosmos will create a typical tiled map structure in that directory, with the zoom level being encoded in the uppermost directory, then the x coordinate in the next directory level, and the y coordinate used for the file name.

Here is an example command, and the output text it generates:

```
C:\Kosmos\Kosmos-2.4.21.1\Console> Kosmos.Console.exe tilegen
"..\..\Daten\basel.kpr" 47.5 7.5 47.65 7.7 0 17 -ts Tiles
Kosmos Console v2.4.21.1 by Igor Brejc

OpenStreetMap rendering application

Loading the project file... (0%)...
Loading project file... (0%)...
Loading rules... (5%)...
Loading rendering rules... (30%)...
Loading data file(s)... (60%)...
Loading data file 'osmxapi_basel.osm'... (5%)...
Loading data file 'ElevationContours_20090220_120555.dat'... (25%)...
Started rendering tiles for zoom level 0.
Started rendering tiles for zoom level 1.
Started rendering tiles for zoom level 2.
Started rendering tiles for zoom level 3.
...
Started rendering tiles for zoom level 17.
Rendered 3008 tiles so far (speed: 64,3 tiles/s).
Rendered 4004 tiles so far (speed: 63,4 tiles/s).
Rendered 5006 tiles so far (speed: 65,2 tiles/s).
Rendered 6002 tiles so far (speed: 61,3 tiles/s).
Rendered 7004 tiles so far (speed: 61,5 tiles/s).
Rendered 8000 tiles so far (speed: 63,4 tiles/s).

C:\Kosmos\Kosmos-2.4.21.1\Console>
```

You can view the generated tiles with a standard OpenLayers installation and a web server, or you can run:

```
Kosmos.Console.exe tileserv tiledir http://localhost/Kosmos/
```

(For tiledir, insert the name of the directory containing the map tiles.) Then you can run a web browser on the given "localhost" URL to view the tiles directly.

☞ *You usually process only small map sections with Kosmos, so expect your whole map to be only a few pixels wide at the low zoom levels. If you accidentally set your browser to show a map on zoom level 4, you could overlook your data.*

18.6 Printing and Exporting Bitmaps with Kosmos

Kosmos has a print function that allows you to tile the image into any number of print pages, so you can create large map posters even with a small printer (and some glue). You only have to specify the desired zoom level and the amount of overlap, and Kosmos computes the number of pages required and splits the image in a suitable way.

Likewise, Kosmos allows you to export bitmaps of arbitrary size. The default setup limits the bitmap size to a width and height of 10,000 pixels but that can be changed in the "Preferences" dialog from the "File" menu. Here you can specify a desired zoom level and have Kosmos determine the image size, or set the image size and have Kosmos determine the zoom level. The current version of Kosmos doesn't allow setting the print resolution (dpi); it always works with a standard screen resolution. But this is scheduled to improve with the upcoming "Maperitive".

18.7 Maperitive

Maperitive (maperitive.net) is scheduled to be released as a successor to Kosmos during late 2010. The user interface is going to be simpler, and Maperitive will have database support to be able to work with large datasets that typically can't be held in memory.

A scripting language will make it possible to group common operations and run the program in command line mode. New rendering options and improved altitude data support are also planned.

19 Navigation and Mobile Use

Navigation devices and route planners have become an essential part of modern modes of personal travel. Since the OSM database now has well-connected road networks in many areas, using the data for navigation is feasible. This chapter presents an overview of using OSM data on some navigation devices and other software available for mobile OSM use.

19.1 Basics

There is no clear distinction between navigation and route planning. When planning a route, people are usually sitting at their desk and wanting to find out the best route for going from A to B by road at some later date; the computing time doesn't matter. Users want the optimum result given a number of constraints, and they might want to change the route interactively to try alternatives. Start and destination are fixed, and the result might simply be a list of roads to travel along. There are already many Internet services offering this kind of route planning.

For navigation, you usually have a fixed destination as well, but the starting location may be variable (often the position currently reported by the GPS receiver). The user is often already driving (or cycling, or walking), and the software has to analyze the changing situation and generate suitable directional instructions. Changes from one road to another need to be announced in advance, and if the driver deviates from the computed route, a new route has to be calculated on the fly. The whole process has to work with as little user interaction as possible, in order not to endanger the driver's safety.

Both situations, navigation and route planning, are often referred to as "routing", a term we use in the following text as well.

Navigation software and matching map data are widely available; you can buy such systems for your mobile phone or PDA, or you can purchase a vehicle navigation system (often called "PNA" or "PND" for "portable navigation assistant" or "device"), which is a hard-ware device that runs the navigation software. Updating the maps for such a system often costs almost as much as a whole new system. Free map data from OpenStreetMap could be an attractive alternative here, but unfortunately it is difficult to install OpenStreetMap data onto most existing navigation systems because the vendors don't publish their file format specifications. Because of this unsatisfactory situation, more and more independent navigation systems are being created to work with OSM data.

There is nothing magic about routing itself. Doing shortest-path searches in networks is a thoroughly researched area of computer science, and the resulting algorithms are known and well-documented. For routing on road networks, a very common algorithm is called A* ("A Star"), it is an improved version of the Dijkstra algorithm. The Dijkstra algorithm is only of interest in routing if you don't have a fixed destination (e. g. "find a way to the nearest gas station"). Wikipedia has very informative articles about both of these algorithms. Much better performance can be achieved with modern algorithms like Contraction Hierarchies or Transit Node Routing.

What sets a good routing software solution apart from the rest is however not so much the choice of routing algorithm, but the quality of its implementation and the way the software deals with complications like turn restrictions or temporary closures. All routing algorithms require intensive "bookkeeping" while they are running (recording which alternatives have been tried already, which nodes have been visited, what interim results have been achieved and so on). An implementation that is done well can make the difference between a program that runs on a mobile phone and one that requires a notebook equipped with a hard disk.

To a certain extent, speed can be bought for memory and vice versa when implementing a routing algorithm. For example, if a lot of storage space is available, standard routings between conurbations can be calculated in advance to speed up long-distance routing requests.

19.2 Pre-Processing OSM Data for Routing

Routing always operates on *graphs* – formations made of nodes (points) that are connected by edges (lines). In theory, OpenStreetMap data is already organized in a graph; you simply have to take each OSM node as a node of the routing graph, and each part of a way connecting two nodes as one of its edges. But this produces an unnecessarily large graph.

Typically all nodes with only one or two adjoining edges can be eliminated from the OSM graph (along with everything that is not a road of course). What remains is a graph where each node represents a road junction.

Figure 19-1 shows such a simplification: The left illustration shows an OSM road network (assume the thin, dashed line to be a river). The right illustration has the same network in a form simplified for routing. Needless to say, any algorithm will run faster if it has less data to work on.

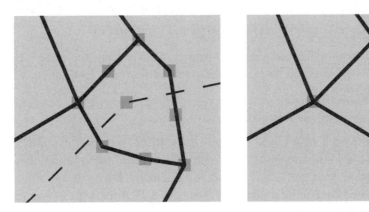

Figure 19-1: Simplification of OSM data into a graph suitable for routing.

19.3 Garmin GPS Units

The GPS units produced by Garmin are now common all over the world, and many of these devices also have the option of displaying a map (see color plate 4). Thus there was high demand for having OSM data on these devices from early in the project. Garmin hasn't documented their data formats, which has made things a bit difficult. But today there are various possibilities for creating these maps from OSM data yourself and installing them onto Garmin devices. Initially it also wasn't possible to use the OSM data with the routing capabilities that some of these devices have built in, but this has now been solved as well.

Further information on Garmin and OSM maps is on the wiki, under OSM Map On Garmin. Some project members as well as some commercial providers create maps of various geographic areas for Garmin devices on a regular basis and offer them for download. The offerings differ in size and richness of features; some are primarily for cyclists, some for walkers, some have a debug overlay for mapping, and so on. A list of such download sites is also on the wiki, under OSM Map On Garmin/Download. If you want to create your own map for a Garmin device, however, then the next few paragraphs describe the Mkgmap software written by Steve Ratcliffe. If on the other hand you are happy just to download a pre-made map, you can skip the following section and continue reading "Installing your Map on the Device".

Creating Garmin Maps

If you want to create your own map for a Garmin device, you first have to download the OpenStreetMap data for the area you are interested in (see chapter 15). You can then use the Java program Mkgmap to convert this into a map image file that can be read by all Garmin devices. Mkgmap can be run under Linux, Mac OS X, and Windows, but it works in command-line mode only and doesn't have a graphical user interface.

First, download and unpack the most recent Mkgmap version from the project page at www.mkgmap.org.uk. Provided you have a working and current Java installation, you can now launch the conversion with

```
java -jar mkgmap.jar osmfile.osm
```

and you will end up with a map image file named 63240001.img. You can also specify more than one OSM file on the command line, resulting in numerous map image files numbered sequentially from 63240001.img onward. Additionally, a map image file named 63240000.img is created containing a map overview, and a TDB file with a description of how the individual files fit together.

You usually want to specify the option --gmapsupp to tell Mkgmap to create an additional file named GMAPSUPP.IMG that has all the map parts combined into one file:

```
java -jar mkgmap.jar --gmapsupp osmfile1.osm osmfile2.osm
```

This file can be loaded directly onto a Garmin device. Mkgmap will attempt to re-map special characters and symbols that can't be displayed on all Garmin devices. If your device does support special characters, you can add the --latin1 option to suppress this mapping. Use the --help-options command line option to see information about other available options.

Installing your Map on the Device

There are two methods for copying map data to a Garmin device. The newer USB models have a Mass Storage Mode, which makes them show up on the PC like a USB stick or external drive. The "classic" Garmin mode, which requires special drivers, will work with all devices, even older ones that have a serial interface.

1) Installing Maps in Mass Storage Mode (all Operating Systems)

Switch the device to Mass Storage Mode by selecting the option "USB Mass Storage" from the "Interface" sub-menu in the "Setup" menu. (This is how the menu items are named on the GPSMap 60CSx, other models may differ in their naming.) After that, the device should show up on your computer like a generic storage device and be accessible on any modern operating system.

The map image file has to be stored under the name GMAPSUPP.IMG in the Garmin directory. You can only have one active map file at a time. You can copy different maps to the device using different names, but you always need a PC to rename the map you want to use to GMAPSUPP.IMG. This can't be done on the device alone.

Remember to "safely disconnect" the device after copying the file. Press the power switch on your GPS to put it back to normal operating mode.

2) Installing Maps in Garmin Mode

Using the proprietary sendmap program, you can copy one or more maps onto the device. Sendmap can be used under Linux and Windows, though under Windows you have to install the Garmin USB drivers first. You can download the program free of charge from http://www.cgpsmapper.com/buy.htm.

The filenames have to be specified on the command line:

```
sendmap20 map1.img [map2.img [...]]
```

Sendmap will then automatically try to detect the correct USB or serial interface to which the Garmin device is connected, and upload the maps. There a few extra options available to control the transfer; these are shown when you call sendmap without any parameters.

If you specify more than one map on the command line, they will automatically be merged into one.

The original Garmin software "Map Source" (Windows only) can also be used for uploading map files to the GPS.

Routable Maps

Mkgmap also creates routeable maps which can be used for navigation on routing-enabled Garmin devices:

```
java -jar mkgmap.jar --gmapsupp --route file.osm
```

Routeable maps take more storage space than normal ones.

Different Map Styles

Mkgmap can create maps in various styles. Styles determine which attributes to show and how to draw them. You can have Mkgmap display a list of built-in styles using

```
java -jar mkgmap.jar --list-styles
```

and you can select one of these styles with the command:

```
java -jar mkgmap.jar --style=mystylename file.osm
```

The definition of these styles can be found under resources/styles in the Mkgmap distribution. If you want to try your hand at a custom map style, it is easiest to start from the
default style you find there. Create an empty directory named styles and below that a
directory with the name of your new style. Copy the contents of the default directory into
that location. On a Linux system this is done with

```
mkdir somewhere/styles
mkdir somewhere/styles/mycustomstyle
cp resources/styles/default/* somewhere/styles/mycustomstyle
```

To use that style in Mkgmap, use the following command line:

```
java -jar mkgmap.jar --style-file=somewhere/styles
    --style=mycustomstyle file.osm
```

Once you have this setup working, you can start modifying the files according to your requirements. The most important files are points, lines, and polygons, which define the
rules about which tags should lead to which display. Details can be found on the wiki pages
Mkgmap/help/Custom_styles, Mkgmap/help/style_rules, and Mkgmap/help/custom.

Splitting Large OSM Files

Mkgmap only works on OSM data files of limited size. If you want to create Garmin maps
for larger areas, you have to split the OSM file into smaller chunks that can then be
processed by Mkgmap. This task can be performed by a program called Splitter (see
http://www.mkgmap.org.uk/page/tile-splitter and the wiki article Splitter). To run it,
use the command:

```
java -Xmx2G -jar splitter.jar britain.osm
```

The software is usually able to determine the correct chunk sizes by itself, but there are
exceptional cases where you may have to specify additional arguments to get it to do the
right thing. These are described on the Splitter website mentioned above.

Splitter needs a lot of memory. Use the Java option -Xmx to allow Java to allocate more
heap space. Processing the whole of Europe, for example, requires several gigabytes of
memory.

There is an alternative to Splitter called osmcut (wiki: Osmcut).

19.4 Web-based Route Planning

In addition to the web-based route planners OpenRouteService and YourNavigation described in section 2.3, there is a routing service run by US-based company CloudMade
(www.cloudmade.com). The service is free of charge (with some conditions attached). End
users can use it without registration, but if you want to use their API in your own appli-

cation you have to register. The service computes routes and creates written instructions for pedestrians, cyclists, or motorists. It can also exclude individual roads from routing.

19.5 Offmaps (iPhone)

The proprietary application Offmaps (www.offmaps.com) is an application for the iPhone (and iPod Touch) and can be bought from Apple's AppStore. OpenStreetMap data can be downloaded to the iPhone to be displayed when the phone is offline. Offmaps can also display POIs and information from Wikipedia.

19.6 Roadee (iPhone)

Roadee (www.roadee.net) is a proprietary application for displaying OSM maps on the iPhone, and routing on them. Roadee downloads map tiles dynamically and uses Cloud-Made's routing service, which means that it requires a connection to the Internet.

19.7 Skobbler (iPhone)

Skobbler (www.skobbler.com, see also color plate 32) is a proprietary application for navigation and map display on the iPhone and (planned) for Android. Skobbler had originally used proprietary map data but switched to OpenStreetMap in March 2010. The platform is intended to be a social networking opportunity for mobile users.

19.8 GpsMid (J2ME)

GpsMid (gpsmid.sourceforge.net) is Open Source software for Java-(J2ME)-based mobile handsets. OSM data has to be prepared at home and then downloaded to the device; prepared data can also be downloaded from the web. GpsMid uses vector rendering, is able to search in the data, and allows for navigation and written instructions, all while offline. It can also record tracks, tag photos, and it has a minimalistic editor that can be used to modify the tags on ways.

19.9 AndNav2 (Android)

AndNav2 (www.andnav.org) is an Open Source navigation software package for Android mobile phones. It is uses OpenStreetMap tiles that are downloaded live (if connected to the Internet) or read from a previously downloaded cache. Navigation is accomplished through OpenRouteService (as discussed in section 2.3), which means that AndNav2 can only calculate routes while connected to the Internet. POI search requires connectivity as well.

AndNav2 finds the shortest or fastest route for cars, cyclists, or pedestrians. It can avoid toll roads, and it can even avoid predefined areas altogether.

19.10 Navit

The routing software Navit (www.navit-project.org) was originally conceived as an alternative viewer for map data distributed with a commercial, Windows-based route planner. It was later adapted to work with OSM data as well, and today is used almost exclusively for OSM.

Navit requires OSM data to be present in a special binary format. There is a web application at http://maps.navit-project.org/download/ that lets you select an area and then download binary data for it. But you can also download raw OSM data from somewhere else and then use the utility osm2navit (part of the Navit download) to convert this into the Navit binary format. The resulting files are approximately half the size of the bz2 compressed OSM files.

Navit is written in C++ and uses GTK+ and SDL for its user interface. The vector-based map view looks good and is reasonably fast. If run on machines supporting OpenGL, Navit can even display a "3D view". Navit can be run on Linux machines (including mobile devices like the Nokia Internet Tablet and the OpenMoko platform), as well as on Mac OS X and Windows Mobile/Windows CE. There are ready-made binaries for some platforms on the Navit web page, but for some platforms you have to compile it from source.

For routing, you can select the start and destination by clicking on the map. Navit works with built-in or otherwise accessible GPS devices, and it has support for providing spoken routing instructions ("turn right now") in different languages.

19.11 Traveling Salesman

The Traveling Salesman software (travelingsales.sf.net) is written in Java. It can use pre-rendered map tiles for its map display, but it can also render vector data itself. After selecting an area on the map, the raw data for the road grid is downloaded from the OpenStreetMap server. Alternatively, OSM files can be read from disk. For searching start and destination locations, Traveling Salesman can access the external Name Finder service. Upon loading data, it is converted into an internal HSQL (a simple Java SQL implementation) storage format.

Traveling Salesman is really just a user interface for the Java library Osmnavigation which does the real work. All components of Traveling Salesman are modular and can be replaced. For example, one module has the task of displaying data on screen, another is there to describe the calculated route to the user.

19.12 pgRouting

The free SQL database PostgreSQL with the PostGIS extension (see section 17.1) has a routing module named pgRouting (`pgrouting.postlbs.org`), which implements shortest-path searches on graphs. Because the algorithms can directly access the database, pgRouting can operate on very large datasets (including the full OpenStreetMap database) without hitting a memory limit. The module implements various search algorithms, among them Dijkstra, A*, and a modified version of A* called Shooting Star, which can also process special cases such as turn restrictions.

In theory, pgRouting doesn't require preprocessing data, because you can supply arbitrary SQL queries to the routing engine which it then uses to build the routing graph. In practice however, searching can be optimized by preparing the data in a way to be easily accessible for the pgRouting algorithms. There is a utility called `osm2pgrouting` (also on pgRouting's project page) which does this for OSM data.

19.13 Gosmore

Gosmore (wiki page: Gosmore) attracted much interest when it was launched in 2007 as at that time it was the first routing application for OpenStreetMap. The program is written in C, and it has a simple user interface for specifying a start and destination location and a reasonably nice vector rendering engine. It can compute routes and generate navigation instructions. It runs on a number of mobile devices as well as on desktop systems.

OSM data needs to be converted into a special file format before you can use it with Gosmore, On a desktop machine, this is done automatically when running Gosmore for the first time. If you are planning to run Gosmore on a mobile device, then perform the preparation step on another computer first, or download ready-made data packages.

Gosmore also has a server mode in which it can be used as a back-end to services like Your-Navigation (see page 14).

20 License Issues When Using Data

All OSM data comes under the "Creative Commons Attribution-Share Alike" license, version 2.0 (CC-BY-SA 2.0 for short).[1] This license says, in a nutshell: You may copy, distribute, process, or make available the data in any way you want, but in doing so you must name the copyright holder, and you must always use the same license for your published work. The idea behind that is that data should always remain freely usable, and it shouldn't be possible for someone to take the free data and add restrictions to it before passing it on. This type of license is also called a "copyleft license".

Over time, it has turned out that the license isn't well suited for geodata because it leaves many questions unanswered. But it isn't easy to change the license because that would require agreement by everyone who ever contributed data, or else their data would have to be removed. At the end of this chapter we will give a short overview about the current plans for a license change, but it can be assumed that data will be made available under CC-BY-SA for some time to come.

> ☞ *Please note: The authors of this book are not lawyers. This chapter documents community practice or the reasoning of the authors. If in doubt, you should consult a lawyer.*

20.1 Who is the Owner of OpenStreetMap Data?

The license requires that the rights owner (the licensor) be attributed in a suitable form. The authors, and therefore rights owners, of the data are the contributors – not the OpenStreetMap project itself, which only collects these contributions. Strictly speaking, anyone who uses an OpenStreetMap map should list every single contributor who took part in

---

1 http://creativecommons.org/licenses/by-sa/2.0/

creating what is visible on the map. That information is available on the server, but not necessarily made publicly available.

Therefore, the license is commonly interpreted in a way that it is sufficient to add a copyright notice like "Copyright © (year) OpenStreetMap Contributors", or a local-language version of the same. Additionally, the license must be given, for example by saying: "License: CC-BY-SA". When making a website, this should be a link to the official license page at http://creativecommons.org/licenses/by-sa/2.0/.

Theoretically it is always possible to ask the rights owners of a CC-BY-SA licensed work for release under a different license. For example, if you want to make a derived work from a CC-BY-SA licensed image but don't want to make your work available under CC-BY-SA, then you can talk to the copyright owner and ask them to license the photo to you differently. For OpenStreetMap, such actions are usually not feasible because it would be difficult to identify all rights owners, and even more difficult to get agreement from them all.

The fact that OpenStreetMap itself isn't the owner of the data also means that OpenStreetMap can't give binding legal advice or permissions. If you buy map data in the commercial market and you have a project in mind for which you want to use it and are unsure whether this is covered by the license, you can always explain your project to the rights owner and ask them whether your use is covered by the license. If you get a positive response, you can continue in the knowledge that should someone later claim that you are operating outside of the license you have official communication to prove otherwise. In contrast to that, if someone comes to OpenStreetMap asking "is this and that use of the data covered by the license?" then while some questions may be clearly answered, the response will often be a collective shrug and a response of: "You will have to consult a lawyer about that."

20.2 Collective Works and Derived Works

The CC-BY-SA license distinguishes between "collective works" and "derived works". This is a very important distinction because it determines how the license will apply to your work.

A collective work is something where the OpenStreetMap content is a more or less independent part of the whole – for example, this book: All OpenStreetMap maps in this book are covered by the CC-BY-SA license and thus you may copy and re-use them just as you can do with data directly loaded from OSM. But this doesn't apply to the rest of the book – which comes under the usual publisher's copyright and may not be copied without permission. The same would apply if you were to distribute a CD that contained some OSM data and some other data files; the OSM data would remain CC-BY-SA and the rest of the CD would have whatever license applied to that part.

Unfortunately not all use cases are that simple. On the Internet, you often have applications where a map is displayed in the background and additional information is shown on top of it on extra layers. We consider these to be collective works as well, where the OSM license applies only to the OSM content.

On the other hand, a derived work is created if you take OpenStreetMap data and other data and combine this into something which can't be separated any more – for example if you were to create a film that has little sports cars racing over an OSM map, or a hand-colored, printed map of your home town where you based the street data on OpenStreet-Map. In cases such as these, the final product must be licensed under CC-BY-SA. This rule is especially important if you want to use data from a third party to draw something on top of OpenStreetMap data.

If you have obtained the third-party data commercially, you have to make sure that the license for that data allows derived works to be under CC-BY-SA.

If your third-party data comes from a "free" source, you must check whether that source itself stipulates that derived works be made available under the same license. Some examples:

- The other dataset is licensed under CC-BY-SA: You can use it and mix it with OSM without problems. You must attribute both sources. Strictly speaking you would have to check if the version numbers of the licenses match but that is really a minor detail.
- The other dataset comes under CC-BY-SA-NC (non-commercial): This license isn't compatible with CC-BY-SA. You must try to convince the rights owner to allow you to release the derived work under CC-BY-SA because this will allow commercial use which the rights owner had opted against.
- The other dataset comes under public domain, the BSD License, the Artistic License or CC-BY: The dataset can be used without problems; naming the source may be required.
- The other dataset is licensed under GNU FDL: This license isn't compatible with CC-BY-SA but quite similar; there is hardly anything that is allowed under the one and not allowed under the other and vice versa. Even so, strictly speaking you have to get permission from the rights owner to license the resulting work under CC-BY-SA.

20.3 Do I Have to Publish?

No. The CC-BY-SA license says that everyone who has something that is CC-BY-SA licensed *may* process, copy, or distribute it – but it doesn't say that they *have to!* Now if you make a fantastic printed map from OpenStreetMap data but then decide not to let anybody access it, then you are fully within your rights, and the map isn't published. If, however, you allow someone to make a copy of the map then you can't stop that person from doing whatever the license allows with that map. Any attempt to restrict that freedom – for example if you were to give the copy to them only under the condition that they sign a contract waiving their rights under CC-BY-SA – would lead to termination of your own right to use OSM data.

20.4 Can I Sell OpenStreetMap Data?

Yes. The CC-BY-SA license doesn't say that you have to make anything you create from OSM data available free of charge. It only says that if you give your work to someone (possibly in exchange for money), that person may then do whatever the license allows, including distributing it for free.

You are perfectly within your rights if you make a beautiful atlas based on OSM data and then sell that for € 100 a piece. But you can't prevent someone who buys your atlas from printing a facsimile and selling that for € 50! (That someone, again, can't prevent their customers from using a color copier to make further copies, and so on.)

20.5 What Happens if I Disregard the License?

If you disregard the CC-BY-SA license, for example by creating a derived work and making that available under a license other than CC-BY-SA (no matter whether that is a more permissive or a more restrictive license than CC-BY-SA), then the legal consequence is the automatic termination of your rights under the license. You are then in the same position as someone who downloads copyrighted works from the Internet and uses them without permission. Rights you have passed on to others may also be terminated.

Whether or not using the data without permission will get you into any kind of trouble, and what kind of trouble, depends very much on the jurisdiction you are in, and perhaps also on the scale of the operation. It may depend on the question whether the data was protected at all (see next section), whether the rights owner complains, and whether you have violated the license on purpose or negligently.

20.6 Is the License Legally Binding?

There is no consensus within the OpenStreetMap project on whether geodata is copyrightable or not (see also the discussion of data sources in chapter 13). Even if geodata isn't copyrightable, it could still be protected by the EU database directive (for those who live in the European Union). Unfortunately, if it is protected by the database directive then the CC-BY-SA license isn't entirely suitable to confer usage rights to anyone because it doesn't explicitly refer to that directive.

In addition, many jurisdictions have some kind of "facts are free" rule regarding copyright – you can't claim copyright on mere facts. That would mean that someone who wants to use OpenStreetMap data in a way that doesn't conform to CC-BY-SA would simply have to base their project in such a jurisdiction.

Finally, the license also can't ensure that work built on top of OpenStreetMap flows back to the project. The CC-BY-SA license was originally meant for works of fiction or art. If someone publishes a story under CC-BY-SA and someone else improves on it, then the license makes sure that the improved story is available to all just like the original work.

OpenStreetMap would like to see a similar rule: If someone, for example, takes an OpenStreetMap map and adds all GSM radio masts to it, then publishes the map in a newspaper, OpenStreetMap would like to have access to the information about the GSM radio masts. But CC-BY-SA doesn't deliver that; CC-BY-SA only makes sure that the final product, the map printed in the newspaper, is available under the free license.

At the end of the day, the license isn't only possibly un-enforceable in some jurisdictions, but also only partially does what many people would like it to do.

20.7 The Open Database License

In the face of the problems discussed in this chapter, a large number of OpenStreetMap contributors would like to release OSM data into the public domain (meaning waiving all restrictions on the data). Many others would prefer to switch to a copyleft license which has similar characteristics as CC-BY-SA but is more suitable for (geo)data.

The authors of this book think that the Public Domain option makes the most sense, but opposition to such complete freedom is strong. Thus, there are concrete plans to switch OpenStreetMap to the "Open Database License". This license isn't exclusively rooted in copyright, like CC-BY-SA is, but instead makes use of the European database law and contract law. It is expected that this will enable OpenStreetMap to control access to the data even if individual data items aren't be worthy of copyright protection. For jurisdictions outside Europe, the ODbL doesn't work like a license but like a contract, allowing use of the data only under the provision that the user first agrees to this contract/license.

Like CC-BY-SA, ODbL is a copyleft license, meaning it is a license that aims at always keeping the data free even if combined with other data. For most real-life applications there will be little change when the old license is replaced by the new one. The major practical differences between both licenses are:

- It would be acknowledged that the database contents aren't protected by copyright.
- ODbL allows the use of "non-substantial" extracts of the database in a completely unrestricted manner. OSM suggests that anything smaller than 100 objects or up to an

area inhabited by 1,000 people is "non-substantial"; such small excerpts could thus be used free of any license restrictions.

- ODbL further allows you to make "produced works" which are derived from the data but aren't a database in themselves, and these may be licensed in any way their producer likes. Unlike with CC-BY-SA, ODbL would allow you to produce the aforementioned atlas, sell it for € 100, and prevent your customers from making copies.

- In exchange for this more liberal rule, ODbL requires that any derived database, even if only used internally in the process of making a produced work, must be released. (Either the full derived database, or a file containing the differences to the original database, or even an algorithm that performs the changes can be released.) In the aforementioned GSM radio mast example, the database with the radio masts would now probably have to be released.

Changing the license of a project as big as OpenStreetMap is, however, a very complex operation, because everyone who has ever contributed data needs to agree. If some contributors don't agree, or can't be reached, then their data can't be used after the license change. If too many refuse to agree, then the whole idea of change has to be scrapped.

At the time of printing this book, it seems likely that the license change could happen in late 2010 or early 2011. All mappers will then be asked to agree to the new license. (In fact new mappers signing up now are already required to accept both the current CC-BY-SA and a possible future ODbL license.) It is likely that, in addition to being asked to explicitly agree to the new license, mappers will also have the option to declare that they don't want to claim any rights in their contribution (the public domain option). For all practical purposes, that option means the same as agreeing to the new license, but it would also count as a voice against too much licensing fuss.

The wiki has more information under Open Database License.

Part IV

Hacking OpenStreetMap

Want to know more than the basics of editing and using OSM? Now let's roll our sleeves up and take a closer look at the OpenStreetMap database server and its Application Programming Interface (API). This part helps you write your own software, work with large datasets and changesets, import and export data, use Osmosis to manipulate and filter data, and revert to earlier versions of the data. Finally we give a quick overview of how to set up your own OSM server.

21 Writing Software for OSM

OpenStreetMap is a young project without rigid rules and hierarchies. We mentioned the "avoiding strict rules" issue when we discussed Map Features. It is the same with all other parts of the infrastructure. This sometimes confounds newcomers. It is often said that OSM is a "brutally pragmatic" project – which means that what works is what counts, and not some high-flying vision of how things could be better with a different data model, a different database engine, or a different programming language. OpenStreetMap isn't a company with a large R&D budget where a team of developers are paid to try out promising future technologies. If someone comes along and says "you should do this differently", the typical response is usually "just implement your idea and demonstrate that it works better than what we have, and we'll use it". Many people think this is just a ploy to get rid of them, but that isn't the case: Once they really start writing code, they are often surprised to find how quickly their contribution is part of "mainstream OSM".

So don't be put off if your first ideas don't exactly meet with an ecstatic reaction on the mailing lists or forums, and you don't get dozens of people offering help. OpenStreetMap has much more programming work than those involved can manage; there aren't hundreds of programmers just waiting for someone to tell them what they should do next. In the previous chapters, this book might have created the impression that some aspects of Open-StreetMap are firmly established or even "finished" – but nothing could be further from the truth. There isn't a single piece of software in the whole project that couldn't do with some improvement or other. And there is great willingness to accept such improvements, no matter whom they come from.

21.1 Working with Large Amounts of Data

A recurring theme in OpenStreetMap programming is working with large amounts of data – whether this is importing datasets comprising hundreds of gigabytes into a database or excerpting an area from such a file. Of course, some of us are used to data sizes like this from our daily work or from other projects, but many people really have to change their way of doing things when they start working on OpenStreetMap projects. Standard methods for problem solving often don't apply to such large amounts of data. Anything that works on the assumption of having all data loaded into memory is especially prone to causing problems with OpenStreetMap.

Currently, all OpenStreetMap data is held in one big, central database. It is likely that this can't go on forever because a single server won't be able to manage the ever-expanding dataset. Also, with the number of mappers rising constantly, the server is having to answer more and more queries. In the future, the workload will probably have to be distributed among several machines in some way. Using the minutely updates described in section 15.2, it is already possible to create an almost current read-only mirror, which can reduce the number of queries put to the main server. However, OSM hasn't yet "officially" established such mirrors; instead those that exist are run by individual project members on their own servers. It would also be possible to split the data by regions.

If you are using OSM data, or writing software for OSM, then you should always keep an eye on the amount of data you are dealing with. Working with XML files of usual OSM dimensions is especially tricky, because many XML libraries are actually geared towards processing small files. The OSM XML format has many recurring elements and thus compresses very well. Many programs directly process compressed OSM XML to avoid unnecessarily using hundreds of gigabytes on the hard disk.

It isn't normally possible to use a DOM (Document Object Model) parser when processing OpenStreetMap data, because DOM parsers read the whole XML file into a tree structure in memory. You have to use SAX (Simple API for XML) parsers instead, which allow you to process the data element by element.

21.2 Finding Your Way through the Subversion Repository

Subversion (SVN) is an Open Source tool for version control. OpenStreetMap has a Subversion repository at svn.openstreetmap.org where you can find almost all programs used in the project. The repository also contains many national websites, advertising material, slides for talks, logos, and icons.

The software that runs the main OSM site, the *rails port*, has its own repository under git.openstreetmap.org using the "git" version control mechanism.

The repositories are readable by anyone; write access to the SVN repository is generally granted on request by an administrator without further ado. For write access to the git repository, see Committing to the rails port on the wiki.

☞ *Before you make changes to central components in SVN like the main style file, you should discuss it on the mailing list or with the relevant server operators. Depending on the extent of your change, they might encourage you to start a "branch" in the repository. Everyone has the same write access to the repository, but your changes will only go live once they are pulled from Subversion by the administrators. Such caution is not necessary for the rails port as it resides in a git repository.*

Accessing the Subversion Repository

There are a few different ways to access the Subversion repository. The easiest is through a web browser: Simply point your browser to `svn.openstreetmap.org` and find your way through the directory hierarchy. A somewhat nicer view is offered by the Trac subsystem at `http://trac.openstreetmap.org/browser`. Trac will show you not only the current version of every file but also older versions, and you can see commit comments and changes between versions.

If you only need individual files from the Subversion repository, you can download them in the web browser. For downloading whole directory hierarchies, or if you want to make changes and upload them, you need to install a Subversion client. Linux distributions generally contain one already or make it easy to install one through their package management. Mac OS X (Leopard and upwards) also has an integrated Subversion client. For other systems, `http://subversion.tigris.org/project_packages.html` has everything you need.

After installing a Subversion client, you can check out the whole OpenStreetMap repository like this:

```
svn checkout http://svn.openstreetmap.org/ osm
```

This will create a subdirectory osm in the current directory and extract the current version of all OSM files there. But because the whole repository is rather large (currently more than 3GB), you probably only want a certain subdirectory. You can specify that directory in the URL to download only that part recursively. Once you have checked out something like this, you can always use

```
svn update
```

in the osm directory to update everything to the newest version.

More information about using Subversion can be found on the Subversion homepage, `subversion.tigris.org`.

Contents of the OSM Repository

The OSM Subversion repository contains a lot of software and is growing steadily. Here is an overview of the directory structure:

applications	Software.
editors	OSM editors (JOSM and plugins, Merkaartor, Potlatch, and others).
etc	Other software.
lib	Libraries.
mobile	Applications for mobile use.
rendering	Rendering software such as Mapnik and Osmarender.
routing	Routing applications.
share	Icons for maps.
utils	Various utility programs.
export	Programs for exporting data and converting it to other formats.
filter	Programs for filtering OSM data.
gps-tracks	Programs working with GPS tracks.
import	Programs that import data into OSM.
osmosis	Osmosis.
viewer	Applications for viewing OSM data or maps.
extensions	Code to integrate OSM into content management systems.
misc	Miscellaneous.
images	Various icons, logos, and images.
lectures	Slides for talks and other presentations.
maps	Various maps.
sites	HTML pages and source code for various web pages.

Many things in the repository aren't current any more. Some programs may have been developed for an earlier version of the API or the OSM data format and won't be usable with the current API; others probably stem from a specific import effort and are unused since that was finished. A glance at the Subversion history for the source code often sheds some light on whether or not the program is still in use or development – to view this type svn log on the command line.

22 The OpenStreetMap API

All access to the OpenStreetMap server goes through a HTTP based API (Application Programming Interface) with an underlying REST architecture.[1]

This API is the OpenStreetMap database's window to the world. Nobody can directly access the SQL database, everybody has to use the API. Thus, the API also determines what kinds of operations are possible with the data.

Every API request has its own specific URL. These URLs all contain a host name and the API version. We are documenting the API version 0.6, which is current at the time of publication, so URLs begin with `http://api.openstreetmap.org/api/0.6/`. When a new API version is introduced, old URLs will become invalid and – as long as the calling syntax isn't changed – be replaced by similar URLs using a higher protocol version. The OSM Protocol wiki page has information about the protocol version that is currently in use.

Data sent to the API or retrieved from there is transferred using the OSM XML format (see chapter 6).

All requests that modify the database in any way require authentication. Two methods of authentication are supported: HTTP Basic Auth and OAuth. The HTTP Basic Auth procedure uses the account information created on the OpenStreetMap website (see section 3.1). Almost all HTTP clients have support for this kind of authentication, as it is the most widely used authentication scheme on the web. If you access a URL requiring authentication in your web browser, it will automatically pop up a password entry dialog. With OAuth on the other hand, an OpenStreetMap user can authorize an application to make edits in their name. The application can then retrieve a secret token from the server and use that to make edits under the user's account until they revoke the authorization (see section 22.9).

---

1 `http://en.wikipedia.org/wiki/Representational_State_Transfer`

Since API 0.6 was introduced, all requests that modify the database also require that a changeset has been opened beforehand, and the changeset ID must be given in the request.

22.1 Creating, Retrieving, Updating, and Deleting Objects

For any of the basic data types – node, way, relation – the API supports the following operations. Replace `<type>` by the data type and `<id>` by the ID of the object affected:

Purpose	HTTP method and URL	Message payload	
		Request	Response
creation	PUT /api/0.6/<type>/create	XML	id
retrieval	GET /api/0.6/<type>/<id>	–	XML
update	PUT /api/0.6/<type>/<id>	XML	version
deletion	DELETE /api/0.6/<type>/<id>	XML	–

With the exception of the GET operation, all methods expect an XML document with the new object as their input. That document must also contain a valid changeset ID (more about changesets on page 254). Each method returns a HTTP status code of 200 OK if it is successful. If something goes wrong, the following error messages could be returned:

400 Bad Request
> The requested geographic area was invalid, or the payload transmitted didn't match the HTTP request. This happens for example if you send an update request for a node, but transmit the XML for a way. This error message also occurs if you try to upload a way that has too many elements, if you omit a changeset ID, or if the XML message isn't well-formed.

401 Unauthorized
> A request that would change data has been sent without authentication, or with bad authentication, or the OAuth access token isn't allowed to perform this operation.

404 Not Found
> The requested object doesn't exist, and has never existed.

405 Method Not Allowed
> The method used did not match the request. For example, a "create" request was sent, but an HTTP method other than PUT was used. "create" requests always require the PUT method.

409 Conflict
> The object that was requested for update or deletion exists on the server in a different (usually newer) version than specified, or something is wrong with the changeset ID (the changeset is already closed, belongs to another user, or has too many changes).

410 Gone

The requested object did once exist, but has been deleted meanwhile. Updating such an object is allowed; this will undelete the object.

412 Precondition Failed

The requested operation would break the referential integrity of the database and thus can't be applied. You will get this message for example if you try to remove a node that is being used by a way, or if you try to create a way that refers to a node that has been deleted.

This error code is also returned if the object given in the XML code contains an ID but the request was for the creation of a new object (where the server will assign a new ID and return that).

500 Internal Server Error

A program error in the server code – usually an exception that hasn't been caught properly.

503 Service Unavailable

The database is offline for maintenance. In these cases you will usually find more information about it on the wiki start page. OSM does not have regular maintenance intervals, so this is really an exceptional situation.

In some cases an additional error header is transmitted that gives you details about the problem. Here is what happens if you request a too large area:

```
HTTP/1.0 400 Bad Request
Content-Type: text/html
Error: The maximum bbox size is 0.25, and your request was too large.
       Either request a smaller area, or use planet.osm
Content-Length: 184
Connection: keep-alive
Date: Wed, 26 May 2010 16:38:12 GMT
Server: lighttpd/1.4.22
```

In API 0.6, OpenStreetMap uses a technique called "optimistic locking" to detect edit conflicts. This means that whenever you delete or update an object, you have to tell the server which version of the object your change is based on. If the server already has a more recent version, your change will be rejected with a 409 error code because it is based on an old dataset. This means that PUT and DELETE requests have to specify the version they intend to affect:

```
DELETE /api/0.6/way/1234
Host: www.openstreetmap.org

<way id="1234" version="7" changeset="888" />
```

(Further object data isn't required for DELETE requests.)

22.2   Creating or Modifying Multiple Objects at once

With API 0.6, you can upload a complete change document that may create, update, or delete a large number of objects. This is also called a "diff upload". All changes in the document are applied to the database in a transaction. This means that either all changes from the document get through, or none do.

A change document can be uploaded with the following request:

```
POST /api/0.6/changeset/<id>/upload
```

A changeset has to be opened to start with. Multiple change documents can be uploaded to the same changeset, however transactionality is only applied to changes in the same document, not all changes that are part of the changeset.

A change document follows the format documented in section 6.2. For the API to process the document, it is important that a version number be specified for every object (except for "create" elements), and the ID of the changeset being used for the upload has to be repeated for every object as well.[2] Where objects in the document need to reference each other, negative IDs must be used.

The following change document creates four nodes and one way built from them:

```
<osmChange version="0.6" generator="JOSM">
<create version="0.6" generator="JOSM">
  <node id="-1" visible="true" changeset="72" lat="69.3023" lon="-30.3511" />
  <node id="-2" visible="true" changeset="72" lat="69.3023" lon="-30.3510" />
  <node id="-3" visible="true" changeset="72" lat="69.3022" lon="-30.3510" />
  <node id="-4" visible="true" changeset="72" lat="69.3011" lon="-30.3508" />
  <way id="-5" action="modify" visible="true" changeset="72">
    <nd ref="-1" />
    <nd ref="-2" />
    <nd ref="-3" />
    <nd ref="-4" />
    <nd ref="-1" />
    <tag k="leisure" v="park" />
  </way>
</create>
</osmChange>
```

A change upload request has a special kind of response – the "diffResult" document. This document matches each ID from the input file with the new ID and version used by the server. For newly created objects the ID will be a new one, and the version will be 1. For deletions or modifications, the ID is the same as used on input, and the version usually one higher.

---

2   If the changeset specified in the object XML is different from the one given in the URL, a "409 Conflict" error will result.

```
<diffResult version="0.6" generator="OpenStreetMap server">
  <node old_id="-1" new_id="340141686" new_version="1"/>
  <node old_id="-2" new_id="340141687" new_version="1"/>
  <node old_id="-3" new_id="340141688" new_version="1"/>
  <node old_id="-4" new_id="340141689" new_version="1"/>
  <way old_id="-5" new_id="30657127" new_version="1"/>
</diffResult>
```

If any of the requests from the change upload can't be processed, an error message is returned. The catalog of error messages is the same as described above for a single object change. Document processing stops when the first problem is encountered, so even if the document contains multiple errors, only the first will be returned.

Note that such uploads are also affected by the size limit for changesets (currently 50,000 changes per changeset, see page 254).

22.3 Requesting all Objects in an Area

There are two API requests that return data within a geographic area (a bounding box), one for OSM data, and one for GPS trackpoints. A bounding box is specified by the upper and lower limits of latitude and longitude.

The "map" call to download nodes, ways, and relations in a bounding box is:

```
GET /api/0.6/map?bbox=<left>,<bottom>,<right>,<top>
```

The bounds are given, as latitudes and longitudes, in the <left>, <bottom>, <right>, and <top> parameters. This request will usually return slightly more than asked for, namely:

- All nodes in the given bounding box.
- All ways using one of these nodes.
- Additionally, all nodes outside of the bounding box that are used by one of the ways.
- All relations that have one of the returned objects as a member.

There is no recursion for relations – if a relation has other members in addition to those that are in the bounding box, these will not be returned. Otherwise this could lead to excessively large return datasets. For example if there were a relations containing all ways that make up the border of each country, and someone were to download a little bounding box on the border between France and Spain, they would get the whole of both country outlines if recursion was used for relations.

If there are no objects in the area requested, an empty message will be returned, but this isn't an error. The error code 400 Bad Request is used for bounding boxes that are larger than the permitted maximum (currently 0.25 degrees squared, see page 119) or where the result would contain over 50,000 nodes. You have to use a smaller bounding box then.

> ☞ *Don't abuse the "map" call by making many repeated, or even parallel, requests in order to download a large area section-by-section. If you need a large area, you must use XAPI, the Planet Dump, or any of the published extracts. Abusing the API will get your application banned. See API_usage_policy on the wiki.*

A similar request is used for requesting GPS trackpoints:

```
GET /api/0.6/trackpoints?bbox=<left>,<bottom>,<right>,<top>&page=<page>
```

The bounding box is given in the same way as for the "map" call. Each request only returns a certain number of GPS points (one page, currently 5,000) After that, the next page can be requested by adding a <page> parameter, incrementing the page number until the request returns no more results.

22.4 Other Methods of Access

In addition to the rather generic methods already mentioned, there are a number of special purpose access methods. All of them are GET requests, and all will return an XML document containing one or more elements, just like the "map" request discussed above.

Change History

Use

```
GET /api/0.6/<type>/<id>/history
```

to download the change history for an object. Put "node", "way", or "relation" in the place of <type> and give the ID of the object in <id>. The response will contain all versions of the object, starting with the earliest, together with the timestamp of their creation. Chapter 25 has an example of such a history on page 287.

This request also works for objects that have been deleted.

You can also access a specific, historic version of an object:

```
GET /api/0.6/<type>/<id>/<version>
```

returns the requested version. For some objects the change history may have become so complex as to result in a timeout error when you try to read the full history (some relations have four-digit version numbers). In these cases you can start with the most recent version that is returned when you ask for the object without a version number, and then go back in history step by step.

Requesting Multiple Objects

A request of the form

```
GET /api/0.6/<type>s?<type>s=<id>,<id>...
```

returns multiple objects of the same type. For <type>, use "node", "way", or "relation" (a plural "s" is required). Add to that a list of object IDs, separated by commas. For example:

```
GET /api/0.6/ways?ways=1123,4452,3428
```

If at least one of the objects can be found, the HTTP status code will be 200 OK, otherwise it is 401 Bad Request.

Resolving Back References

You can find out which other objects use a given object:

```
GET /api/0.6/node/<id>/ways
GET /api/0.6/<type>/<id>/relations
```

The first call returns all ways using the node with the given ID. The second call returns all relations that contain the given object; <type> may be any of "node", "way", or "relation".

Resolving Forward References

An extension of the normal object read request will return the object itself plus all other objects referenced by it:

```
GET /api/0.6/<type>/<id>/full
```

This request only works with a <type> of "way" or "relation" – nodes can't reference other objects. If you request a way like this, then the way and all its nodes are returned. If you request a relation, the following objects are returned:

- The relation itself.
- All nodes, ways, and relations that are members of the relation.
- All nodes that are used by ways returned in the preceding step.

Searching by Tags

The API has a method to find objects with a given tag (either with a given key or with a given value):

```
GET /api/0.6/ways/search?type=<key>&value=<value>
GET /api/0.6/nodes/search?type=<key>&value=<value>
GET /api/0.6/relations/search?type=<key>&value=<value>
GET /api/0.6/search?type=<key>&value=<value>
```

The first three requests search for a way, a node, or a relation with a tag of <key>=<value> (e. g. you have to use type=amenity&value=fuel to find gas stations). The fourth request doesn't specify an object type, and may return any of the three.

The <key> specification may be omitted to search for objects that have any key with the given value (so searching for value=hotel will find objects tagged tourism=hotel as well as those unusually tagged amenity=hotel). Omitting <value> was once possible but is currently disabled due to high server loads.

The search is case insensitive, and search terms have to be given in UTF-8 encoding. It will return a maximum of 2,000 nodes, 100 ways, and 100 relations. For any way found, all nodes will also be returned (even if that brings the total node count above 2,000).

> ☞ *This search function can't be used to limit the search to a geographic area, and it is rather slow. We suggest using the XAPI (see section 23.1) instead. If you want to search for objects with a specific name, you should also consider Nominatim or the Name Finder (section 23.2).*

22.5 Working with Changesets

The API version 0.6 has introduced a method to group multiple changes. This was done in the hope of giving users the opportunity to describe their change as a whole, much like you would do in a software revision control system. Instead of seeing lots of individual object changes, someone could now see a group of changes titled "fixed A67/B22 ramp" or "completed central Goatstown". This makes it easier for other users to get an idea of what has been changed in an area.

The introduction of changesets brought with it a number of API calls to create, retrieve, and update a changeset. Also, the XML representation of objects had to be extended to add the "changeset" attribute. When uploading a change with a PUT or DELETE method, you always have to give the ID of a previously created changeset.

Changesets can hold up to 50,000 changes, and they may remain open for up to 24 hours. If one of these limits is reached, or if no changes have been added to the changeset for the last 60 minutes, then the changeset is considered closed, and it can't be modified or appended to any longer. It isn't possible to re-open a changeset once it is closed; a new changeset has to be created if further changes are to be uploaded. Multiple changesets can be open simultaneously for the same user.

The API records which area is affected by a changeset to allow fast access; however this is only done for a rectangular area so that a changeset that encompasses small changes on several continents will have a very large affected area.

Changesets are not *atomic*, i. e. there can be multiple changesets open at the same time that all modify the same object. Changesets are also not transactional; every change in the changeset is written to the database independently. The "diff upload" described in section 22.2 is an exception to this rule.

Creating, Updating, and Closing Changesets

The API request

```
PUT /api/0.6/changeset/create
```

creates a new changeset. An XML message containing changeset data must be transmitted with this request:

```
<osm>
  <changeset>
    <tag k="created_by" v="JOSM 1.61"/>
    <tag k="comment" v="Just adding some street names"/>
    ...
  </changeset>
</osm>
```

The changeset may have any number of tags. The return value is the ID of the newly created changeset, given as a plain text message. While the changeset is still open, the tags can be modified by sending a new XML document with this request:

```
PUT /api/0.6/changeset/<id>
```

Other data that the API stores for the changeset internally, such as the affected area or the time when the changeset was created, can't be modified. This call returns the current XML version of the changeset (or 409 Conflict if the changeset is already closed, or belongs to another user).

A changeset can also be closed explicitly:

```
PUT /api/0.6/changeset/<id>/close
```

This request closes the changeset if it exists, is open, and belongs to the user making the request. The potential HTTP return codes are 200 (all fine), 404 (the changeset doesn't exist), or 400 (another problem).

Once created, a changeset can't be deleted, not even if it contains no changes. But it is conceivable that a periodic cleanup job will remove empty changesets from the database in the future.

Using the request

```
POST /api/0.6/changeset/<id>/expand_bbox
```

you can extend the affected area stored internally for the changeset. A document like

```
<osm>
  <node lat=".." lon=".."/>
  <node lat=".." lon=".."/>
  ...
</osm>
```

has to be transmitted. The affected area is enlarged to contain all the node positions given. You don't have to use real OSM nodes for the node objects in this document – they are just used as a transport wrapper for the latitude and longitude values. This call returns the updated changeset document. The idea behind this call is to give editors the chance to influence the affected area for complex edits where what the API computes automatically may not be sufficient. Details about the algorithm used by the API can be found on the wiki: OSM Protocol Version 0.6.

Retrieving Changesets

The request

GET /api/0.6/changeset/<id>

returns all meta data stored about a specific changeset. The response document looks like this:

```
<osm version="0.6" generator="OpenStreetMap server">
  <changeset id="1234" user="fred" uid="1234"
      created_at="2009-02-02T11:47:10Z" closed_at="2009-02-02T11:47:10Z"
      open="false" min_lon="7.0191821" min_lat="49.2785426"
      max_lon="7.0197485" max_lat="49.2793101">
    <tag k="comment" v="Some changes"/>
    <tag k="created_by" v="JOSM"/>
  </changeset>
</osm>
```

The rectangular area described by min_lat, min_lon, max_lat, and max_lon is the area affected by this changeset. As stated before, this area may be large even if the changeset contains only a small number of changes. It is also not necessarily the smallest possible area that contains all the changes because the API may include a small buffer around objects. If an object is moved, the area will normally cover the old and new positions.

To see the full list of changes made as part of a changeset, use the API request:

GET /api/0.6/changeset/<id>/download

This produces a change document (see section 6.2) containing all changes that are associated with that changeset.

Remember that the return data of the calls described in this section may change while the changeset is still open.

Finding Changesets

The search request

```
GET /api/0.6/changesets?<search_criteria>
```

can be used to find changesets that match the given search criteria. The following are al-lowed for `<search_criteria>`:

- A geographic area: `bbox=minlon,minlat,maxlon,maxlat`.
- A time range: `time=T` (all changesets closed at or after T) or `time=T1,T2` (all changesets opened at or after T1 and closed at or before T2). The timestamp has to be formatted as YYYY-MM-DD followed by a "T" and then HH:MM:SS followed by a "Z", e. g. 2009-02-02T11:54:14Z.
- A user ID: `user=uid`.
- A user's screen name: `display_name=name`.
- All changesets that are currently still open: `open` (without a value).

Multiple criteria can be combined using an ampersand (&). The return message consists of at most 100 <changeset> elements, which each describe the changeset and its tags; the full content of individual changesets can then be retrieved with the download request mentioned above.

Information About Changed Areas

Software that needs to work with a very current dataset can request from the API a list of areas that have recently changed:

```
GET /api/0.6/changes?zoom=12&hours=1
```

This request returns a list of all map tiles on which there has been a node change in the given time span. (Changes to ways or relations are ignored because it would take too long to compute them.) The zoom parameter can be used to specify the tile zoom level of interest, and hours tells the API which period the caller is interested in (a maximum of 24 hours into the past is allowed). Alternatively the period can also be given in the form of a start and end parameter, each containing a timestamp formatted as shown above.

This call returns a document like this:

```xml
<?xml version="1.0" encoding="UTF-8"?>
<osm version="0.6" generator="OpenStreetMap server">
  <changes starttime="2007-12-18T22:24:54+00:00Z"
           endtime="2007-12-18T23:24:54+00:00Z">
    <tile x="683" y="1629" z="12" changes="1"/>
    <tile x="684" y="1629" z="12" changes="8"/>
    ...
  </changes>
</osm>
```

The important information is stored in the <tile> tags. The x, y, and z attributes are the zoom level and coordinates of a particular tile (see also section 14.1), and the changes attribute counts the number of node changes in the area covered by that tile.

This API call was invented at a time when minutely downloads weren't yet possible (see section 15.2). Today, most applications that are interested in tracking current changes simply download minutely or hourly updates from OpenStreetMap and analyze these to remain current.

22.6 Uploading and Downloading GPS Tracks

The following POST request can be used to send GPX data to the server:

POST /api/0.6/gpx/create

This request uses an HTTP message of the type multipart/form-data containing the following parameters:

file

> The GPX file containing the track. The track must be encoded in trackpoints (<trkpt>) inside the GPX file. See also the GPX description on page 35. All trackpoints must carry a timestamp or they won't be processed.

description

> A description of the GPS track (for example "New Forest hike, 23rd June 2010").

tags

> A list of keywords describing the track, separated by spaces. Don't confuse these tags with the key-value combinations that OSM otherwise uses for tagging. It makes sense to list the important places visited and perhaps the mode of transport so that people can easily find tracks that are relevant to them.

public

> This parameter was used to describe whether or not the track was public. It has been superseded by the "visibility" parameter.

visibility

> One of the three values "private", "trackable", or "identifiable". This parameter specifies to what level of detail others may access the track data. An explanation of the different values is on page 20. There is also a deprecated fourth option, "public", which was used in earlier API versions.

The API responds to this POST message with a plain text message containing only the ID under which the new track has been stored. The track won't be inserted into the database directly; instead, a periodic background process analyzes the files and inserts them into the database. An e-mail is sent to the uploading user upon completion.

Uploading GPS tracks isn't an operation covered by changesets, and doesn't require an open changeset or the specification of a changeset ID.

Individual points from GPS tracks can be requested using the `trackpoints` call discussed on page 252.

You can download meta data for a given GPX file with the request:

```
GET /api/0.6/gpx/<id>/details
```

(Specify the number assigned by the API upon upload for <id>.) The full file can be downloaded with:

```
GET /api/0.6/gpx/<id>/data
```

Both of these requests require authentication. "Private" and "trackable" tracks can only be downloaded by the person who has uploaded them; all others can be downloaded by anyone.

The response to a "details" request might look like this:

```
<osm version="0.6" generator="OpenStreetMap server">
  <gpx_file id="38698"
    name="rathfarnham_churchtown_nutgrove.gpx"
    lat="53.285644054" lon="-6.238367558"
    user="robfitz" visibility="identifiable" pending="false"
    timestamp="2007-09-13T23:28:41+01:00"/>
</osm>
```

The response to a "data" request is the uploaded GPX file.

22.7 Accessing User Data

The request

```
GET /api/0.6/user/details
```

can be used by members to retrieve information about their own account. (It only ever works for the logged-in user, thus the username doesn't have to be given.) Currently the response contains the screen name, the home coordinates, the self-description, and the preferred language(s):

```
<osm version="0.6" generator="OpenStreetMap server">
  <user display_name="woodpeck" account_created="2006-12-13T11:06:24+00:00">
    <home lat="49.0025" lon="8.3925" zoom="3"/>
    <description>I am an example user, and this is how I
    describe myself on my profile page.</description>
    <languages> <lang>en</lang> <lang>de-DE</lang> </languages>
  </user>
</osm>
```

The request

```
GET /api/0.6/user/gpx_files
```

returns a list of all GPX files uploaded by the logged-in user. The request

```
GET /api/0.6/user/preferences
```

returns a list of custom user settings (in the form of key=value pairs) for the logged-in user. The same request used with the HTTP PUT method can be used to upload a full set of new user settings, replacing all existing ones. The request

```
PUT /api/0.6/user/preferences/key
```

uploads a new value for one setting only and doesn't require an XML document, but just a plain text string when uploading.

These user settings aren't used for anything by the API. The facility is meant to allow third-party applications, for example an editor applet, to store user preferences directly in the OSM database.

22.8 Capabilities Request

The simplest API call of them all is the "capabilities" request, akin to a "who are you" directed at the OSM server. This is the only request that doesn't carry a version number in the URL:

```
GET /api/capabilities
```

The response lists the API versions currently supported by the server, plus some other server limitations like the maximum area (in degrees squared) that may be requested in one "map" call:

```
<osm version="0.6" generator="OpenStreetMap server">
  <api>
    <version minimum="0.6" maximum="0.6"/>
    <area maximum="0.25"/>
    <tracepoints per_page="5000"/>
    <waynodes maximum="2000"/>
  </api>
</osm>
```

A current list of API calls is available in the `config/routes.rb` file in the server source code, also known as the *Rails Port* (because it was initially written in another programming language, and then ported to Ruby on Rails). This file matches API URLs and the parts of the program responsible for answering them.

22.9 Authorization with OAuth

Until the end of 2009, the only authentication mechanism supported by OpenStreetMap was the standard way of transmitting passwords in the HTTP protocol (HTTP Basic Auth). There was no authorization – if you had the password you were allowed to do everything, and if you didn't have it, you weren't allowed to do anything.

More and more tools and utilities were created by third parties, software that wasn't running on the OSM servers but which was meant to help users make changes to OSM data – for example a simple, web based POI editor. Such services either had to use their own user account (but that meant that the changes couldn't later be associated with the user who really made them) or the user had to reveal their OSM password to the third-party application, which would then log in and commit the changes in their name (but that required a great level of trust and is generally not considered good practice on the Internet). Because neither of these solutions was satisfactory, OAuth was introduced.

OAuth is a cryptographically secured method that allows someone to create, in simple terms, a number of additional passwords for their account that aren't as powerful as the main password. In OAuth jargon these are called *access tokens*. You can therefore create an access token for a third-party application which enables this application to upload new data or change existing data in your name, but, for example, not download your private GPS tracks or modify your profile, and of course not to set a new password for your account.

OAuth works in three basic steps, we go through below.

Registering an Application

An application that wants to use OAuth must first be registered with the OSM server. When registering an application, you have to specify a name for it, and choose which permissions the application would like the user to grant it. Currently, the following permissions are supported:

- Read their user preferences.
- Modify their user preferences.
- Create diary entries and comments and make friends.
- Modify the map.
- Read their private GPS traces.
- Upload GPS traces.

During registration, the application receives a *consumer key* and a *consumer secret*. An application only has to be registered once, usually by its author.

Granting Authorization

Before a registered application can become active in your name, you have to grant the desired permissions to the application. To achieve this, the application needs to send you to the OSM server, transmitting its consumer key. You have to identify yourself to the OSM server using username and password, and are then shown a message that says something like: "Application XYZ would like you to grant it the following permissions: ... Do you agree?". If you agree (and you may also agree only to a subset of requested permissions), the application receives an access token and a matching secret that it can later use to act in your name.

There is a page in the user preferences section on the OSM server where users can always see which applications they have granted which permissions, and they can also revoke them.

Using Authorization

When the application wants to use a previously granted authorization, it simply uses the normal API calls, but instead of setting the classic "HTTP Basic Auth" Authorization header, it now sets a header that contains, among other things, the application's consumer key, the access token, and a cryptographic checksum, called the *nonce*. On the server side, such access is then treated exactly like an access with username and password – provided that the access token is valid and the application actually is authorized for the action it is attempting.

Further information on OAuth can be found on the OAuth wiki page and in the web links collected there.

22.10   Development and Testing APIs

If you are writing software that has to communicate with the OpenStreetMap API, but are unwilling or unable to set up your own API server for testing, have a look at the web page apis.dev.openstreetmap.org. This page lists a number of active "play instances" of various API versions where you can register and play with the data in any way you want without breaking anything. Data on these servers is deleted at regular intervals. Depending on what you want to do you may have to upload some test data first, or ask an administrator to pre-load one of the instances with a small dataset.

23 Other APIs and Web Services

In addition to the core OpenStreetMap API we presented in the previous chapter, there are a number of other services that use OSM data and are part of, or used by, OSM.

23.1 XAPI

The "OSM Extended API", or XAPI (pronounced "zappy"), is a modified form of the standard API. It runs on its own copy of the full database, which is usually updated every minute. This means that XAPI data may be a few minutes old compared to "live" data.

XAPI only offers read requests, and answers with the same data format used by the standard API.[1] XAPI's big advantage is that it allows complex search requests, and is able to return more data at once than the standard API.

XAPI requests always take the form of HTTP GET requests like this:

```
http://www.informationfreeway.org/api/0.6/...
```

There are various XAPI servers, and the above URL will always redirect to the one best suited for the request. XAPI supports these types of requests:

```
GET /api/0.6/node[condition]
```

```
GET /api/0.6/way[condition]
```

```
GET /api/0.6/relation[condition]
```

```
GET /api/0.6/*[condition]
```

(The square brackets have to be given as part of the request.)

---

1 In addition to the usual attributes, XAPI adds an attribute named xapi:users to every returned object, containing a list of all users who have ever modified the object.

The first three request types fetch only nodes, ways, or relations respectively; the fourth fetches anything that matches the given condition.

Inside the square brackets, you can give a condition regarding the tags and/or a condition regarding a geographic bounding box.

A tag condition looks like this: [key=value]. An asterisk (*) can be used to denote arbitrary keys or values. Different values can be joined with a pipe character (|) to form a logical "or" condition.

A bounding box condition looks like this: [bbox=left,bottom,right,top], where the limits are specified using degrees of latitude (for bottom and top) and longitude (for left and right).

Examples

The first example command downloads the whole of the coastline of southern England (the example uses wget, which takes the name of the file to save to in the -O argument, but you can use any other web client too):

```
wget -O coast.osm
    'http://www.informationfreeway.org/api/0.6/way[bbox=-6,50,1.5,51] ⤶
    [natural=coastline]'
```

The resulting file currently is around 10 MB and contains all ways (and nodes used by them) that are in the given geographic area and tagged natural=coastline.

The next example request returns all restaurants in Scotland (and then some):

```
wget -O fuel.osm
    'http://www.informationfreeway.org/api/0.6/node[bbox=-8,54.5,0,61] ⤶
    [amenity=restaurant]'
```

This is a request without a tag filter which downloads the whole of Iceland:

```
wget -O iceland.osm
    'http://www.informationfreeway.org/api/0.6/*[bbox=-25,63,-13,67]'
```

And finally a request for all motorways and trunk roads worldwide (which will be a long download):

```
wget -O trunk.osm
    'http://www.informationfreeway.org/api/0.6/*[highway=motorway|trunk]'
```

Pseudo Keys and API Compatibility

In addition to the usual tags, XAPI also supports three pseudo keys in the search condition: "@user" (for the user who last edited the object), "@users" (for a list of users who have ever edited an object), and "@timestamp" (for the time when the object was last changed).

For example the request

```
wget -O iceland.osm
   'http://www.informationfreeway.org/api/0.6/*[bbox=-25,63,-13,67] ↙
   [@user=woodpeck]'
```

returns all objects in Iceland that have been last edited by the user "woodpeck".

Instead of retrieving a rectangular area as described above with a [bbox=...] condition, you can also request an area using the same syntax understood by the central API:

```
wget -O iceland.osm
   'http://www.informationfreeway.org/api/0.6/map?bbox=-25,63,-13,67'
```

That means that any software written for direct API access can also use the XAPI instead – if you simply replace api.openstreetmap.org by www.informationfreeway.org. That way you can take advantage of the less stringent size restrictions and often faster response time of XAPI. Of course XAPI only supports a small subset of API requests and thus isn't suitable as a general replacement for the standard API.

Historic Data

The XAPI server has a special type of request for historic versions of an object with matching historic versions of referenced objects that isn't available from the API. A request like

```
http://www.informationfreeway.org/api/0.6/way/<id>/<version>/full
```

retrieves the given way in the given version with all nodes the way is using, and returns the version of each node that was current at the time the given way version was current. The standard API can *either* retrieve a historic version *or* the current version with all current nodes, but not an old version with matching nodes.

Other Special XAPI Features

XAPI has a number of highly specialized functions, for example it can search for ways without nodes or nodes that aren't part of any way (and similar requests for relations). XAPI can also keep a personal "watchlist" for you, and inform you of changes to any of the objects you are watching by means of an RSS feed.

Details about these functions, and latest XAPI developments, are on the Xapi wiki page.

23.2 Name Finder

The Name Finder, developed by David Earl, used to be the main search engine for the OpenStreetMap database and website. It is still operational but has been replaced on the main site with Nominatim (see next section). The Name Finder can be accessed from `http://gazetteer.openstreetmap.org/namefinder/`.

The Name Finder uses its own copy of the OSM database for searching and thus may not always be current; if you can't find an entry that is present in the main database, you may simply have to wait a few days until the Name Finder database has caught up. A detailed description can be found in the Name Finder article on the wiki, and the source code is in SVN under `http://svn.openstreetmap.org/sites/namefinder`.

The Name Finder API

The Name Finder can be used as a web service. Requests can be directed to the URL `http://gazetteer.openstreetmap.org/namefinder/search.xml?find=...` and will be answered with an XML document that contains the data found.

The XML document uses a root element called `<searchresults>`. If an error occurs, it will be given in the "error" attribute, as in this example:

```
<searchresults date="..." error="updating index, back soon"/>
```

If everything went well, the root element will contain a lot of `<named>` elements with the individual search results. Below these elements there will be further information about the place. A (simplified) response to a query for "Abbey Road, London" might look like this:

```
<searchresults find="Abbey Road, London">
  <named type="way" id="4235869" lat="51.537326" lon="-0.183789"
  name="Abbey Road" category="highway" rank="0" region="51280" zoom="16">
    <description>secondary road <strong>Abbey Road</strong> found less than 1km
    north-east of middle of suburb <strong>Maida Vale</strong> (which is about
    1km south-east of middle of town <strong>Kilburn</strong> and about 5km
    north-west of city <strong>London [fr:Londres] [nl:Londen]</strong> in
    England, United Kingdom, UK)</description>
      <place>
        <named type="node" id="107775" lat="51.507245" lon="-0.127806"
        name="London [fr:Londres] [nl:Londen]" category="place" rank="60"
        region="51280" is_in=" in England, United Kingdom, UK" info="city"
        distance="5.107711" approxdistance="5" direction="319" zoom="10">
        <nearestplaces>
          ...
        </nearestplaces>
      </named>
    </place>
  </named>
</searchresults>
```

In reality, a lot more information is returned about places in the vicinity. Which information the Name Finder returns also depends on the type of query. Details about query and response types are in the Name Finder wiki article.

23.3 **Nominatim**

Just like the Name Finder, Nominatim is an Open Source Geocoding engine for OpenStreetMap. It has been developed by Brian Quinion. The Nominatim source code is available from the OpenStreetMap SVN (`applications/utils/export/osm2pgsql/gazetteer`). You can run a search query directly on `http://nominatim.openstreetmap.org/`.

Nominatim uses a PostGIS database that is kept current using the "gazetteer" output option of the Osm2pgsql tool. This database has a structure wholly different from the rendering database that Osm2pgsql creates for use with Mapnik.

The Nominatim API

The URL `http://nominatim.openstreetmap.org/search`, followed by a question mark and a number of URL parameters, is the entry point for the Nominatim API.

Parameter	Usage
`format=[html|xml|json]`	The desired return format. Use "html" for a complete website, or "xml" or "json" to transmit only the search results encoded in one of these formats.
`accept-language=code`	The language code used for sorting the result set, and also for selecting names where multiple languages are given in OpenStreetMap.
`q=query`	The search word(s).
`polygon=[0|1]`	1 if you want outline polygons with your search results, where available.
`addressdetails=[0,1]`	1 if you want individual components of an address listed.
`viewbox=l,t,r,b`	The geographic area in which to perform the search (left, top, right, bottom, in latitude/longitude).

Nominatim isn't as verbose as the Name Finder in its search results. The following request:

`http://nominatim.openstreetmap.org/search?q=Abbey Road&format=xml&accept-language=en`

will for example yield a response like this:

```
<searchresults timestamp="Mon, 31 May 10 23:52:34 +0100" attribution="Data
  Copyright OpenStreetMap Contributors, Some Rights Reserved. CC-BY-SA 2.0."
  querystring="Abbey Road, London" polygon="false">

<place place_id="47216631" osm_type="way" osm_id="4235869"
  boundingbox="51.53166,51.54134,-0.19298,-0.17694"
  lat="51.540658" lon="-0.18961" display_name="Abbey Road, Maida Vale, Kilburn,
  City of Westminster, Greater London, NW8 6AG, United Kingdom"
  class="highway" type="secondary"/>
```

```
<place place_id="67673871" osm_type="way" osm_id="48865463"
  boundingbox="51.53166,51.539360,-0.18689,-0.17694" lat="51.5357003471959"
  lon="-0.18177" display_name="Abbey Road, Maida Vale, Kilburn, City of
  Westminster, Greater London, NW8 6AG, United Kingdom"
  class="highway" type="secondary"/>

<place place_id="47106053" osm_type="way" osm_id="2953911"
  boundingbox="51.64185,51.64600,-0.07492,-0.07056"
  lat="51.64434" lon="-0.072538" display_name="Abbey Road, Enfield, London
  Borough of Enfield, Greater London, N21 2AU, United Kingdom" class="highway"
  type="residential"/>

...
</searchresults>
```

Further information about Nominatim can be found on the wiki under Nominatim.

23.4 GeoNames

GeoNames (www.geonames.org) is a collection of free and open geodata that can be queried through a web interface or a web service, or even downloaded in its entirety. GeoNames collects information about the location of countries, regions, and cities, about postal codes and administrative hierarchies. If you search for "Washington" for example, you will find one that is classed "capital of a political entity", one that is a "first-order administrative division" (the state), numerous "second-order administrative divisions" (counties) and so on. GeoNames doesn't collect polygons, only points, but it is strong on proper classification and hierarchy, something that isn't always consistent in OpenStreetMap.

GeoNames isn't in any way affiliated with OpenStreetMap, but because it, too, collects free data and makes them available through a web interface, GeoNames can sometimes be used in addition to OSM. On the main OpenStreetMap website (www.openstreetmap.org), both GeoNames and Nominatim are queried if you search for a place name.

24 Osmosis, the Universal Tool

Osmosis (wiki: Osmosis) is a universal filtering and conversion program for OpenStreetMap data, developed in Java by Brett Henderson. Among other things, Osmosis offers much more advanced methods for downloading and updating OSM data than we have discussed earlier in chapter 15, namely going through the API or the Planet Dump.

The source code is in the OSM SVN repository under applications/utils/osmosis and requires Java 6 to run. You can also download a compiled version of Osmosis as a zip or tgz archive and then unpack it in any directory. The directory structure contains a subdirectory named bin, and this has ready-made scripts that call Osmosis with the required settings for Windows (bin\osmosis.bat) as well as Unix (bin/osmosis). If you modify your system search path (PATH) to include that directory, then you can run Osmosis just by entering osmosis at the command line. Otherwise you'll have to change to the installation directory before using Osmosis and always call it with bin in the name.

Osmosis generally uses a pipeline model when processing data: You have to specify a data source, then optionally a number of filtering or processing tasks, and then a destination; the data then flows through that "pipe" you have constructed. Osmosis doesn't read the data fully into memory, but processes it piece by piece, which allows most of Osmosis's tasks to process arbitrarily large datasets.

A typical data source, for example, is the --read-xml task, which reads an OpenStreetMap XML file. A typical destination, or *sink,* task is --write-xml, which writes a data stream into an XML file. Osmosis supports the gzip and bzip2 compression methods (file extensions .gz and .bz2). A simple, but admittedly rather useless, Osmosis command line uses these two tasks to copy from one file into another:

```
osmosis --read-xml file=sourcefile.osm
        --write-xml file=targetfile.osm
```

Pipeline tasks have full and shorthand names. Most tasks take one or more arguments that are given in the form `parameter=value` after the task name. Many tasks also have one default argument for which you can enter a value without needing to name the argument.

For the read and write tasks, the default argument is the file name, so you can omit `file=` and just write:

```
osmosis --read-xml sourcefile.osm
        --write-xml targetfile.osm
```

Tasks are connected by data streams. Generally, all data streams issued by a task will be put onto a stack in the proper order, and any task that consumes a data stream will take the top-most one from the stack. This method allows the modeling of very complex data flows on the command line. Figure 24-1 gives an example for such a stack operation.

For very complex command lines, this stack-based connecting of task inputs and outputs is not always sufficient, as you might want to have a task read from a different output than the one last added to the stack. If that is the case, you can explicitly assign names to the pipelines by adding an `outPipe.n=name` or `inPipe.n=name` argument (where n counts up from 0, for tasks that have more than one input or output pipe). The above example would then be written:

```
osmosis --read-xml sourcefile.osm outPipe.0=my-pipeline
        --write-xml targetfile.osm inPipe.0=my-pipeline
```

There are two major kinds of data streams: *Entity* streams, which transport the OSM data objects way, node, and relation; and *change streams,* which transport changes to such objects. Both kinds of streams can under certain circumstances transport several versions of the same OSM object. A change stream is called a *delta change stream* if it only contains the smallest amount of information that makes it possible to change an object from state A to state B, whereas a *history* or *replication change stream* also contains any intermediate states.

Some tasks consume or create multiple data streams. On the following pages we will describe the most important tasks, together with their arguments and input and output streams. The tables use "ES" for entity streams, and "CS" for change streams. Timestamps always use the form YYYY-MM-DD_HH:MM:SS.

Besides the streams there is also the concept of a *dataset*. A dataset isn't accessed in a streaming fashion but instead offers random access. It is typically provided by a database, and is denoted with "DS" in our tables.

The OpenStreetMap wiki has more details and examples on the Osmosis page, as well as links to installable packages.

24.1 Common Command Line Options

The common command line options start with a single dash, whereas tasks are given with two leading dashes.

Short	Long	Description
-v	-verbose	Show more messages about what Osmosis is doing (when followed by a number: Larger number = more).
-q	-quiet	Show fewer messages (can also be followed by a number).
-p	-plugin	Loads the given Java class as a plugin.

24.2 Reading and Writing XML Files

The following tasks can be used to read data from a file or from the OSM server or to write data to a file:

Short	Long	Description	Input	Output
--rx	--read-xml	Load an XML file.	XML file	1x ES
--wx	--write-xml	Write to an XML file.	1x ES	XML file
--ra	--read-api	Load data from the OSM server.	OSM server	1x ES

The --rx and --wx tasks take the file name as their argument. Compression is denoted by the file name extension (.osm for uncompressed files, .osm.gz or .osm.bz2 if the file is, or is to be, compressed with gzip or bzip2 respectively). You can also use a dash ("–") as the file name, which makes Osmosis read from standard input, or write to standard output. In these cases an additional parameter compressionMethod=gzip or bzip2 can be used to specify compression.[1] The --read-api task can load data directly from the OpenStreetMap API. It requires a bounding box to be specified via the parameters left, right, top, and bottom.

Some versions of Osmosis have a task called --fast-read-xml, which uses a different, faster XML parser compared to --rx, but otherwise works the same.

24.3 Reading and Writing Databases

Osmosis isn't limited to reading and writing files; it can also access a MySQL or PostgreSQL/PostGIS database in read or write mode.

---

1 The Java implementation of the bzip2 algorithm, which is used in Osmosis, is rather slow. If you are processing large files it is advisable to use an external program (bzcat, bzip2) for (de)compression and then let Osmosis read uncompressed data from standard input or write uncompressed data to standard output.

Database Access using the APIDB Schema

For MySQL and PostgreSQL, Osmosis supports the APIDB database schema, which is also used by the API server (see section 27.2 for a detailed description). This schema can hold historic versions of all objects, enabling Osmosis to perform operations like reporting all changes within a specified time frame. The APIDB schema doesn't make use of geometry objects.

Short	Long	Description	Input	Output
--rd	--read-apidb	Read data from database.	database	1x ES
--rdcur	--read-apidb-current	Read latest data from database.	database	1x ES
--wd	--write-apidb	Write data to (empty) database.	1x ES	database
--rdc	--read-apidb-change	Read changes between two timestamps from database.	database	1x CS
--wdc	--write-apidb-change	Apply changes to database.	1x CS	database
--td	--truncate-apidb	Empty database.	-	database

Several pieces of database access information (server name, database name, username, password, and the type of database) have to be given on the command line:

```
osmosis --rd host=localhost database=openstreetmap user=openstreetmap
            password=openstreetmap dbtype=mysql --wx output.osm.bz2
```

If you'd prefer not to pass access information on the command line for security reasons, you can use the authFile argument instead to specify a file containing that information.

When reading from an APIDB database, Osmosis looks at the full tables that contain all historic versions of every object, and retrieves the version of the object that was current when the program was started. This means that things stay consistent even if the data is changed while Osmosis is running. Alternatively, a timestamp can be given with the snapshotInstant argument to make --rd extract information for a different time. If you use --rdcur instead of --rd, Osmosis reads data from the "current" tables instead. This is faster, but may lead to an inconsistent snapshot if changes are made while Osmosis is running; only use it if no other processes access the database in parallel.

All database write access requires that the database schema has been set up beforehand. (For details of the schema see section 27.2.) When Osmosis writes to the database it will lock all tables against access by others. If you run Osmosis on a system where other processes have to access the database in parallel, you can ask it not to do that by specifying lockTables=no. If the database isn't intended to serve an OSM API server but only as an intermediate data storage, then the import speed can be increased greatly by adding the populateCurrentTables=no argument. This saves Osmosis from having to copy the most recent version of every object from the full tables to the "current" tables.

Database Access Using the PostGIS "Simple" Schema

When using a PostGIS database, Osmosis can also use the Simple schema. This is a hybrid of the original APIDB schema and the schema generated by osm2pgsql (see section 17.2). In the Simple schema, database geometry values are created for the OpenStreetMap objects. Osmosis can then execute some geometry operations, for example retrieving data for a given bounding box, with help from the database engine.

The Simple schema doesn't store historic versions.

The schema is contained in the `pgsql_simple_schema_0.6.sql` file in the script subdirectory of the Osmosis distribution. The Osmosis_PostGIS_Setup wiki article explains in detail how PostGIS is used with Osmosis.

Short	Long	Description	Input	Output
--rp	--read-pgsql	Load data from database.	database	1x DS
--wp	--write-pgsql	Write data to (empty) database.	1x ES	database
--fwp	--fast-write-pgsql	Like --wp but uses COPY commands (faster).	1x ES	database
--wpd	--write-pgsql-dump	Create dump files that can be loaded into database with COPY.	1x ES	files
--wpc	--write-pgsql-change	Apply changes to database.	1x CS	database
--tp	--truncate-pgsql	Empty database.	-	database

Database access information has to be provided in the same way as with the tasks using the APIDB schema. The introduction of --fwp is a recent development, and this task is likely to supersede both --wp and --wpd in the long run.

When data for a is written to a Simple schema database, Osmosis can either have the database compute a bounding box (the smallest enclosing rectangle) or a proper geometry object (or *linestring*, which describes the exact geometry of the way and takes longer to create). Bounding boxes are created automatically if a "bbox" column is present in the target table; linestrings are built if a "linestring" column is present. If you use the alternate options enableBboxBuilder=yes and enableLinestringBuilder=yes for the --write-psql task instead, Osmosis will compute these extra values in Java rather than have PostGIS do the job. Java is usually faster.

Setting Osmosis to read from a Simple schema database does not directly create an entity stream, but rather a dataset. The following tasks are defined for datasets:

Short	Long	Description	Input	Output
--dbb	--dataset-bounding-box	Extract rectangular area.	DS	ES
--dd	--dataset-dump	Convert dataset to entity stream.	DS	ES

24.4 Creating and Processing Change Files

The following tasks can create or process changes to OSM data:

Short	Long	Description	Input	Output
--dc	--derive-change	Find out changes.	2x ES	1x CS
--ac	--apply-change	Apply changes.	1x ES + 1x CS	1x ES
--rxc	--read-xml-change	Read a change file.	XML file	1x CS
--wxc	--write-xml-change	Save a change file.	1x CS	XML file
--rdc	--read-apidb-change	Find changes between two timestamps in a MySQL or PostGIS database.	database	1x CS
--wdc	--write-apidb-change	Apply changes to a MySQL or PostGIS database.	1x CS + database	(modified) database
--rri	--read-replication-interval	Read all changes since last call from the server.	OSM server	1x CS
--rrii	--read-replication-interval-init	Initialize a working directory for the task above.	-	-
--simc	--simplify-change	Create a simplified delta change stream from a history change stream.	1x CS	1x CS

A typical use of Osmosis is applying a daily (or hourly or minutely) change file from the OpenStreetMap server to a locally held data file. The following command applies the file changes.osc.gz to the existing planet-old.osm.gz and create a planet-new.osm.gz:

```
osmosis --rxc changes.osc.gz --rx planet-old.osm.gz --ac
        --wx planet-new.osm.gz
```

A valid Osmosis command line has to be written in such a way that all streams created by some task are also consumed by a task. You can visualize that by thinking of the internal stack where tasks place their output streams, and from where they take their input streams (see figure 24-1).

Applying a change file to a running APIDB database works in a similar fashion, but doesn't require the --ac task as you don't need to deal with an entity stream:

```
osmosis --rxc changes.osc.gz
        --wdc host=localhost database=openstreetmap user=openstreetmap
              password=openstreetmap dbtype=mysql
```

Again this requires database access information, which can be given on the command line or through a file named in the authFile argument.

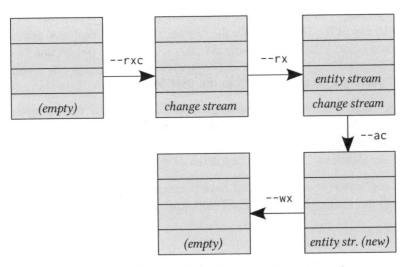

Figure 24-1: The Osmosis stack is changed by various tasks.

When applying a change file, Osmosis only applies those changes that aren't already known. Applying an older change file, or applying the same change file twice, won't normally cause any damage.[2]

If you are planning to start a continuously updated database by applying daily change files to a downloaded a Planet Dump, then it is a good idea to start with the change file from the day before the Planet Dump was created. This makes sure that your data is complete, as the Planet Dump generation and update file generation aren't synchronous. For example, if you initialize your database with a Planet Dump dated 22nd July 2010, first apply the change file containing the changes from 21st to 22nd July. Use a similar method (apply one extra file to ensure overlap) if you want to apply hourly or minutely changes.

To create a change file that contains the differences between two datasets stored in local files, run:

```
osmosis --rx file1.osm --rx file2.osm --dc --wxc changes.osc
```

The --rdc task can be used to determine changes between two timestamps in an APIDB database. You have to pass the timestamps in the usual format as the parameters intervalBegin and intervalEnd:

```
osmosis --rdc host=...
        intervalBegin=2010-07-01_00:00:00 intervalEnd=2010-07-31_23:59:59
        --wxc changes.osc.bz2
```

---

2 There are, however, exceptional cases where applying an old change file will re-create an already deleted object.

The --ac and --dc tasks rely on both input streams being sorted by type (node, way, relation), and then by object ID. This is already the case for the Planet File, but if you have an unsorted file you can sort a data stream using the tasks --s and --sc (see section 24.7).

Continuously Updating a Local Dataset from the OSM Server

Osmosis can be used to continuously update a local dataset from the OpenStreetMap server. Osmosis can determine which change files have been added at the server side since it was last run, and download them all. They can then be saved to a file for later processing with programs like Osm2pgsql, or applied to a database directly.

In order to run continuous updates, you first have to create a working directory by running the --rrii (short for: read-replication-interval-initialize) task:

```
mkdir ~/osm-update
osmosis --rrii ~/osm-update
```

Osmosis creates a file named configuration.txt in the given directory. That file can be changed to influence the download behavior. Among other things, the baseURL directive can be changed to control where Osmosis loads updates from. By default this will be http://planet.openstreetmap.org/minute-replicate, meaning that Osmosis reads minutely change files from the OSM server. You can change this to load hourly or daily change files (see section 15.2 for more on change files). Once this is set up, Osmosis can be run at regular intervals, for example through a "cron" job on Unix:

```
osmosis --rri ~/osm-update --simc --wxc changes.osc
```

The file so created contains all changes since Osmosis has last been run in that fashion, and can be used to update a local database. Osmosis saves its current state (the time and database transaction ID of the last synchronization) in a file named state.txt in the working directory, so that it will always download only the required files no matter how often or how seldom you call it. Even if the availability of change files was delayed on the server, that would simply delay the update process but not derail it. The file is created when you run Osmosis with --rri for the first time. If you want replication to start not at the current time but in the past, for example to match a downloaded dataset, you need to place a state.txt file in the working directory that matches the desired replication start time. You can download that file from the download directory specified in the configuration file (for example http://planet.openstreetmap.org/minute-replicate).

In addition to --rrii and --rri there is also an older set of tasks named --rcii and --rci, which store the current state in timestamp.txt and not in state.txt. These can only be used for daily updates, not for hourly or minutely ones.

A more detailed discussion of storing and updating OSM data in a local database can be found in chapter 27.

24.5 Filtering by Geography or Tags

Osmosis can extract a geographic area from a data stream, or select objects that match certain conditions:

Short	Long	Description	Input	Output
--bb	--bounding-box	Extract rectangular area.	1x ES	1x ES
--bp	--bounding-polygon	Extract polygon.	1x ES + polygon file	1x ES
--nk	--node-key	Copy nodes with certain keys only.	1x ES	1x ES
--nkv	--node-key-value	Copy nodes with certain key-value combinations only.	1x ES	1x ES
--wk	--way-key	Copy ways with certain keys only.	1x ES	1x ES
--wkv	--way-key-value	Copy ways with certain key-value combinations only.	1x ES	1x ES
--un	--used-nodes	Copy only those nodes that are used by ways.	1x ES	1x ES

The --bb task takes the arguments left, bottom, right, and top (in any order) using latitude and longitude to determine the rectangular area to be extracted:

```
osmosis --rx planet.osm.bz2
        --bb left=-73.9 right=-73.3 top=45.7 bottom=45.3
        --wx montreal.osm.bz2
```

If you use the --bp task, you have to specify a polygon definition through the file parameter:

```
osmosis --rx planet.osm.bz2 --bp file=illinois.poly
        --wx illinois.osm.bz2
```

The polygon definition file is a plain text file that may contain one or more polygons, including polygons that have holes. You can see some examples of such polygon files on the website for this book (www.openstreetmap.info).

Both --bp and --bb normally only copy nodes that lie inside the requested area. Ways are copied if at least one of their nodes is inside the requested area. Relations are copied if one of their members is copied. This means that the output file will normally contain unmodified, original OSM objects; but the file might not have referential integrity because there might be ways using nodes that are outside of the area, and thus not present in the file.

There are two ways to deal with such potential inconsistencies. The simplest solution is to use the extra argument clipIncompleteEntities=yes. This will remove references to objects that aren't contained in the output. The result is a consistent output file, but one in which some ways or relations may have lost some members. The alternative is to use the arguments `completeWays=yes` and `completeRelations=yes` (the latter includes the former). With these, Osmosis copies all nodes and ways to a temporary file. Later, when a way or relation is copied that includes one of these objects outside of the requested area, they can be added in from the file. This procedure goes against the pipeline concept normally used by Osmosis, and it is much slower than running Osmosis in the usual way.

With `--nk`, `--nkv`, `--wk`, and `--wkv`, you can tell Osmosis to copy only objects that have certain tags. You have to pass an additional argument called `keyList` or `keyValueList` respectively, which is the list of keys (or key/value combinations). If an object matches one of the items in the list, it will be copied. List items have to be separated by commas, and a dot has to be used to separate keys from values. The `--nk` and `--nkv` tasks only act on nodes and don't copy anything else. The `--wk` and `--wkv` tasks will only act on ways and copy all nodes and relations, unless you specify `--un` afterward, which will copy only those nodes which are referenced by a way. The command

```
osmosis --rx england.osm --wkv highway.motorway,highway.motorway_link
        --un --wx motorway.osm
```

reads the input file `england.osm` and selects from it all ways tagged either with `highway=motorway` or with `highway=motorway_link`. It then removes all nodes not used by any of these ways, and writes the result to `motorway.osm`.

24.6 Merging and Multiplying Data Streams

The following tasks can merge or multiply data streams:

Short	Long	Description	Input	Output
`--m`	`--merge`	Merge entity streams.	2x ES	1x ES
`--mc`	`--merge-change`	Merge change streams.	2x CS	1x CS
`--apc`	`--append-change`	Concatenate change streams.	2x CS	1x CS
`--t`	`--tee`	Multiply entity stream.	1x ES	n x ES
`--tc`	`--tee-change`	Multiply change stream.	1x CS	n x CS

You can use `--m` for example to merge multiple OSM files saved with JOSM into one large file for rendering or other processing:

```
osmosis --rx part1.osm --rx part2.osm
        --m --wx result.osm
```

Conversely, the `--t` task duplicates an entity stream (or a numeric argument can be given with the command to create more than two streams). This makes sense if you want to apply a number of different filters to the same input file, because it is faster to read the file once and then do several things with the data than having to read it again and again. The following command cuts out three different polygons from the same input file:

```
osmosis --rx planet.osm --t 3
        --bp file=p1.poly --wx output1.osm
        --bp file=p2.poly --wx output2.osm
        --bp file=p3.poly --wx output3.osm
```

This multiplies the input stream by three, and runs a polygon filter and an XML writer task on each of the resulting streams. It is important to specify the polygon filters and write operations in this order, otherwise Osmosis would try to run the second polygon filter on the output of the first. If you find this too difficult and error-prone, you can assign symbolic names to all the data streams:

```
osmosis --rx planet.osm outPipe.0=planet
        --t 3 inPipe.0=planet outPipe.0=duplicate1
            outPipe.1=duplicate2 outPipe.2=duplicate3
        --bp file=p1.poly inPipe.0=duplicate1 outPipe.0=excerpt1
        --wx output1.osm inPipe.0=excerpt1
        --bp file=p2.poly inPipe.0=duplicate2 outPipe.0=excerpt2
        --wx output2.osm inPipe.0=excerpt2
        --bp file=p3.poly inPipe.0=duplicate3 outPipe.0=excerpt3
        --wx output3.osm inPipe.0=excerpt3
```

If you use this explicit naming, the order of the tasks isn't relevant any more.

The --tc and --mc tasks work in a similar fashion, but they apply to change streams rather than entity streams. This, for example, allows you to combine multiple change files into one and then apply that to another dataset. The difference between --mc and --apc is that --mc only keeps the newest version of every object, whereas --apc simply joins the files and may thereby also keep intermediate versions. The output of --apc is unsorted.

24.7 Other Tasks

The following is a list of other tasks that can be useful:

Short	Long	Description	Input	Output
--re	--report-entity	List of processed objects.	1x ES	text file
--ri	--report-integrity	Analyze data integrity.	1x ES	text file
--lp	--log-progress	Display progress information.	1x ES	1x ES
--lpc	--log-progress-change	Display progress information.	1x CS	1x CS
--wn	--write-null	Do nothing.	1x ES	-
--wnc	--write-null-change	Do nothing.	1x CS	-
--s	--sort	Sort an entity stream.	1x ES	1x ES
--sc	--sort-change	Sort a change stream.	1x CS	1x CS
--b	--buffer	Buffer an entity stream.	1x ES	1x ES
--bc	--buffer-change	Buffer a change stream.	1x CS	1x CS

The --re and --ri tasks each create a textual report about the data that has been read. If you specify --lp or --lpc then Osmosis gives you a progress update at regular intervals while processing data. If you want to play with Osmosis command line options you can use the data sinks (they aren't really output tasks) --wn or --wnc to suppress output.

The --s and --sc sorting tasks are required if you want to process unsorted input data with --derive-change or if you want to apply a change file to an unsorted entity stream using --apply-change. Some older Osmosis versions required that you write --sort-0.6 to process version 0.6 data but that has been fixed in newer versions.

The --b and --bc tasks implement a data buffer of configurable size between two tasks. This is likely to speed up processing on multiprocessor machines, because without a buffer data can only be processed sequentially even if additional processors are available. In the case of the simple copying example

```
osmosis --rx input.osm.bz2 --wx output.osm.bz2
```

this would mean: While an object is read and decompressed, the output task sits idle; and then while the object is compressed and written, the input task is idle. On a machine with one processor this doesn't make a difference, but if more than one processor is available, then one could already be reading the next object while the other is still busy writing the previous one. And this requires a buffer:

```
osmosis --rx input.osm.bz2 --b --wx output.osm.bz2
```

This little change may yield a 20% performance increase on a multiprocessor machine, and using --b in more complex command lines can improve processing speed even more.

24.8 Processing Old Data Files

Until March 2009 OpenStreetMap used the API version 0.5, and therefore all OSM files saved at that time still use the 0.5 format, which is slightly different from that used for 0.6. Most importantly, 0.5 files don't have a changeset ID and a version number for each object.

For a transition period, Osmosis still supports both data formats; the default data format is the current 0.6, but all tasks for which it makes a difference are also available in a version that works with 0.5 files (just add -0.5 to the full name of the task, e. g. --read-xml-0.5).

There are two special tasks called --migrate and --migrate-change that you can use to convert a 0.5 data stream into its 0.6 equivalent.

If you need to load a 0.5 file into a 0.6 database for example, you can write:

```
osmosis --read-xml-0.5 input.osm --migrate --write-apidb host=localhost
        dbtype=mysql user=osm password=osm database=osm
```

24.9 Osmosis Plugins

Osmosis has a plugin interface that allows the addition of arbitrary tasks without having to compile Osmosis. Plugins are added to Osmosis by placing a zip file into the user directory ~/.openstreetmap/osmosis/plugins (or the equivalent directory under "application data" on a Windows system). The Osmosis wiki page has up-to-date information about available plugins.

One widely used plugin is TagTransform, which supports mapping from one set of tags to another set, which helps with normalizing an OSM file. TagTransform could for example replace every oneway=true tag with oneway=yes.

24.10 Alternatives to Osmosis

When Osmosis was less developed, many of the tasks now routinely executed by Osmosis were being done using small individual utilities. Although we expect that Osmosis will sooner or later make all of them redundant, some of these programs still make sense for niche tasks, so they are mentioned here. All programs are in the SVN repository.

Filtering by Tags

The Perl script planetosm-excerpt-tags.pl (to be found in the SVN repository under applications/utils/osm-extract/) can make "thematic" excerpts from an OSM file, i. e. filter by tags. The first lines of the program configure which tags to select. For ways, such a selection would look like:

```
my @way_sel_tags = (
    ['railway', undef],
    ['highway', 'motorway']
);
```

This would create an OSM file which has all ways with any kind of railway tag and all ways tagged with highway=motorway.

Osmosis has almost the same functionality (see section 24.5) but cannot yet select relations according to their tags, something that this Perl script is capable of.

Filtering by Geography

The planetosm-excerpt-bbox.pl utility can cut out a rectangular area from an OSM file (comparable to Osmosis's –bb task):

```
perl planetosm-excerpt-bbox.pl -bbox=bottom,left,top,right in.osm >out.osm
```

Both filtering programs work very much like the Osmosis filter tasks, but they always copy all referenced nodes, just as if you were to use completeWays=yes with Osmosis. The Perl scripts don't however use temporary files; they store everything in memory.

In the directory applications/utils/osm-extract/osmcut there is a program that can be used to split an OSM file into rectangles of constant size.

If you want to cut out polygons from OSM data (comparable to Osmosis's --bp task) you can use a C implementation from applications/utils/osm-extract/extract-polygon-c or a Perl program from applications/utils/osm-extract/polygons; the Perl program has more options (for example it supports polygons with holes), but it is slower and more memory hungry.

25 Advanced Editing

Any technically savvy person working with OpenStreetMap will quickly reach the point where they want to make more significant changes that require more sophisticated techniques. This could be the large-scale fixing of a tagging mistake, repairing an import that has gone awry, or the cleaning up of a case of vandalism.

Before we start discussing various "power editing" techniques, a note of caution. Whatever you do with OpenStreetMap, always consider that this is a project made by people for people, and always respect the work of others. The overwhelming majority of mappers want to make OpenStreetMap better; if someone breaks something it's usually a misunderstanding or an operator error, and rarely an act of deliberate vandalism. Also, many mappers have their own style – they may interpret different aspects of the "map features" page differently, or pay more attention to certain details. It would be wrong to patronize them by "fixing" their work on a large scale.

Every now and again someone in OpenStreetMap picks some rule from the wiki at random and writes a script that enforces that rule with blanket coverage, causing consternation among others in the project. Of course this is always done with the best intentions, but still it upsets others, who may have deviated from common usage for a good reason. Before you start making any large-scale changes or an (assumed) "correction", you should always make an attempt to contact those whose data you are planning to change, or discuss the issue on one of the relevant mailing lists (see section 3.2). The wiki Automated Edits page has a suggestion for a code of conduct for automated edits.

This chapter discusses some techniques to make complex or large-scale changes to the OpenStreetMap database with little or no programming effort, and offers some advice for those writing software that performs such tasks.

25.1 Large-Scale Changes Using the Editor

A lot of complicated changes can be effected using the sophisticated OSM editors, with no programming required at all. For example, if you want to take all post boxes in a large area and add operator=United States Postal Service to them where they don't yet have an operator tag, you can do this in JOSM as follows:

- Download the area in question.
- Search for "amenity:post_box" to select all post boxes.
- Search for "selected -operator". This will reduce the selection to all post boxes without an operator tag.
- Use the properties dialog to add the operator=United States Postal Service tag. The change will be applied to all selected objects.
- Upload your changes.

If you need more information on searching with JOSM look back at section 10.4.

If you want to execute similar changes on an area which is too large to be loaded from the server in one go, you can also use JOSM to open a file that you have downloaded via XAPI (see section 23.1). Let us assume that all "Kiwi Fried Chicken" fast food outlets were acquired by rival chain McMonroe's; then you could use this URL to download all fast food restaurants in England:

```
http://www.informationfreeway.org/api/0.6/node[amenity=fast_food]
    [bbox=-6.5,49.6,2.2,55.9]
```

Save the resulting file, and open it in JOSM or another editor. You can then search for name:Kiwi Fried Chicken and replace that globally. Alternatively, you could have instructed XAPI to search for objects with the right name tag but then you would have had to be careful not to modify something that wasn't a fast food restaurant – XAPI can use only one condition at a time.

This technique has its limitations where the total amount of data is larger than that which can be sensibly loaded into the editor, or where the modification rules are so complex that they can't be processed by searching and replacing.

25.2 Undeleting Objects

There is currently no API call that returns a list of all deleted objects in an area. If an object's ID is known, it can be used to access the full history of the object. But some research is required if you don't have an ID.

... With Potlatch

Potlatch has the capability of showing all deleted ways in the current map view and undeleting them on request. This includes all nodes used by the way. Undeleting single nodes
that aren't part of a way, and undeleting relations, isn't possible. Potlatch uses a special
private API call to access deleted objects in an area. There is more about undeleting data
with Potlatch in section 9.6.

... Using an Old Planet Dump

The web server planet.openstreetmap.org has a complete database dump for almost
every week from the past few years. Thus it is possible to download an older data dump
and extract a region of interest from it with suitable tools (e. g. Osmosis, as discussed in
chapter 24). However it won't be possible to simply take some objects from an old dump
and upload them because uploading only works if the current version number of an object
is known. You have to request the history of every recovered object from the API and
modify the recovered objects to match the highest version number on the API. You can also
download one of the infrequently published Full History Planets, which contain the full history of all objects, to find out about the ones that have been deleted. There are no tools yet
that work with these files because that concept is still relatively young.

... With Change Files

If the time of deletion is known, even approximately, you can also check the daily change
file for the day in question. These files are on http://planet.openstreetmap.org/daily/
and contain all changes that have been made during the day. The oscgrep.pl utility from
the SVN repository can find certain edits in these files. It is called like this:

```
perl oscgrep.pl [-a action] [-r regex] [-t type] [file] [file...]
```

For action you can put one of create, modify, or delete. For type, put node, way, or
relation. Finally regex may be any Perl compatible regular expression, which oscgrep.pl
will apply to the full XML of the object. The program reads files from standard input, or
from file names supplied on the command line. The command

```
perl oscgrep.pl -a delete -t node -r 'user="Ben78"' 20090126-20090127.osc.gz
```

extracts all deletions of nodes performed by user "Ben78" from the given file. The output
looks like this:

```
<delete>
    <node id="247314838" version="7" timestamp="2009-01-26T21:46:09Z" uid="2274"
        user="Ben78" lat="52.2145611" lon="-1.1367269">
      <tag k="created_by" v="JOSM"/>
    </node>
</delete>
```

```
<delete>
    <node id="247314841" version="2" timestamp="2009-01-26T21:46:09Z" uid="2274"
        user="Ben78" lat="52.2146191" lon="-1.1368981">
      <tag k="created_by" v="JOSM"/>
    </node>
</delete>
...
```

In this special case (when nodes are deleted), the OSC file really contains all data for the node, even though the ID and version would be sufficient to effect a deletion. A script that takes these nodes and uploads them to the server with the same node ID and a version number increased by one would be trivial to write. In other cases, when for example a way has been deleted or a node has been moved, things are a little more challenging, and you have to do a history request against the API first to find out the previous state of the object before you can upload it.

Daily change files are archived for about two weeks on the server. If you think that you will often want to analyze such files, it makes sense to keep a local mirror.

... From Changesets

Since API 0.6 changes are combined into changesets, and there are API calls to retrieve all changesets affecting a given area or time span (see section 22.5). It is also possible to download all changes made within a changeset; the result of such a query is an OsmChange document much like the code example shown above.

25.3 Making Automated Changes

A program that commits changes automatically – perhaps even on a regular basis – is called a *bot* (short for: *robot*). Bots aren't an established tradition in OpenStreetMap. While projects like Wikipedia have fixed procedures describing what to do if someone wants to set up a bot, and what the bot may and may not do, all this is still in its infancy within OpenStreetMap.

The aforementioned Automated Edits wiki page is a good starting point. It has links to software that may be useful as a basis for writing bots, and information about existing bots and their operators. Let us however stress again: Everything you program a bot to do has to be discussed with the affected community at least on one of the relevant mailing lists, before it is run. Otherwise you risk far-reaching opposition, and may create discord in the community.

A typical bot will process an input file with OSM data – a Planet Dump, or an excerpt from it, or even an update file – and find those objects it wants to change. It will then prepare an OsmChange document (see section 6.2) and upload that to the server, either directly or using a third-party upload script. If some of the objects that the bot wants to modify have been changed by someone else in the mean time, the API returns error messages that the bot has to process suitably. If the bot wants to reduce the risk of such conflicts, it can download every object again shortly before attempting to change them.

It is considered good practise to make bot edits obvious, for example by creating a special OSM user account or at least add a proper created_by tag to all changesets. A bot should also use a custom User Agent header when accessing the API.

25.4 Reverting Changes

The Potlatch editor can revert a single way to a previous version (see section 9.6). Now that changesets are ubiquitous, we will surely soon see end-user tools for reverting whole changesets or even larger groups of edits – but we aren't quite there yet. As things stand, you still have to apply some programming knowledge if you want to revert edits. This section explains the basics, and potential pitfalls.

Reverting to a Previous Version

To change an object back to a previous version, you usually have to download the object's history first:

```
http://www.openstreetmap.org/api/0.6/way/4888299/history
```

The result of such a request is a list of all versions of the node, way, or relation in question, sorted by time:

```
<osm version="0.6" generator="OpenStreetMap server">
  <way id="22726557" visible="true" timestamp="2008-01-27T22:23:16Z"
user="dolphinpix" uid="25096" version="1" changeset="702425">
    <nd ref="243770748"/>
    <nd ref="243770120"/>
...
    <nd ref="243770799"/>
    <tag k="created_by" v="Potlatch 0.6c"/>
    <tag k="highway" v="secondary"/>
  </way>
...
  <way id="22726557" visible="true" timestamp="2008-08-08T19:08:26Z" user="tommg"
uid="6637" version="3" changeset="139894">
    <nd ref="243770120"/>
    <nd ref="243770749"/>
...
    <nd ref="243770799"/>
    <tag k="created_by" v="Potlatch 0.6c"/>
    <tag k="highway" v="secondary"/>
  </way>
```

```
   <way id="22726557" visible="true" timestamp="2009-07-09T19:34:48Z" user="tim"
uid="2919" version="5" changeset="1783233">
      <nd ref="243770120"/>
      <nd ref="243770749"/>
   ...
      <nd ref="286296047"/>
      <tag k="created_by" v="JOSM"/>
      <tag k="highway" v="tertiary"/>
   </way>
   ...
   <way id="22726557" visible="false" timestamp="2009-08-08T07:47:53Z" user="greg"
uid="7037" version="6" changeset="2072245"/>
</osm>
```

In this example, a way has been created as a secondary road with Potlatch, later changed into a tertiary road using JOSM, and finally deleted. You can see some created_by tags in the output: They aren't used in that fashion any more since we now place them on changesets, but you still find them in history data.

If you want to go back to a previous version, you first have to find out which version that is. Sometimes someone will have said "something has been broken on <date>, we need the last good version before that", or "user X has committed vandalism in this area and we need the last good version before their edit"; in these cases you can find the requested "last good version" from the history. A special case of this is of course where the first element in the history is actually not wanted – then the object has to be deleted in order to go back to the "last good version".

Once it is clear which version needs to be restored, the data for that version can simply be uploaded to the API using the matching upload URL (with the PUT method, and after having adjusted the version number to the latest version, see chapter 22). Going back to an old version is really not any different to making a new edit. The Potlatch editor has started the convention of adding the tag history=retrieved from v# (where # = old version number) in these cases.

Sequencing Revert Operations

Often you want to change more than one object back to a previous state, perhaps even roll back a whole area to the state it was a day or so previously. To effect the desired reversion, some objects have to be undeleted, some have to be deleted, and some changed back. This can cause dependency problems between different operations: A node can't be deleted if a way is still using it; a way can't be created if it tries to use a non-existent node. Combining all these changes in one changeset upload doesn't automatically solve the problem; the order of operations must still be such that the database is consistent all the time.

Dependency problems can largely be avoided by dividing all changes into three groups. Firstly, undelete everything that has been deleted (nodes first, then ways, then relations).

Next, restore all modified objects (again first the nodes, then the ways, then the relations). Finally, delete everything that has been created (this time starting with relations, then ways, then nodes).

Finding Out What to Revert

Reverting something to an earlier state is a more general form of undeleting, which we have discussed earlier. On the whole, you can use the same range of methods to find out which changes you need to revert. If the changes to be reverted all belong to the same changeset, or at least to a small number of known changesets, then the list of modified objects can be read from those changesets. If changes are spread across too many changesets, it may be better to evaluate the daily change files with the oscgrep.pl script as discussed earlier, or extract an old version from a Planet Dump.

Utilities

The OpenStreetMap SVN has a range of helpful programs for reversions and other tasks, at applications/utils/revert. You will find programs to manually open changesets, upload changes, undelete (or delete) objects, and revert whole changesets.

These programs are only meant to be used by experienced mappers. They are useful in many situations, but don't work in all cases. For example, while they can fully revert a changeset, things can become difficult if some objects have meanwhile been changed by others.

We advise you not to use these programs if you are uncertain about any aspect of the API, or if you don't understand Perl (the programming language in which they are written). You need to be confident that you can repair any damage should things go wrong.

26 Import and Export

OpenStreetMap doesn't exist in a vacuum: There are other collections of geodata, some of which can be imported, if it is under a free license or has been freed specifically for OpenStreetMap. Also people want to export OSM data to use it in non-related programs and projects.

26.1 General Data Import Issues

As with other aspects of OpenStreetMap, a general rule is to get in touch with the community first if you are planning something large, so that people won't be surprised. Discuss beforehand how much data you want to import, what kind of data it is, and when you are planning to do it. Also, get community buy-in for whatever postprocessing or review might be needed afterward. In many cases it makes sense to test the import on a small area to gain experience.

There is no standard way that geodata can be imported into OpenStreetMap. In most cases you need to write your own converter program or perhaps use an existing converter customized to the data being imported.

Read the remarks about automated edits of OSM data in section 25.3, as they apply to imports as well.

Bulk Import

One approach often used for imports is to create OSM files from the source data in a format compatible with JOSM. All objects must be given negative IDs (see section 10.6). When uploading the data to the server JOSM automatically converts the negative numbers to the ones assigned by the server and makes sure all references work.

In the SVN directory `applications/utils/import/bulk_import` you can find a Perl script that basically does the same; it is very suitable for imports. Documentation is on the Bulk import.pl wiki page. The program doesn't expect JOSM files but wants OsmChange documents as input.

For every such import you need some conversion rules that describe which attributes in the original data should be converted to which OSM tags. You have to be extra careful when there are conflicts with existing data. In these cases you could exclude such areas from your import, or you could import the new data with special tags and let interested people re-tag them with the right tags as they consolidate the two datasets.

GPX Imports

Depending on the type and size of the source data it might make sense to convert the data into the GPX format and treat it like GPS tracks. That way no objects are created automatically, but mappers can use those fake GPS tracks as a background in their editors and create objects based on them. This approach is especially good in areas where there is a lot of data in OSM already.

Many editors allow you to convert GPX data into OSM geometries automatically. For point data (Points of Interest) this is easy and efficient, but for lines and areas it generally leads to a lot of work afterward.

Tracing from Printed Maps or Images

Tracing from printed maps or images takes considerable preparation. The source first must be scanned and the resulting image orthorectified (i. e. warped) so that it conforms to the map, before you can use it as a background image in an editor. You can find some notes about this in the JOSM chapter on page 137. The free GIS program QGIS also has some functions for aligning images and now even has an experimental OSM editor included.

Some images' sources are available as a WMS service. In this case you can already use them as background images in some editors. Some editors have special functions to help with tracing detail – like the JOSM Lakewalker plugin.

26.2 Importing Shapefiles

Lots of geodata uses the shapefile format or can be converted into it. There are two import programs for OpenStreetMap that you can use, after suitable adaptation, to create OSM files from shapefiles. Both are in SVN under `applications/utils/import/shp2osm`.

Shapefiles can use an arbitrary projection and map datum. If you have shapefiles in a projection other than WGS 84 (EPSG:4326), you have to convert the coordinates before you can import them into OSM. One way to do this is through the `ogr2ogr` utility from the free GDAL library.

The shp2osm Program

You can use this Perl program to extract linear features (for instance roads or rivers) from shapefiles. It will convert all attributes in the shapefile into OSM tags. Because you probably have very different attributes in your shapefile, you either have to edit the shapefile to have the right attributes beforehand or edit the resulting OSM file.

Please note that shapefiles don't contain a topology. If you import a road network, for instance, there will be no common node at a crossroads as is needed for OpenStreetMap. Depending on the source data you instead have either no node at all at that location or possibly several (one for each line geometry).

It is possible to clean up the resulting data in JOSM using the Validator plugin, which will combine multiple nodes at the same spot. Adding missing nodes at intersections has to be done manually though.

The polyshp2osm Program

The `polyshp2osm` Python program is intended for importing areas such as lakes, forests, or buildings. It has a conversion table from shapefile attributes into OpenStreetMap tags. The comments in the source code tell you how to customize it for your needs.

Import of Point Geometries

There is no import program for point geometries but shapefiles with point geometries can easily be converted to GPX (for instance with `ogr2ogr`) and then into OSM using a suitable OSM editor.

26.3 Data Export

There are several ways to convert OSM data into other formats. But because most other formats don't have the flexibility inherent in the OSM tagging schema you have to customize the export for each case. Inevitably you will lose some data. For instance the shapefiles common in the GIS world can't reproduce the topology in the OSM data and they can't work with arbitrary tags, but need a fixed attribute list. For that reason, there is no simple conversion software that will "just work" without configuration.

If you want to export the data into typical GIS formats (shapefiles, PostGIS, ...), the use of a PostgreSQL database as an intermediate stage may be the solution. You can either use Osmosis (see section 24.3) or Osm2pgsql (see section 17.2) to import the data into the database. Depending on what you want to do with the data, either approach could have its advantages. In any case you probably need to do more conversion steps inside the PostgreSQL database.

Some other export programs can be found the `applications/utils/export` directory of the Subversion repository. Unfortunately most of those scripts are out of date and badly maintained.

Export using Osmexport

Osmexport (`osmlib.rubyforge.org`) is a Ruby library for exporting OSM data into several formats. Currently shapefiles, KML and CSV are supported. The tool reads an OSM file and a file with rules, converts the data according to the rules, and writes them into one or more output files.

The rules are necessary because the different data formats have very different structures and a direct mapping between formats isn't possible. You have to decide which format is best suited for your needs and how you want to convert the data and customize the rules accordingly.

Osmexport is a very flexible tool but can be slow. It is not suitable for converting large amounts of data.

It is easiest to use the Rubygems tool to install Osmexport:

```
gem install osmlib-export
```

This will put the `osmexport` program in your path. (On Debian the executable will be installed into `/var/lib/gems/<RUBY-VERSION>/bin`. You have to add this directory into your path or add a symlink for instance from `/usr/local/bin/osmexport`.)

Osmexport is called with:

```
osmexport rule.oxr data.osm outputfile
```

In this case the rule file `rule.oxr` is read, the OSM data comes from the file `data.osm`, and the output goes into `outputfile`. It depends on your rule file which output format you are converting into. If the output format is shapefile or CSV you won't get one output file but a directory containing several files instead.

There are some example rules files in the Osmexport package, or you can browse them at `http://osmlib.rubyforge.org/svn/osmlib-export/trunk/examples/`.

26.4   Exporting Bitmap and Vector Images

For further processing in graphics programs outside the GIS world or for printing you probably want to export OpenStreetMap maps as bitmap or vector images. Some of that can be done with the Export tab on the OpenStreetMap website – we have covered that in section 2.1 already.

Bitmap Exports

If you want to export an OSM into a bitmap file larger than that which the OpenStreetMap Export tab allows, you can use a utility called Bigmap. You can assemble a map of any size from the website http://openstreetmap.gryph.de/bigmap.cgi, starting from the URL of a central map tile, or based on tile coordinates. The website doesn't directly create the map but produces a small Perl script. You can run this script on your computer to load the necessary map tiles from the server and assemble them into one large image. For this to be possible you need a working Perl installation with the GD library on your computer. Note, however, that this procedure downloads a large number of tiles and thus may, if the image is too big, fall foul of the tile server usage policy.

An alternate solution for creating large bitmaps is the Windows renderer Kosmos (or its successor Maperitive), which we have covered in chapter 18. Kosmos can export bitmaps up to a size of 10,000 by 10,000 pixels and can render for configurable print resolutions.

It is often difficult to print high resolution bitmaps when the font sizes and line widths are optimized for the screen. Either you have to enlarge the image for printing to get readable letters, which may result in the images being pixelated, or the font may be too small if you use the full resolution.

Vector Exports

If you want more than the Export tab on the website has to offer for a Vector export you have to use Osmarender (see chapter 16) or the Mapnik renderer (see chapter 17). Both can output vector data, Mapnik can create PDF or SVG files, Osmarender can only create SVG files, which can then be converted into PDF with a program like Inkscape. In any case you have to use suitable rendering rules: If you create a map for a whole country including every dirt road you won't be able to process this huge and highly complex file in any application.

If you want to postprocess the vector file, it is probably easier to have used Osmarender because it exports texts labels as real text whereas Mapnik exports the texts as curves, which makes them very hard to edit.

There is also an "osm2ai" utility in SVN, which creates very basic Adobe Illustrator files from OpenStreetMap data. This utility doesn't export any styling information, so all you get is the bare grid of lines.

Printing high resolution images from vector data generally yields good-looking results but bear in mind that the vector files will be huge, which places great demands on the graphic programs you use.

The Open Source service MapOSMatic (www.maposmatic.org) offers the automated production of PDF city maps including a street index. You only have to choose a place or make a map selection and after a few minutes you get the generated PDF file. An example MapOSMatic map is shown in color plate 23.

WMS Servers

OpenStreetMap doesn't operate a WMS server. If you want to access OSM data through a WMS, you can either make use of a third-party service, or set up your own WMS.

Third-party WMS servers are available from a variety of providers. There are limited free services (most don't cover the whole world, or are updated infrequently, or have reduced image quality because they are based on pre-rendered bitmaps), and there are commercial services that offer a wider range of features but cost money. A list of WMS providers is on the WMS wiki page.

If you want to set up your own WMS, you can either use a product like UMN Map Server and load it with OSM shapefiles, or you can set up the ogcserver component that is part of the Mapnik package. Details on this are at http://trac.mapnik.org/wiki/OgcServer.

27 Running an OSM Server

In this chapter we explain the steps needed to run your own, regularly updated, OpenStreetMap API or tile server.

27.1 Running Your Own API Server

There are many reasons for running your own OpenStreetMap server, for instance to:

- Do software development and testing on the API.
- Use OSM software on computers without (or with limited) Internet access.
- Have really fast read access for many requests.

If you install an OSM server with the software from the repository, you can do everything the "real" OSM server can do.

Requirements

If you want to run your own OpenStreetMap server system, you need the web framework Ruby on Rails (rubyonrails.org) and a suitable database (ideally PostgreSQL, but running the server with MySQL is possible with some restrictions). These components are available for Windows, Linux, and OS X. You can expect the fewest hurdles on Ubuntu Linux, because the central OSM server itself uses that operating system.

The use of web server software is optional, Ruby on Rails comes with its own little web server, which is sufficient for testing purposes.

Installation and Configuration

Platform specific installation tips for the Ruby on Rails environment are available from the wiki page The Rails Port. Generally the steps are as follows:

- Install the PostgreSQL database.
- Install Ruby, Rubygems, and Rails (for most distributions its recommended to install Rails not from a distribution package, but through the Ruby package mechanism where packages are called Gems).
- Change into a suitable directory and download the OSM server from the git repository and some more Gems after that:

```
cd my_directory
git clone git://git.openstreetmap.org/rails.git
cd rails
rake gems:install
```

- Create a database instance by running the PostgreSQL commands `createdb` and `createuser`, make sure the user can access the database, and create a `database.yml` file in the config subdirectory based on the provided `postgres.example.database.yml`, configuring your database and user name. Then initialize the database using

```
rake db:migrate
```

At this point you can use

```
rake test
```

to test your installation.

Unless you want to start with an empty database, you can now load an OSM file (for instance a complete Planet Dump or an extract) into your new database. Use the Osmosis program, which we have covered in chapter 24:

```
osmosis --rx my-osm-file.osm --wd host=localhost user=openstreetmap
        password=openstreetmap database=openstreetmap dbType=postgresql
```

Make sure PostgreSQL has enough disk space for all the data. As a rule of thumb you need about 15 to 20 times the amount of the bzip2 compressed input file. The import can take a long time – expect something like two days for the full Planet Dump on modern hardware.

Once the import is finished, run the `script/server` program. You can then address requests to the local API. By default the port 3000 is used, so you should get an answer at `http://localhost:3000/api/capabilities`. Experienced users can also run the server using an Apache web server with the "passenger" module, or using lighttpd, instead of the built-in Rails web server.

Of course, you can choose not to import any OpenStreetMap data and run the server with your own data instead.

If you want to run a server that always has the current OpenStreetMap data, look at section 24.4 for a description of how to keep a database current with incremental updates.

Alternatives to the API Server: XAPI, ROMA, TRAPI

If you need a local server that simply provides OSM data but doesn't allow local edits, you can use one of the alternatives to the standard OSM server.

The XAPI server is written in the unusual computer language "M" (used to be "MUMPS") and uses the matching database "GT.M". This is a largely unstructured database system that doesn't follow the usual relational model. The source for XAPI is freely available (see the Xapi wiki page), but there are limited installation instructions. XAPI doesn't try to implement the standard API requests, it only allows searching for objects by tags or region. You can find more about XAPI in section 23.1.

The ROMA server ("Read-Only Map API") is a Perl CGI script using a PostGIS database filled with OSM data and kept current through Osmosis. It only supports the "map" request (so it does even less than the XAPI server), but this request can be answered very quickly because of the PostGIS indexes. There are installation instructions for Linux systems on the ROMA wiki page.

The TRAPI system ("Tiles Read-Only API") stores OpenStreetMap data not in a database but, in reduced form, directly in the file system. Therefore the system is relatively space efficient, using only about 20% of the size of the Planet Dump (or about 5 times as much as the bzip2 compressed input file) to store its entire contents. The TRAPI server also supports the "map" request, but always returns the data for a complete tile at zoom level 11, 12, 13, or 14. Further to that TRAPI offers (non-standard) API calls for getting single nodes, ways, or relations. TRAPI is (like ROMA) written in Perl and works as a CGI script. Details and installation instructions are in the Trapi wiki article.

27.2 The API SQL Schema

The table structure of the database more or less directly results from the data model (see chapter 6). But because we not only want to store the current data but also all historic data, the SQL schema is a bit more complex. Additionally there are the tables for storing the GPS tracks and for user data.

Historic Data

For nodes, ways, and relations, all tables exist twice, once with the prefix "current" and once without. The "current" tables contain only the current version of all objects, and the "visible" flag denotes whether this object is visible in this version. For deleted objects this flag is unset. The tables without "current" contain the current and all older versions of an object.

Nodes and Ways

Figure 27-1 shows the table structure for storing nodes and ways. Nodes and ways are linked through the way_nodes table. It relates each way to its two or more nodes. The order of the nodes inside the way is established by the sequence_id field.

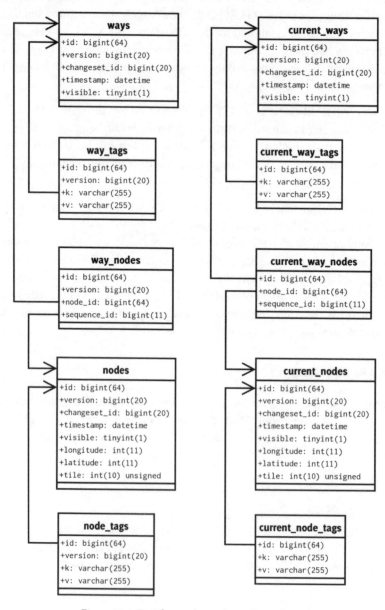

Figure 27-1: Database schema for nodes and ways.

For nodes the field `tile` contains the quadtile index number described below. The longitude and latitude are stored as integers (after multiplying the real value by 10,000,000).

The `version` field is used together with the `id` to be able to reference a specific version of an object. The `timestamp` field contains the date and time of the last change of the object, and `changeset_id` references the changeset in which the change occurred.

Quadtile Indexes

Because the MySQL database system that was used in earlier versions of the Open-StreetMap database doesn't support spatial indexes, the search for nodes in a geographic area (with longitude > lon1 and longitude < lon2, latitude > lat1 and latitude < lat2) was very inefficient. When processing those requests MySQL would only use an index for one axis and had to scan all datasets for the other one.

For OpenStreetMap this problem was solved using a quadtile index. This converts the geographic longitude and latitude of a node into a 16 bit integer and the two resulting numbers are then combined bit by bit into a 32 bit number (first bit of the first number, first bit of the second number, second bit of the first number, and so on). In the resulting range, neighboring nodes are usually mapped to close index numbers in this one-dimensional index. When searching for data in a specific geographic area you only have to calculate the index value range and MySQL can answer the resulting query of the form "quadtile > t1 and quadtile < t2" efficiently. There is a more detailed explanation on the Quadtiles wiki page.

Because the database has since been switched to PostgreSQL which does support spatial indexes, this technique is now superfluous. But it is still used to keep compatibility with the MySQL installations used by some users.

Relations

Relations are modeled almost identically to ways, but the connection between a relation and its members is made through the `relation_members` table, which has a field named `role` in addition to the `sequence_id`. Figure 27-2 shows the table structure.

In contrast to the `way_nodes` table, the table `relation_members` not only stores the ID of the referenced object but also its type (node, way, or relation). This is necessary because ways, nodes, and relations each have their own ID space, so there can be an object of each type with the ID 1.

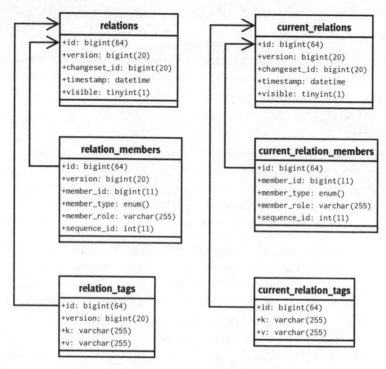

Figure 27-2: Database schema for relations.

Changesets

A changeset entry has a bounding box (min_lon, min_lat, max_lon, max_lat) as well as a timestamp for its creation and closing. Changesets can also have arbitrary tags. Figure 27-3 shows the structure used for storing changesets.

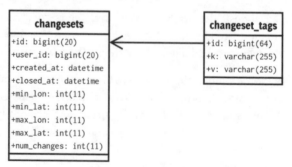

Figure 27-3: Database schema for changesets.

The number of changes in the changeset is stored in num_changes.

When a changeset is created, the closed_at timestamp will be set to a suitable value in the future, and it is pushed further forward each time the changeset is updated. If this time-stamp is reached, however, then the changeset is assumed to be closed. This way no special processing is required to clean up changesets that haven't been closed explicitly.

GPS Tracks

Uploaded GPX files aren't stored in the database but in the file system. Only a filtered ex-tract of these files is imported into the database. The extract contains only the timestamp and position of the trackpoints from the file.

Figure 27-4 shows the database schema for GPS tracks. There is one entry in the gpx_files table for each GPX file, which contains, among other things, the file name under which the file was stored when the user uploaded it. The flag inserted tells a background process whether this file has already been processed. If not, it adds the trackpoints from the file to the gps_points table.

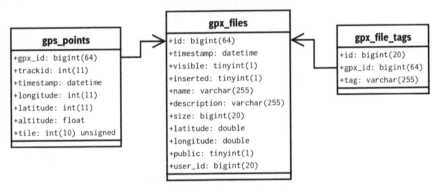

Figure 27-4: Database schema for GPS tracks.

User Data

The remaining tables in the OpenStreetMap database schema are used to store the user data (see figure 27-5). The users table contains data like username and e-mail address. In ad-dition users can add their "home coordinates", so that others can see who is mapping in their area. The users table is referenced from the changeset table, to show which user committed a particular change.

The messages table stores messages that users can send to each other through the web interface. If you marked another user as your friend, this is stored in the friends table. Currently this doesn't do any more than display your friends; maybe there will be further uses in the future.

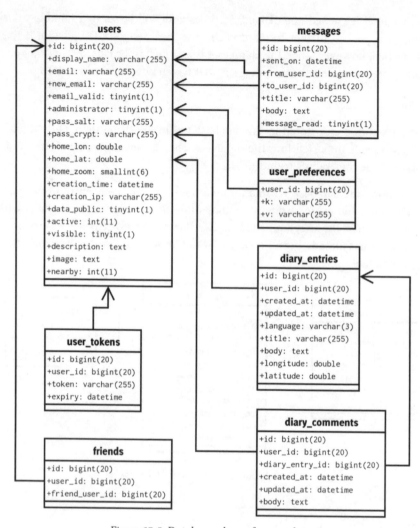

Figure 27-5: Database schema for user data.

OpenStreetMap users can create blog or mapping diary entries on the OSM website. The entries are stored in the diary_entries table. Other users can write comments on those entries, which are stored in the diary_comments table.

The user_preferences table is used for storing the user settings that aren't kept in the users table itself. The user_tokens table is used for temporary access codes for the registration and the "lost password" process.

27.3 Running Your Own Tile Server

There are many different ways to run your own tile server that delivers map tiles to, for example, an OpenLayers interface. The simplest way is to install a web server and use a directory with pre-rendered PNG tiles.

In this section we show you briefly how to run a server that can render map tiles on the fly and can be updated regularly, just like the public OpenStreetMap tile server. This short explanation can't replace a detailed study of the relevant wiki and manual pages, but it gives you an overview of the general approach.

PostGIS

The core of a tile server is a PostGIS database populated with OSM data by the Osm2pgsql program. Platform specific information on how to install PostGIS can be found in the wiki under Mapnik/PostGIS, and the basics have already been covered in section 17.1. Before importing the data you have to decide whether you want to update the database regularly in the future (in that case you need to use the --slim option of Osm2pgsql and you need to install the IntArray module for PostgreSQL; see section 17.4) or if you just want to import the complete data if you need an update.

You need to add a suitable user account in the database and load an initial dataset with Osm2pgsql.

Mapnik

The next step is to install Mapnik as described in section 17.5. In addition to the Mapnik software itself you need the map style file and map icons as described there, and you also have to download and install the shapefiles for coastlines as described in section 17.8.

Finally you have to install the Apache web server, the Apache mod_tile module, and the renderd rendering server (available in SVN under /applications/utils/mod_tile). You can configure the web server using the file mod_tile.conf that comes with mod_tile as a template. It is very important to ensure that there is a line looking something like this:

```
AddTileConfig /mytiles mystyle
```

This tells mod_tile to work on URLs starting with /mytiles.

Configure the renderd so that it can find your map style file. For this add an entry to /etc/renderd.conf in the following form:

```
[mystyle]
XML=/path/to/my/stylefile.xml
```

In this file you also have to configure where Mapnik should look for its input plugins and fonts (the paths can vary for different Linux distributions and also depend on the installed Mapnik version):

```
[mapnik]
plugins_dir=/usr/lib/mapnik/0.7/input
font_dir=/usr/share/fonts/truetype/ttf-dejavu
```

After a restart of Apache and renderd, you should be able to request URLs of the form http://servername/mytiles/0/0/0.png, which should return a map tile. If it doesn't work, you can start renderd manually (as the www-data user) with the option -f, to see debugging output at the console. Typical problems when installing for the first time are missing database authorizations, or style, symbol, or shapefiles that can't be found.

Data Updates

You can use Osmosis to do regular data updates (see section 24.4). You can directly send the update streams from Osmosis to osm2pgsql like this:

```
osmosis --rci ~/osm-update --simc --wxc - | osm2pgsql ...
```

Depending on the specification of your computer, processing the updates can use so many resources that the parallel rendering of map tiles is slowed down considerably.

You can always do a complete data re-import with osm2pgsql. If you want to continue tile rendering while the import is happening, you have to set the import to make a new database and then rename it after the import has finished.

Pre-rendering and Deleting Tiles

You can pre-render a larger area using the render_list helper program. Tiles in smaller zoom levels often need considerable time for rendering and you don't want your users to wait too long.

You also have to ensure that your system isn't keeping old tiles in your cache for too long if you do regular data updates. You can either re-render old tiles regularly or just delete them. Another option is to use Osmosis to find out from the downloaded update streams which tiles need updating because something has changed within them. There are different ways of doing that. On the OpenStreetMap tile server, a Ruby script named expire.rb is used (in SVN under /applications/utils/export/tile_expiry), but Osm2pgsql can also generate a list of tiles that need updating. The render_expired program (from the renderd package) can then be used to process that list and re-render the tiles.

Tirex – the Renderd Successor

The Tirex program (developed by the authors of this book and available from SVN at /applications/utils/tirex) is likely to be the successor of the currently much-used renderd. In contrast to renderd, Tirex splits the management of the rendering queue from the actual rendering, and has many more options for influencing the tile rendering. Read more about Tirex on the wiki.

27.4 The Osm2pgsql SQL Schema

If you import OSM data with Osm2pgsql, four important database tables are created. Each of these tables contains a column called "way" containing the geometry of the object as well as a large number of additional columns for the tags.

Table	Content
planet_osm_point	All POIs, address points, etc.
planet_osm_line	All lines (like roads etc.), also "artificial" line geometries created from route relations.
planet_osm_polygon	All areas including those created from multipolygon relations.
planet_osm_roads	A subset of the lines already found in the planet_osm_line table in simplified form. This speeds up rendering on smaller zoom levels. The table name is misleading in that it contains much more than just roads.

All tables are organized in a similar fashion. The column osm_id contains the ID of the original object, and the column way holds the object geometry. The number given in z_order determines a drawing order for objects; it is computed from the highway type, the layer tag and a few other things. All other columns are named after tag keys and contain the respective tag value, or NULL if the object in question doesn't have the tag.

Which attribute columns are present is configured through the Osm2pgsql style file, usually called default.style.

If you use the "slim mode" of Osm2pgsql (the --slim option), additional tables are created: planet_osm_nodes, planet_osm_ways, and planet_osm_rels contain the raw OSM data. They are used exclusively for later updates of the data, and not for rendering.

Appendix

A. Introduction to Geodesy

Geodesy is the scientific discipline dealing with the measurement and representation of the Earth. Due to the shape of the Earth, which is almost – but not quite – a sphere, this is an amazingly complex subject. In this appendix we cover just a few basics of Geodesy that sometimes are significant in the OSM project.

Geographic Coordinates

Let's simplify things and assume the Earth is a sphere. To indicate a position on the Earth's surface we will need a defined point of origin for our coordinate system and two angles measured from this point. The angles are measured in degrees, a full circle corresponds to 360 degrees. Mathematical formulae sometimes need the angles in radians, a full circle then corresponds to 2π.

The geographic latitude is the angle to the equator. So the equator itself is at 0°, the North Pole at 90° N (+90°), the South Pole at 90° S (-90°).

The geographic longitude is the angle to the prime meridian, for which there is (unlike the equator) no obvious candidate. For a long time, different countries used different prime meridians, but in 1884 everybody agreed on using the Greenwich meridian running through the astronomical observatory in Greenwich, just south-east of Central London. Starting from Greenwich, there are 180 degrees of longitude to the East (180° E or +180°) and 180 degrees to the West (180° W or -180°).

Degrees of longitude and latitude are each divided into 60 minutes and these again into 60 seconds. They are written like this: 49° 17' 46". But in the age of computers you also often encounter a simpler decimal notation which just uses degrees and fractions of degrees: 49.2961°. And instead of specifying North and South or East and West, respectively, positive and negative signs are often used.

Unfortunately, there is no standard giving the order of the geographic coordinates. Often you see the latitude first and then the longitude. But because of the usual mathematical notation where the X coordinate comes before the Y coordinate, GIS professionals will often write the longitude first.

The Geodetic Datum

So that is simple then – but there are a few complications, because the Earth might be round, but it isn't quite a sphere. The Earth is flattened at the poles and it has other little deformations here and there. If you assumed the Earth to be a sphere the potential error would be too large. Therefore the Earth is modeled as an ellipsoid (the correct name for an ellipse in 3D). The ellipsoid used for surveying is called a reference ellipsoid.

Different reference ellipsoids and reference datum points.

When people began surveying the Earth accurately in the 18th century, each country did the work in isolation. As with the different prime meridians, surveyors used different reference ellipsoids with slightly different radii – best suited to the local situation. Different countries also used different reference datum points – the points from where the surveying started. In the US, for instance, the reference datum was for a long time at Meades Ranch, Kansas, near the geographic center of the 48 contiguous states.

The combination of reference ellipsoid and reference datum point is called a geodetic datum. Over the years the geodetic datums were often adjusted, unified or changed, so now there is a huge number of those datums, but only a few of them are of practical importance.

Today it is possible to use satellites for global surveying. For this, globally fitting reference ellipsoids are used instead of locally fitting ones. The geodetic datum used for GPS is called WGS 84. It is used for instance by Google and Yahoo Maps and also by OpenStreetMap. Most GPS devices can be configured to use a different geodetic datum, and the device will then convert the coordinates internally. You should make sure that your device is set to WGS 84, otherwise coordinates might be misplaced by 100 meters or more. Printed maps often use a different datum (for instance Ordnance Survey maps use the OSGB36 datum).

Geographic Projection

The Earth is roughly a sphere, but a paper map (or a computer screen) is flat. To display the 3D data it has to be converted into two dimensions. This conversion is done using one of many mathematical calculations, called projections. Each projection distorts reality in some way or other, with the character and degree of distortion at different points of the Earth being different for different projections.

If you want to draw a map for a specific region or a specific use, you have to choose the right projection. For world maps (like the OSM web maps) the Mercator projection is often used. This projection works well for lower latitudes, but the distortion gets bigger the nearer you come to the poles. Greenland appears much too big in comparison and the poles themselves don't appear at all in this projection.

Depending on the projection, longitude and latitude of a point are mapped to different projected coordinates. Many projections use meters to the right (i. e. to the East) and up (i. e. to the North) of a reference point. These are also called Eastings and Northings.

EPSG Numbers

In order not to get too confused with the many different geodetic datums and coordinate systems used around the world, the European Petroleum Survey Group (EPSG) has created a catalog.[1] Instead of talking about a reference ellipsoid and coordinate systems, a prime meridian or a reference datum and so on, you can simply use the EPSG number from this catalog. Those EPSG numbers have become established as a standard in the GIS world and nearly all software will understand them and can work with them. You shouldn't blindly trust the EPSG definitions though, because they sometimes don't give the maximum possible accuracy.

The already mentioned WGS 84 datum with geographic (non-projected) coordinates is cataloged as EPSG:4326.

At www.epsg-registry.org and www.spatialreference.org you can find EPSG numbers and other information about many geodetic datums and coordinate systems.

To get some idea of the complexity, consider the position in the UK. The national mapping agency Ordnance Survey (OS) uses three coordinate systems:[2]

1. The National GPS Network uses ETRS89 datum as the basis for the OS control survey.

2. The National Grid (a traditional horizontal coordinate system) consists of: A traditional geodetic datum using the Airy ellipsoid; a Terrestrial Reference Frame called OSGB36; and a Transverse Mercator Projection.

---

1 The role of the EPSG has since been taken over by the OGP Surveying and Positioning Committee.
2 http://www.ordnancesurvey.co.uk/oswebsite/gps/information/
   coordinatesystemsinfo/guidecontents/guide5.html

3. Ordnance Datum Newlyn (ODN) is a traditional vertical coordinate system, based on tide gauge datum at Newlyn (Cornwall).

The last two together are signified by EPSG:7405.

The Proj.4 Library

For the conversion between different projections and from one geodetic datum into another, you can use the Proj.4 library (`proj.maptools.org`). Proj.4 is a C library, and there are adapters for the most important computer languages. Many Open Source programs (such as the PostgreSQL extension PostGIS) use this library.

Proj.4 understands detailed descriptions of the desired geodetic datums and projections or the above mentioned EPSG numbers. WGS 84 for instance can be written in short as

```
+init=EPSG:4326
```

or detailed as

```
+proj=longlat +ellps=WGS84 +datum=WGS84 +no_defs
```

You can use the program `cs2cs` to do conversions on the command line. For instance from WGS 84 to OSGB36, British National Grid, Ordnance Datum Newlyn:

```
cs2cs +init=epsg:4326 +to +init=epsg:7405
```

The program reads coordinates from standard input and prints the converted coordinates on standard output.

For JavaScript there is the Proj4js library (`proj4js.org`), but it isn't as powerful as the C one.

B. Mapping the World

OpenStreetMap is an international project, and the community spans the globe. But there are local differences in the way the community is organized, where its mapping emphasis is, or what kind of data has been imported. Even though the same data model and the same tagging system is used all over the world, there are many national or regional differences. This appendix gives some information specific to particular regions. Because of the limited space available in this book, we have had to choose only a few countries for this section. This doesn't mean that nothing is happening in other countries. Please see the wiki for those places and contact the local community to find out more. If there is no OpenStreet-Map community in your part of the world, maybe you should get something started!

For each region we have listed the primary wiki entry point, the local web page (if available), the mailing list[1], and the IRC channel[2].

Please note that there are countries where using a GPS is illegal or where you need a permit to create a map. We don't necessarily know where such problems could occur, so we can't go into them here. Make sure you know what applies in your country.

This appendix is released under the Creative Commons Attribution Share-Alike 2.0 license. This allows you to copy and re-use the whole or parts of this appendix at will. Please add the following, or a similar, attribution:

Based on the book, "OpenStreetMap. Using and Enhancing the Free Map of the World", by Ramm, Topf, and Chilton.

The appendix is available for download at `www.openstreetmap.info` and, in a possibly edited and updated form, from `/misc/documents/osmbook` in the OpenStreetMap Subversion repository.

---

1 Go to `lists.openstreetmap.org` to find the mailing lists.
2 See section 3.4 for information about IRC.

The following people contributed further local knowledge to this appendix: Shoaib Burq, Nicolas Chavent, Steve Chilton, Elizabeth Dodd, Mikel Maron, Ivan Sanchez Ortega, Pieren, Richard Weait, and Harry Wood.

Australia

Wiki	WikiProject_Australia
Website	openstreetmap.org.au
Mailing list	talk-au
IRC	#osm-au

Work has started to establish a non-profit organization as the local OSMF chapter, see Foundation/Local_Chapters/Australia. There are regular mapping parties in Canberra and Brisbane.

Tagging

Some Australian states use an alphanumeric system for labeling roads; in others the official road classification can be deduced from the type of signs used.

Australian road tagging reflects the importance of the road, and not the physical form of the road itself. There are many unpaved roads that are nonetheless important; tag these roads according to the usual scheme and add surface=unpaved. Don't be tempted to tag them as highway=track just because they are unpaved; this tag should be used for gravel fire trails, forest drives, 4WD tracks, and similar roads only.

Remember that Australia has left-hand drive traffic.

Much more information can be found on Australian_Tagging_Guidelines.

Government Data Imports

The Australian government has released many datasets including geodata under a Creative Commons license. Data is available for download at data.australia.gov.au. See the wiki category Category:Data.australia.gov.au_projects for some projects to import this data. Major imports have covered the coastline, as well as suburb boundaries and postal code areas.

NearMap Aerial Imagery

The Australian company NearMap has released some of their high resolution aerial images for OSM use, mostly of urban areas and surroundings. Information about coverage and use of the images is on NearMap PhotoMaps.

Canada

Wiki	WikiProject_Canada
Website	www.openstreetmap.ca
Mailing list	talk-ca
IRC	#osm-ca

Government Support

Canadian government agencies Natural Resources Canada (www.nrcan.gc.ca) and the Centre for Topographic Information – Sherbrooke (CTI-S, www.cits.rncan.gc.ca) participate in the Canadian OpenStreetMap community. CTI-S publishes several sets of Canadian geodata including the CanVec dataset, which they publish in OSM format (see CanVec).

Imports

The CanVec, GeoBase, and other Canadian public geodata sets are being converted and imported by the OSM community. They include boundaries, First Nations' lands, national protected areas, and the national road network. Refer to the GeoBase_Import, CanVec and Canada_Import_Status wiki pages for details.

Tagging

Some guidelines for tagging Canadian roads and other features are documented on the wiki under Canadian_tagging_guidelines.

Local Groups

Local groups in Canada are still relatively thin on the ground:

- Toronto ON – http://www.meetup.com/OpenStreetMap-Toronto/
- Waterloo Region ON – http://www.meetup.com/Waterloo-OSM/

France

Wiki	WikiProject_France
Website	www.openstreetmap.fr
Mailing list	talk-fr
IRC	#osm-fr

Cadastre

The OSM community is permitted to use the official French cadastre (land register) for deriving data. This allows mapping to a great level of detail. WikiProject_France/Cadastre has more information. A special JOSM plugin is available to work with cadastre data, and JOSM has been enhanced to support a number of special French map projections.

Tagging

See FR:France roads tagging for information about tagging roads in France.

The French community is running the Osmose data quality checking tool (see Osmose on the wiki) at osmose.openstreetmap.fr.

Corine Land Cover

The Corine Land Cover project of the European Union collects land cover data for its member states. The data for France has been released under an OSM-compatible license and it was mostly imported into OSM in 2009. See WikiProject_Corine_Land_Cover and WikiProject_France/Corine_Land_Cover.

Germany

Wiki	WikiProject_Germany
Website	www.openstreetmap.de
Mailing list	talk-de
IRC	#osm-de

Germany has a vibrant OSM community and is among the best-mapped countries in OpenStreetMap. There are many regular regional meetings (see www.openstreetmap.de). The German community has chosen not to found a national OpenStreetMap Foundation chapter, but rather to let OpenStreetMap affairs be handled by an existing organization, FOSSGIS e.V. (www.fossgis.de)

FOSSGIS e.V. is also the German chapter of OSGeo and is expected to become the German chapter of OSMF. Initially dealing mainly with Free and Open Source software in the GIS field, FOSSGIS e.V. now also concerns itself with Open Data.

FOSSGIS Conference and LinuxTag

There is an annual conference also called FOSSGIS. In 2010 this conference featured an OpenStreetMap track for the first time. It is expected to continue being the main German-language OpenStreetMap event.

OpenStreetMap traditionally also has a strong presence at LinuxTag, Europe's largest Open Source event held in Germany every year.

Imports and Aerial Imagery

The German community hasn't benefited from any large-scale imports, but smaller donations of various kinds have been processed, for example building data for Rostock, or sets of administrative boundaries.

There have also been many small-to-medium-scale donations of aerial imagery, most notably a "trial" project agreed with the government of the German state of Bavaria in 2008. The community was given permission to use official aerial imagery for a period of three months (see DE:Luftbilder_aus_Bayern on the wiki). AeroWest GmbH, a commercial provider of aerial imagery, made their imagery for the city of Dortmund available in 2010, which has led to Dortmund being mapped very well (DE:Luftbilder_aus_Dortmund).

Yahoo aerial imagery with good resolution is available in some German conurbations but doesn't comprehensively cover rural areas.

Other Donations and Sponsorship

FOSSGIS operates a number of servers that have been sponsored by German hosting provider STRATO AG. They are available for all project members (see FOSSGIS/Servers on the wiki).

The German community has also been given a number of GPS devices that are available for mapping parties and related projects.

Tagging

Germany is a hotbed of experimental features in OpenStreetMap. Some ideas that were started in Germany are now used worldwide (e. g. the "Karlsruhe Schema" for addressing, see section 8.3), but many more are still considered exotic by others. With basic road tags, land use, and POI information already captured in many areas, mappers in Germany turn their attention to details, adding extra information such as track types, surface quality, and access restrictions. Germans are also diligent when mapping public transport routes, stops, and stations – all using relations, of course.

Haiti

Wiki WikiProject_Haiti

Mailing list talk-ht

In January 2010 a 7.0 earthquake struck Haiti, devastating the capital, its metropolitan region, some of the major Haitian urban centers, and several rural areas. In the aftermath hundreds of OSMers worked on the Haiti map using aerial imagery supplied by several companies and importing public domain baseline and humanitarian specific datasets. As a result, within a few days of the earthquake, the OSM map of Haiti's capital Port-au-Prince and its surroundings quickly became the most detailed one available. OSM maps were used on mobile devices by search and rescue teams in the days immediately following the earthquake.

The remote mapping is being complemented by advisory field missions of OSMers working with the World Bank and by capacity-building field missions of the Humanitarian OpenStreetMap Team (HOT). The first HOT mission resulted in plugging OSM into the geodata management solutions in place in Haiti among humanitarian international responders, ongoing development projects, and Haitian national and local authorities, primarily the *Centre National d'Information Geomatique et Spatial (CNIGS)*, the Haitian national mapping agency.

There is plenty of information about how you can get involved on the wiki (see Wiki-Project_Haiti and HOT). There is still lots to do as Haiti is trying to get back on its feet again.

India

Wiki WikiProject_India

Mailing list talk-in

The OSM coverage of Chennai on the East coast of India has long been an example of wonderful mapping dedication, but we are now starting to see India's OSM community taking off elsewhere as well. There remains plenty of mapping to do, which as yet untraced Yahoo aerial imagery available for several large cities.

Tagging

For rules on tagging roads in India see Tagging_Roads_in_India.

Remember that India has left-hand drive traffic.

Italy

Wiki WikiProject_Italy

Website www.openstreetmap.it

Mailing list talk-it

IRC #osm-it

At blog.openstreetmap.it there is an Italian language OSM community blog.

OSMit Conference

A national OSM conference is planned, see http://www.dicat.unige.it/osmit2010/.

Imports

Some data has been imported, for instance buildings in the region of Friuli Venezia Giulia.

Japan

Wiki	WikiProject_Japan
Website	www.openstreetmap.jp
Mailing list	talk-ja

Tagging

There is lots of information on local tagging rules on Japan_tagging.

Remember that Japan has left-hand drive traffic.

The Netherlands

Wiki	WikiProject_Netherlands
Website	www.openstreetmap.nl
Mailing list	talk-nl
IRC	#osm-nl

Host to the State of the Map conference in 2009, the Netherlands has always had an active OpenStreetMap community, though the AND import (see below) has left them with less mapping to do. Mapping footpaths and POIs is now the priority.

There is a blog about Dutch OSM activities at blog.openstreetmap.nl.

AND Import

In 2007 the AND company donated data for the road network of the Netherlands as well as some other data to OSM. It was subsequently imported into OSM. See AND_Data for more information.

Spain

Wiki WikiProject_Spain

Website www.openstreetmap.es

Mailing list talk-es

The "Asociación OpenStreetMap España" was founded in Spain early in 2009. It is planned to make this into a chapter of the OSMF.

Tagging

The Spanish community is still deciding about some highway tags. Politically speaking, Spain is divided into 17 regions, and most of them classify their roads in a different way. You can find the latest information on the Spanish way of tagging roads at Normalización. Most Spanish maps depict national roads in red. These are tagged as highway=trunk.

Data Imports

Spain has more than 20 regional and national mapping agencies, with several of them interested in sharing their data.

At the time of writing, several mapping agencies already allowed their data to be imported or used in OSM:

Instituto Geográfico Nacional: Geodetic network and political boundaries.

Instituto de Tecnologías Agrarias de Castilla-León: 95000 km^2 of 25cm/px orthophotos.

Consellería d'Infrastructures i Transport de la Comunitat Valenciana: Valencia roads.

Instituto Cartográfico de Andalucía: Half a gigabyte worth of street and road network.

Eusko Jaurlaritza – Gobierno Vasco: Orthophotos, topographic maps, land use.

United Kingdom

Wiki United_Kingdom

Mailing list talk-gb

The UK community is active at several levels. There are frequent local mapping parties to try to fill in details in less well mapped areas (noted on the project's event calendar). Several regions have separate mailing lists (e. g. West Midlands) and an active social calendar (e. g. London). Work has just started to incorporate a local OSMF chapter for the UK.

Ordnance Survey

The restrictive licensing policy from the UK national mapping agency (Ordnance Survey) was one of the driving forces in starting the OpenStreetMap project. Due to a major change in government policy, the Ordnance Survey released some geodata under a liberal license in April 2010. Members of the community have looked at the various datasets (such as Meridian, StreetView, and VectorMap District) to see if they provide significant and usable data for adding detail to OSM. See the wiki page at Ordnance_Survey_Opendata for the current status.

Imports

The UK community has tended not to consider data imports, mostly because UK datasets are often derived from Ordnance Survey data. The one major exception to this has been that of importing data from NaPTAN. This is the UK official dataset for bus stops, which the UK Department for Transport and Traveline have jointly offered to make available to the OpenStreetMap project. There is a wiki page for this at Naptan.

Tagging

Because of the project's origins in the UK, much of the tagging schema has a distinctly UK bias. For instance, the highway tagging schema is explicitly based on the highway classification from the UK (motorway, trunk, primary, secondary, tertiary, etc).

Remember that the UK has left-hand drive traffic.

Aerial Imagery

There is good aerial imagery available from Yahoo for some urban areas in the UK, with the subsequent right to derive data from it. There is a UK Yahoo coverage map at: `http://steve8.dev.openstreetmap.org/yahoo.html`. Recently high resolution aerial imagery of the whole of the county of Surrey was released to the project, see Surrey_Air_Survey.

Out-of-copyright Maps

Copyright expires for maps in the UK after 50 years from publication. Various editions of Ordnance Survey maps come into this category. Nearly all *1" New Popular Edition* maps are available, as are many *2.5" Provisional Edition* maps, and many of the *1" 7th Series* maps. Where they are out-of-copyright they have been scanned, rectified, and tiled before being made available as a layer to work from in the main OSM editors. See Out-Of-Copyright.

United States of America

Wiki	WikiProject_United_States
Mailing list	talk-us
IRC	#osm-us

American OSMers have founded OpenStreetMap U.S. Inc., a non-profit organization to support OSM, which is going to be an OSMF local chapter (see Foundation/Local_Chapters/United_States). The community is also planning to hold a State of the Map US Conference (see www.stateofthemap.us and WikiProject_United_States/US_SOTM).

Local Groups

Some local groups have formed in the US:

- Albany, NY: http://www.meetup.com/CapitalDistrict-OpenStreetMap/
- Atlanta, GA: http://www.meetup.com/Atlanta-OpenStreetMap/
- Columbus, OH: http://www.meetup.com/OpenStreetMap-Columbus/
- San Francisco, CA: http://www.meetup.com/Bay-Area-OpenStreetMappers/
- Washington, DC: mappingdc.org

TIGER Import and Fixup

The US Census Bureau publishes geodata for the US under the name TIGER (Topologically Integrated Geographic Encoding and Referencing) including a complete road network. The data is in the public domain, so there are no legal problems with using it for OSM. The data is often old and incorrect, but still useful. Between October 2007 and January 2008 the data was converted and imported into the OSM database. More information about the import is available on the TIGER wiki page.

Although this gives us a complete road network, there is much work to be done to fix this data in OSM. The data is wildly inaccurate in places. See the wiki page TIGER_fixup for information on how you can help.

Other Imports

More detailed data for Massachusetts from the Commonwealth's Office of Geographic and Environmental Information was imported, too. See MassGIS for details.

Land cover data has been imported for the whole state of Georgia, and there are several other imports.

Units

OSM is an international project and generally uses the metric system for measurements in tags like maxspeed or maxheight. Americans can use the numbers they are used to if they add the unit: maxspeed=55 mph.

Availability of Aerial Imagery

There are good aerial images available from Yahoo covering the whole of the US.

Tagging

There is exhaustive information on tagging United States highways on the wiki under United_States_roads_tagging. Note that many highways weren't classified correctly when the TIGER import was being done.

Index

3D fix 28
account
    for OSM contributions 19
    for Subversion repository 22
address
    mapping 86
    search (Name Finder) 265
    search (Nominatim) 267
administrative boundaries 85
aerial imagery
    in JOSM 136
    in Merkaartor 144
    in Potlatch 108
    suitability for mapping 49
    usability (license) 160
altitude
    measuring with GPS device 29
AndNav2 231
Android 231
API 247, 269
API
    changes in 0.6 59
    downloading data 177
    size limit 178
API key (Google Maps) 171
API methods
    finding references 253
    objects in bbox 251
    reading and changing objects 248
    searching for objects 253
area
    creating in Potlatch 104
    mapping in OSM 57
    special data type 59
    with holes 84
ATM 77
attribution (license) 235
Australia 316
authentication
    HTTP Basic Auth 247
    OAuth 261

automated changes 286
bank 75
barrier 71
Bing Maps 4
bitmap data
    exporting 295
blog 19, 304
bollard 71
bookmark (JOSM) 118
border 76
bot (robot) 286
boundary 85
bounding box 251
bounds
    in XML file 56
    Osmarender 189
bridge 67
    modeling with relations 96
bridleway 64
bug tracking 22
building
    GPS shadowing 30
    mapping in OSM 74
    mapping using relations 97
bus route 88
business park 74
cadastre 318
Canada 317
car navigation systems
    for mapping 32
car park 74
cartography 5
Cascadenik 218
CC-BY-SA license
    applicability for geodata 238
    attribution 236
    compatible data 157
    for illustrations in the book VI
    publication 237
    showing in Osmarender 189
    violations 238

Directory of OSM Tags

The following is a list of tags discussed in this book:

More about this book

Register your book: receive updates, notifications about author appearances, and announcements about new editions. *www.uit.co.uk/register*

News: forthcoming titles, events, reviews, interviews, podcasts, etc. *www.uit.co.uk/news*

Join our mailing lists: get email newsletters on topics of interest. *www.uit.co.uk/subscribe*

How to order: get details of stockists and online bookstores. If you are a bookstore, find out about our distributors or contact us to discuss your particular requirements. *www.uit.co.uk/order*

Send us a book proposal: if you want to write – even if you have just the kernel of an idea at present – we'd love to hear from you. We pride ourselves on supporting our authors and making the process of book-writing as satisfying and as easy as possible. *www.uit.co.uk/for-authors*

UIT Cambridge Ltd.
PO Box 145
Cambridge
CB4 1GQ
England

Email: *inquiries@uit.co.uk*
Phone: **+44 1223 302 041**